Smart Cards

For a complete listing of the *Artech House Telecommunications Library*, turn to the back of this book

Smart Cards

José Luis Zoreda
José Manuel Otón

Artech House
Boston • London

Library of Congress Cataloging-in-Publication Data
Zoreda, José Luis.
Smart cards / José Luis Zoreda
Includes bibliographical references and index.
ISBN 0-89006-687-6
1. Smart cards. I. Otón, José Manuel. II. Title.
TK7895.S62O86   1994   94-7671
006–dc20   CIP

A catalogue record for this book is available from the British Library

© 1994 ARTECH HOUSE, INC.
685 Canton Street
Norwood, MA 02062

International Standard Book Number: 0-89006-687-6
Library of Congress Catalog Card Number: 94-7671

10 9 8 7 6 5 4 3 2 1

To Choni, María, Roberto, and Eva

Contents

Preface

Plastic cards, usually provided with magnetic stripe and embossed characters, have been used for many years in financial applications. Smart cards, credit-card-size devices with microelectronic circuits embedded in them, have recently joined the world of plastic cards, covering an amazingly high number of different areas both in financial and nonfinancial applications.

Microcircuit cards, or chip cards, range from humble wired-logic cards used as debit cards in public phones to powerful microprocessor cards, which are essentially computers embedded in plastic. They include a CPU, permanent and volatile memory, a communications port, and, occasionally, power supply, display, and keyboard. To compare a smart card to having a computer in one's wallet or purse is not an exaggeration.

Security is one of the main features of smart cards. Data stored in card memory are managed by the microprocessor, which continuously supervises data flow and access restrictions. Card memory may be divided among different files whose access rules are separately established. Smart cards may also be able to test (or ''challenge'') the eligibility of the external device being used for data reading. Unauthorized access is avoided by the card, by reversible self-blocking or even by self-destruction. Moreover, built-in data enciphering is included in many cases. These features make smart cards the best solution for carrying sensitive information and for applications in restricted environments. Card fraud is decreasing in countries (e.g., France) where smart cards are extensively used, while it is steadily increasing, in countries with magnetic stripe-based credit cards.

As data security is provided by the card itself, off-line operations and transactions (i.e., transactions conducted without a connection to a centralized system) can be safely carried out. This opens up the number of applications, as off-line transactions can be performed in many places and situations where on-line transactions are not applicable, such as vending machines, phones, parking lots, public transports, and the like. Several independent applications may be implemented in the same card.

This book is not just a technical book; it is intended to be used by two different groups of readers. One of these groups is made up of electronic and computer experts, software developers, hardware designers and manufacturers, and persons involved in data communications and networks. For these people, the hardware and software used in smart cards are analyzed in depth, both as independent devices and as computer peripherals. The development of actual smart cards applications is explained, and programming examples are given.

The second, more heterogenous group is made up of the technical staffs of several kinds of organizations, especially financial companies, health-care management, shopping centers, government departments, and public services such as telephone, gas, electricity, and transportation. This group may use the book to identify specific applications of smart cards within their areas of interest. Smart cards are compared to other similar media, such as laser optical cards and magnetic stripe cards. A comprehensive review of current smart card applications in different areas is also included, as well as a selection of the most interesting trends in this field, including biometric identification, plug-in cards in cellular phones, and multipurpose cards.

As mentioned in the book, smart cards are here to stay. This book has been prepared not only as an introduction to the smart card world but also as a succinct, state-of-the-art guide to current and eventual possibilities of smart cards.

ACKNOWLEDGMENTS

No technical book is the sole creation of its authors, and this one is no exception. Indeed, many people deserve thanks for their contributions to the book. At the top of the list are the members of the Grupo Universitario de Tarjeta Inteligente (GUTI). Special thanks go to Covandonga Rodrigo and Jaime de Pereda, designers of the C programs shown in Chapter 6. Thanks also to Octavio Nieto and Enrique Fenoll, who have applied their experience in electronics to all the questions related to card hardware.

Support on the issues concerning standards has been given by Gemma Déler and Julián Caballero, from the Asociación Española de Normalización (AENOR, Spanish section of CEN). Personal contributions from a number of card experts, Ángel Sierra, Ángel Viñolo, Josep Masana, and especially Javier Pérez-García, are also appreciated. Whether it was correcting the manuscript or bringing up useful technical information, their contribution has been an asset to the final completion of the book.

Many card-related companies have brought technical information of their products and/or kindly offered graphic material for publication. At each company were one or two persons who patiently answered our questions and provided the requested information. Thanks to Pedro L. Sánchez-Gontán (Telefónica), José L. Adanero (Amper), Sébastien Tormos (Schlumberger Technologies), Xavier Libret and Youri Bebic (Gemplus), Antonio González (Philips), Joan Navarro and Jesús Peña (Telesincro), Fernando Álvarez de Lara (2IS/McCorquodale), José L. Fernández (Alcatel), and Carlos Montes (Fábrica Nacional de Moneda y Timbre).

Santiago Matey from Rafael S.L. applied his expertise in preparing and mounting photographs and artwork. Last but not least, Mark Hallett from Mark Hallett Associates was able to transform our rudimentary English into an attractive text. Any remaining misuse of the language is our fault, not his.

The authors also wish to thank the advice and technical support of Artech House personnel during the preparation of the manuscript.

José Manuel Otón
José Luis Zoreda
April 1994

Chapter 1
Old Cards and New Cards

People have used cards for many years. As just a simple form of identification or a matter of social status, cards were included in the civilized world in the old days when paper was the preferred medium for communication. Calling cards with names, addresses, and short notices printed on paper were the only cards for decades. However, in the second half of this century, and notably in the last twenty years, these humble paper rectangles have been overridden by the arrival of plastic-based cards featuring new attributes, such as embossing, holograms, magnetic stripes, or golden contacts (Figure 1.1). It would not be unusual for a person to carry half-a-dozen plastic cards in a wallet or purse. The amazing spread of plastic cards, especially as a business tool in finance-related services, must be analyzed in terms of social phenomena rather than as yet another offspring of modern times.

1.1 CONTENTS OF THE BOOK

This book focuses on the most recent achievement in plastic-based cards, namely, *chip cards*. The continuous progress of microelectronics with ever increasing performance and the smashing of prices reached cards in the 1970s, when electronic circuits began to be embedded in plastic cards. Since then, technology improvements have turned these early circuits into tiny computers that include microprocessor and reusable memory. This enables these cards to be programmed for specific duties, as well as to dialog with an external device while controlling the data flow. A new term, *smart cards*, was coined to distinguish these intelligent devices from other chip-embedded, nonprogrammable memory cards, such as those employed in many countries as a prepaid medium for public phone calls.

Smart cards are currently used in many areas. Paradoxically, financial institutions, which played a major role in the development of this technology, have made modest progress in their implementation. Instead, smart cards have found niches in many nonfinan-

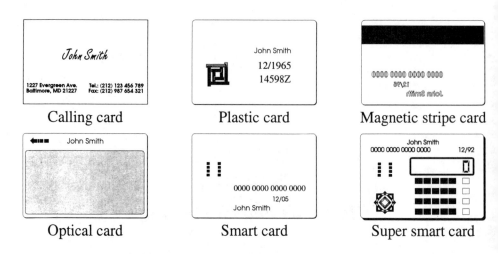

Figure 1.1 From calling cards to super smart cards.

cial areas, especially health care, universities, and telecommunications. There have also been remarkable differences in the level of implementation and in the preferred technology (magstripe, optical, smart) in highly developed countries. European countries, especially France, have introduced the smart card technology in many financial and nonfinancial areas. Japan is mainly using nonsmart, high-storage *optical cards*. Little activity is detected in the United States.

This book is divided into three sections. The first three chapters are a general review of smart cards, related devices, and peripherals. The history and evolution of smart cards are analyzed, as well as the pros and cons of applying these devices in different areas. Alternative technologies such as magnetic stripe and laser optical cards are reviewed and compared to smart cards. This will allow the reader to achieve a better understanding of the facts that should be taken into account when deciding on the best type of card for a given application.

Chapters 4 to 6 explore the hardware and software features of current smart cards. In the hardware section we will learn the kinds of memory employed by chip cards, as well as their communication protocols, power supply, and timing attributes. The software section will show the so-called operating systems or *masks* used by cards to accept external commands and/or be programmed for specific duties. A complete example of card programming, including program listings, is given.

The final three chapters of the book focus on applications. After the fundamentals of application design are reviewed, examples of actual applications in different countries and working areas are given, including the latest trends and techniques.

Standardization is a crucial issue in the smart card arena. Cards from different manufacturers must work with alien peripherals and computers; compatibility is achieved through the guidance of numerous standards ranging from physical dimensions to electrical signals. Card-related standards will be mentioned throughout the book, and supplementary data are included in the appendix.

1.2 BASIC CARD TYPES

As usually happens, standardization in the card world was as a consequence of market trends rather than a previously agreed-on framework. Card standards, mainly developed by the International Standards Organization (ISO) and the *Comité Européen de Normalisation* (CEN, European Committee for Standardization), are in most instances adaptations of *de facto* standards already employed by the manufacturers.* As the card market grew, many different types of cardlike devices were produced, and the need for widely accepted standards became apparent. The first card-related standards, concerning the card's physical dimensions and embossing area, were published as ISO 7810 and ISO 7811. Other features, like issuer's ID, location of elements, coding, and recording techniques are further mentioned in ISO 7812 and ISO 7813. Finally, ISO 7816 is specifically devoted to chip cards.

The following sections discuss the basic concepts of the current main plastic card technologies. All these cards share the same plastic substrate, their performance being conditioned by extra items added to the plastic surface or embedded inside the plastic body. It must be mentioned that other, less relevant, card technologies are used as well; also, it is important to realize that many cards may include several features. In particular, smart cards often contain magnetic stripes.

1.2.1 Magnetic Stripe Cards

ISO 7811 includes a description of the position, size, and writing/reading characteristics of a 0.5-in magnetic stripe located either in the front or rear surface of the card. Magnetic stripes in cards are divided into three longitudinal parallel tracks (Figure 1.2). Tracks are numbered starting from the nearest card edge. First and second tracks hold read-only information, whereas the third track may be rewritten.

- The *first track* was developed by the International Air Transportation Association (IATA) for automating airline ticketing applications, and it is still reserved for them. Its 210-bpi storage density makes room for 79 alphanumeric characters. The track is divided into two fields for the primary account number (up to 18 digits) and the name (up to 26 alphanumeric characters), respectively. The remaining bytes are used for additional data such as expiry date, restrictions, or card type.
- The *second track* was first suggested by the American Bankers Association (ABA) to allow on-line financial transactions. Storage density is 75 bpi, which corresponds

---

*CEN is composed of the national standards organizations of 18 European countries: the twelve countries belonging to the European Community plus Austria, Finland, Iceland, Norway, Sweden, and Switzerland.

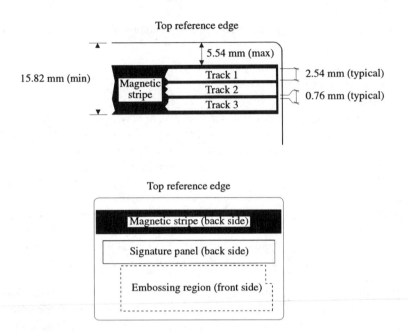

Figure 1.2 Location and dimensions of magnetic stripe track (top); the most common location of the magnetic stripe, signature panel, and embossing area in a credit card (bottom).

to 40 numeric characters. As above, the first field contains the account number (up to 19 digits). Additional information is stored in the remaining bytes.

- The *third track* is used for financial transactions. It includes an enciphered version of the user's personal identification number (PIN), country code, currency units, amount authorized per cycle, subsidiary account, and restrictions. The track may only contain digits (up to 107; storage density is 210 bpi). It is rewritten every time the track is used.

Many issues concerning reliability and security of magnetic stripes are often mentioned in the mass media. It is relatively easy to read and/or amend a magnetic stripe, in spite of new protection systems already included in current cards. Comparisons of the properties of smart cards and magnetic cards are presented in several places throughout the book. A less mentioned area is data management and storage capacity. In fact, the limited storage of present magnetic stripe cards deters issuers from proposing new applications.

1.2.2 Optical Cards

Optical cards, or laser cards, consist of two layers: one very thin, highly reflective layer covering a second, nonreflective layer (or the other way round: a nonreflective layer on a highly reflective one). These two layers are in turn covered by transparent plastic protective outer layers and placed on an opaque substrate.

The first optical cards were commercialized by Drexler Technology Corporation in 1981 (Drexler is the parent company of LaserCard Systems Corporation, a major optical card manufacturer). At present, Japan is also highly active in optical cards (about 20 electronic manufacturers are involved), the most widespread probably being Canon cards.

These optical cards are not erasable; instead, they work on a write-once, read-many-times (WORM) basis. Laser diodes (LD) are used for reading or writing. A high-power LD is focused on the active surface, producing a tiny spot (a few microns). The power is enough to melt the surface, digging a hole that shows the nonreflective back surface. By moving the spot on predefined linear tracks over the surface, digital coding of information can be achieved, the bits being represented by the presence or absence of holes. Reading is performed by a low-power LD. Data remain throughout the entire card life span (though information may be destroyed, if necessary, by burning new holes in the data files). Data files are updated by flagging old files and writing new files on unused areas. The main advantage of this technique is the large amount of memory that can be obtained. A typical optical card is able to store over 4 MB of data, which are reduced to 2.86 MB if data correction algorithms are included. This huge capacity has demonstrated its usefulness in several nonfinancial fields, especially in health care.

1.2.3 Chip Cards

The third type of card features one or several electronic circuits embedded in the plastic substrate. The generic term *chip cards* is used throughout the book to designate such circuit-containing cards. These cards always contain a certain amount of erasable or nonerasable memory, and possibly a microprocessor. The presence of this device modifies the performance, applications range, and price of chip cards to the extent that two different families must be considered.

Memory Cards, Without Microprocessor. Again, several subfamilies may be considered. The most typical memory cards hold less than 1K of nonrewritable memory. Its management is performed by a simple circuit capable of executing some preprogrammed instructions. The circuit cannot be reprogrammed, since the instructions are built into the circuit itself. For this reason, this card system is called *wired logic*. Wired logic cards are chiefly used as prepaid cards for public phones. Other integrated circuit (IC) memory cards holding kilobytes or megabytes are used as data banks or memory extensions for computers. As shown in the following chapters, these cards may have no control over data flow.

Smart Cards, With Microprocessor. These cards are, in practice, small microcomputers lacking power supply, display, and keyboard. Besides the microprocessor, the cards usually have several kilobytes of permanent (either rewritable or nonrewritable) memory. Data stored in this memory cannot be directly accessed. The microprocessor looks after data handling while controlling the access to different memory areas according to a given set of conditions (passwords, ID of external devices, encryption, etc.). Current models feature rewritable memory and built-in encryption algorithms. Some smart card models (active cards or super smart cards) are provided with battery, keyboard, and display, thus being self-sufficient systems.

1.3 COMMUNICATING WITH CARDS

Any card, regardless of its type, is used for communicating information to other people or to electronic devices. In most instances, this information includes data concerning the cardholder's identity and/or eligibility for obtaining specific services or privileges. The card holds the information in different formats (printed as text or pictures; embossed; magnetically, electronically, or optically stored, etc.). Two main points regarding information storage are relevant in assessing cards.

- *Capacity.* The volume of information that can be stored in a card is quite variable. Translated to common units, calling cards store tens of bytes, plastic cards (including cardholder's signature) and magnetic stripe cards hold hundreds of bytes, smart cards usually have a number of kilobytes, and current optical cards may reach several megabytes.
- *Security.* Quite often, cards are used to hold sensitive data whose access must be restricted to selected persons or electronic systems. Calling and plastic cards offer no protection for their data. Magnetic stripe and optical cards may give limited protection by enciphering the information (since reading these cards is relatively simple). Therefore, data protection is achieved by external devices. Smart cards are self-protecting units, since access to the stored information is controlled by their internal microprocessor. Security is indeed one of the most important characteristics of smart cards.

Every card, moreover, has its own language. Figure 1.3, taken from a 60-year-old Spanish encyclopedia, is a romantic example of the rich language developed for calling cards by our grandparents. Notches and holes punched in paper or plastic cards were, and still are, used for automatic detection of owners' privileges in low-security environments (e.g., in room keys of many hotels). Formerly, plastic cards identified their owners with embossed names and written signatures. Currently, cards store digital information using various media, thus requiring specific peripherals and computer systems for retrieving the information.

1.4 PLASTIC CARDS AND MAGNETIC STRIPE CARDS

Paper or cardboard-based cards are intrinsically not reliable for long-term utilization. Metal plates employed in some countries, such as the U.S. charge-a-plate, were also clumsy. The first application of plastics in cards was the protection of paper cards by soft materials. Such plasticized paper cards, still heavily used, are much better protected against mechanical stress and weather.

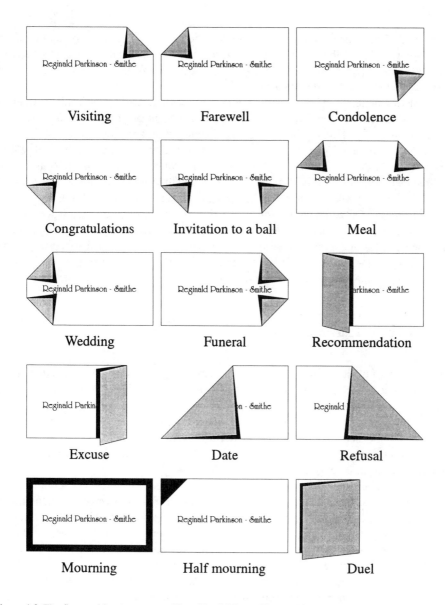

Figure 1.3 The first card language was achieved by folding calling cards.

1.4.1 Origin of Plastic Credit Cards

In plastic cards, hard plastics like polyvinyl chloride (PVC) are used as the substrate, where information is printed. Hard plastics also have two valuable properties: endurance in harsh environments and feasibility of embossing. The first major application of all-plastic cards was Diners Club in 1950. This charge card was used as a symbol of social status, allowing its cardholders to obtain services in restaurants and hotels without having to carry money. By the end of the 1950s, two other companies joined Diners Club: American Express and Carte Blanche.

The first nationwide initiative for credit cards was launched by the Bank of America. The Bank Americard would eventually become VISA; meanwhile, Interbank prepared another system, Mastercard. Soon, both companies extended their business overseas. Europe had little activity in the first few years of credit card development. The first European credit card was issued by Barclays in the United Kingdom in 1966, following an agreement with VISA. The major European banks had joined in by the beginning of the 1970s, creating Access. Other banks decided to license VISA or Mastercard.

Information in these credit cards was restricted to the embossed area, where ID data of the customer and several registration numbers were included. The cardholder's signature was employed for authentication at the point of sale (often a second ID document like a driver's license was requested). When the transaction was larger than a previously established amount, an authorization was solicited by phone to the credit card issuer.

1.4.2 Automatic Teller Machines

The plastic card business increased sharply when a magnetic stripe was included on the card. The first application of this magnetic stripe was in airlines, developed by IATA. By the end of the 1970s, banks realized that services to their customers could be improved and, in some cases, extended to 24 hours a day by installing automatic devices providing the most typical bank services, rather than increasing their office network. Besides improved services, of course, there were big savings in staff and premises that overcame the huge investment of such a nationwide electronic system.

The automatic teller machines (ATM) took advantage of the then recent implementation of magnetic stripes on cards. The first simple models just delivered a certain amount of money to their customers after they identified themselves through a PIN, usually a four- or six-digit number entered by the cardholder using the ATM keyboard. Present ATMs (Figure 1.4) have many more services, such as account balance, cash, and check deposits, and PIN change. At the same time, efforts toward compatibility of different ATM systems have led to a widespread offer of electronic services that are not restricted to the customer's area, not even to the customer's country of origin.

ATMs usually work on line, which means that the decision to deliver the requested service is taken by a centralized system, which holds the customer information and a list of canceled cards. Should the network fail, the ATM terminal "hangs up," displaying an "out of order" message on the screen. In some instances, it delivers a limited amount of money while working off line; the remaining services, which require data from the central system, become inaccessible.

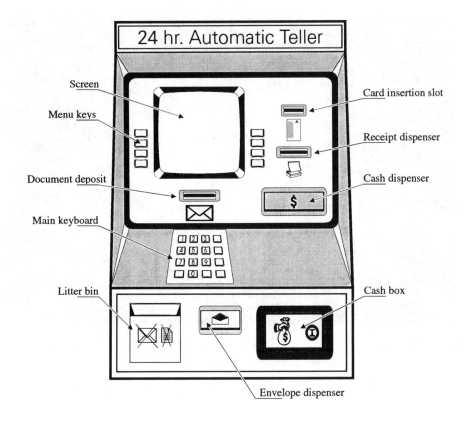

Figure 1.4 Layout of a modern automatic teller machine.

1.4.3 Electronic Points of Sale

Magnetic stripe cards were eventually used by retailers. Traditionally, card transactions used to be confirmed by the customer's signature on a receipt, where the card data were mechanically printed using the card's embossed characters. Current points of sale have card readers that automatically perform the transactions by calling the card issuer through regular or dedicated phone lines. Once the purchase is authorized, the device prints the receipt. The complete operation usually takes less than one minute.

This system is called *electronic point of sale* (EPOS) (Figure 1.5). A more involved system, not yet fully accepted in many countries, is the electronic fund transfer at the point of sale (EFT-POS). In this case, the transaction initiates an automatic transfer of money from the customer's account to the retailer's bank. From the customer's point of view, EPOSs are used with *credit* cards; that is, cards allow the cardholder to spend up to a certain limit of credit, the customer being periodically (e.g., monthly) charged for

Figure 1.5 Electronic point of sale for magnetic stripe and smart cards. The PIN pad may be used for off-line transactions (courtesy of Schlumberger Technologies).

the expenditure. In the EFT-POS case, the card is used as a *debit* card, since no credit is given.

1.4.4 On-Line and Off-Line Systems

Both EPOS and EFT-POS card management used to be on line (i.e., with remote confirmation from a central computer). This led to some problems when the phone service was unreliable or overloaded, or no local issuer premises were available. In some low-population countries, like Norway, off-line solutions based on smart cards were adopted to avoid high-cost communications. In other cases, off-line magnetic stripe systems were introduced. Upon the retailer's request, the customer authenticates the transaction by keying in his/her PIN using a separate keypad (Figure 1.5). The terminal, or a centralized system within the store, accumulates the transactions until they are transferred to the card issuer (e.g., every evening).

Strictly speaking, the PIN should be requested for every off-line transaction, though sometimes it is not solicited for low-value purchases in order to speed up the operation. It is important to realize that, in these transactions, the terminal must be smart enough to read and decipher the user PIN, to compare it to a keyed-in PIN, and to approve the transaction when correct matching is found. Off-line magnetic stripe card transactions are often called *track-3* operations, as opposed to *track-2*-based on-line transactions. However, the track is seldom rewritten by retailers, because track recording requires expensive mechanical, rather than manual, card readers like those of ATMs.

1.4.5 Interchangeability

Both ATMs and EPOSs are currently offered by many different providers. Soon banks and financial companies realized that they could improve their service with little investment by allowing their customers to use anybody else's ATMs. At the same time, retailers wanted to use their EPOS for different credit cards, instead of having as many terminals as card types they accepted. Indeed, such a proliferation of terminals would have certainly caused many retailers to refrain from accepting electronic card payments.

Let us analyze each problem separately. ATMs always work on line. The customer ID is checked by a central system; therefore, if two financial organizations (e.g., two banks) decide to share their ATMs, their systems must be interconnected to allow reciprocal authorizations at each other's terminals. However, they need not share sensitive information, such as the algorithm employed for enciphering their customers' PINs.

The EPOS case is more involved. Tracks can be read by any standard reader; therefore, the simplest solution is to use the same reader for all the cards, selecting the card issuer by phone number (either manually or automatically). This solution does not work, however, if off-line transactions are attempted. Here, the terminal must contain the tools required for deciphering the PIN or any other encoded information. For the system to have reasonable security, it is also necessary to store in the terminal a list of invalidated cards. The list should be as exhaustive as the terminal memory permits.

1.4.6 Point-of-Sale Dilemma

Choosing between on-line and off-line systems in magnetic stripe card applications for EPOS is always a trade-off between functionality and security. Heavy-duty checkouts like those of supermarkets cannot possibly accept the delays introduced by on-line systems. Perhaps the best solution in these cases is a hybrid system working off line for low-value transactions and requesting remote authorization above a certain purchase limit.

Smart cards are very suitable for offering a high security level in off-line transactions. PIN recognition and payment authorization may be assumed by the card itself, with no external confirmation. Nonsmart chip cards like wired logic cards may also be used as *prepaid* cards for low-value transactions. While credit cards perform electronic *loans* and debit cards are used as electronic *checks*, prepaid chip cards are rapidly being accepted as electronic *cash*. As shown throughout the book, these prepaid cards may easily be implemented as applications in multifunction smart cards that simultaneously hold other independent financial and nonfinancial applications. Moreover, magnetic stripes can be attached to smart cards, thus maintaining the compatibility with present ATMs and EPOS.

1.5 COSTS

When deciding the best card for an application, or when analyzing the card market trends, there are obviously two main considerations, namely, performance and costs. The performance of most common card types is studied in the following chapters.

Costs have been traditionally been adduced as the main reason for smart cards not replacing magnetic stripe cards in massive applications such as credit cards. The numbers given in Table 1.1 are unit prices for volume production of both cards and peripherals required to handle them. Some different peripheral prices are given, since these devices may vary considerably in cost, depending on their format: standalone units, standalone readers connected to a computer, or writing/reading units attached to or embedded in other devices (e.g., phones).

Costs given for chip card peripherals in the table apply to all types of chip cards except contactless. Contactless cards are special memory cards or special smart cards whose data flow is effected by inductive or capacitive coupling of embedded components with an external electromagnetic field.

As seen in the table, magnetic stripe cards are quite inexpensive, even when other security features, such as holograms, are included. Memory chip cards with a few hundred bits are quite inexpensive, too. The price of these chips, including embedding, is about $0.25. Smart cards are more expensive: the simplest models range from $3 to $10, and the most sophisticated models vary from $10 to $15 or more. A typical smart card of the second group is equipped with 2K to 8K of rewritable memory, an 8-bit microprocessor, and a built-in encryption algorithm such as the Data Encryption Standard (DES). Optical card prices compare to low-performance smart cards; of course, these cards have the lowest cost per byte.

On the other hand, smart card peripherals are the simplest and least expensive. These units have no mobile parts, since chip cards are connected through eight contacts

Table 1.1
Cost per Card and Peripheral Cost for Different Card Types (in dollars)

	Card Unit Price	*Attached Reader*	*Standalone Reader*
Magnetic stripe	0.15–0.60	15–20 (2 tracks)	150–600 (PC)
		25–50 (3 tracks)	300–1,000 (POS)
			10,000 (ATM)
Optical	4–8	N/A	800–3,000
Chip cards:		3–10	100–200 (PC)
Memory	0.5–5		300–800 (POS)
Smart	3–15		
Super smart	20–50		
Contactless	5–20	N/A	500–900
Note: N/A = not applicable			

located on the card surface. Optical cards require mechanical positioning which increases the peripheral cost. Magnetic stripe cards in POS readers are manually passed through a slot where the magnetic head is located. ATM magnetic stripe readers are mechanically handled, since track writing requires higher reliability than that provided by hand dragging.

1.6 CONCLUSIONS

In this chapter, we have reviewed the basic concepts of some of the most common current cards. New materials (plastics) and features (magnetic stripes, optical surfaces, chips) have created an impressive market of credit, debit, prepaid, and nonfinancial applications, where cards are counted in billions.

We have also reviewed some problems concerning the security and performance of popular card types, especially magnetic stripe cards. As a rule of thumb, the security level of a system is the same as the security level of its weakest point. Magnetic stripe cards are menaced by severe security pitfalls, as demonstrated by the increasing card fraud in financial applications. Most countermeasures rely on external devices, thus producing new difficulties for off-line applications.

Smart cards' built-in security features are the best candidate for overcoming these problems. Although their unit price is higher than magnetic stripes, the financial companies of several countries have already decided on their implementation on an ever larger scale. In the meantime, smart cards have found specific niches in a wide variety of nonfinancial applications where some of their unique characteristics are required. The smart card market is steadily growing; this trend may be boosted in a few years as card costs drop and security arguments make smart cards more competitive for financial applications.

In the next chapter, the primary applications for and new advances in nonsmart (e.g., magnetic stripe and optical) cards are reviewed, allowing a comparison of the solutions offered by these technologies with the smart card approach. Dissimilar application areas demand specific requirements that must be fulfilled by versatile cards. On the other hand, as the number of card applications increases, so does the number of cards in customers' wallets or purses. Multifunction cards are the solution in the foreseeable future.

Chapter 2
Data Storage Cards

The card world is presently populated by old-style cards and newcomers sharing the existing markets and opening new ones. In this chapter, the principal application areas of the main nonsmart card types are reviewed. The purpose is to analyze the pros and cons of each technology; no extensive listings of applications are given, just representative examples where specific features of each card type have proved to be advantageous for its implementation. In addition, other sections summarize relevant technical details for each technology.

The chapter focuses on the two principal competitors in the smart card market, namely, magnetic stripe and laser optical cards; these could be grouped together as *chipless cards*. For the sake of completeness, let us look at some other chipless card types. Plastic cards have already been discussed in the previous chapter. Microfilm cards store text and graphic information in photographic form attached to a plastic substrate. Many kinds of badges containing ID information (e.g., pictures, signatures, text, bar codes, punched holes, magnetic inks) are also used. As a rule, these badges are permanently or semipermanently displayed by their owners. Plastic or cardboard-based magnetic stripe tickets are routinely employed in several areas, especially public transportation.

Large-capacity memory cards will also be mentioned in the chapter. Of course, these cards are not chipless, but they should not be considered chip cards like those studied in the next chapter, simply because their purpose is mainly confined to computer support; that is, they are not usually employed as independent devices. Additionally, there is a whole family of memory banks, data cartridges, and other card-shaped storage devices associated with electronic devices such as portable computers, electronic musical instruments, and home video games; this group is beyond the scope of the book.

2.1 MAGNETIC STRIPE CARDS

Magnetic stripes work on the same basis as conventional audio tapes. The magnetic medium (typically gamma ferric oxide) is made of tiny needle-shape particles dispersed in a binder on a flexible substrate. During manufacturing, these needles are oriented parallel with the longest dimension of the stripe. When an external magnetic field along this direction is applied to the magnetic medium, the particles develop permanent magnetization. One of the tips of each needle becomes a magnetic north pole, and the opposite end becomes a magnetic south pole. Therefore, the needles behave as microscopic magnets oriented along the length of the stripe. The magnetization may be either N-S (north pointing to the beginning of the stripe) or S-N, depending on the polarity of the external magnetic field. This in turn is brought about by an electromagnet (encoding head), whose *magnetic* polarity is determined by the direction of the electric current flowing through the coil (i.e., by the *electric* polarity of the current).

In the following sections, we look at the main issues concerning magnetic stripe recording and data retrieval. Different kinds of card fraud and proposed countermeasures are also discussed. Technical matters are intended to be unbiased; we have tried to keep our opinions as impartial as possible. Bear in mind, however, that only economic factors maintain the privileged position of magnetic stripe cards in financial applications. From a technological point of view, magnetic stripes are far from the best solution in most of these applications.

2.1.1 Coercivity

If the external magnetic field H is plotted versus the material magnetization (or any related quantity describing the material response to the field, like the magnetic induction B), a typical double S-shaped curve, called a *hysteresis loop*, is obtained (Figure 2.1). This curve reveals two important facts about magnetic materials:

- The material magnetization does not increase steadily when the magnetic field is increased. Instead, it reaches a saturation value.
- If an opposite magnetic field is applied, the magnetization remains until a certain value of H is reached. If the field is further increased, the magnetization sign changes, achieving saturation again, but in the opposite direction. If the field is removed after this, the material magnetization remains.

The physical magnitude that measures the magnetic field required for magnetizing any given material (strictly speaking, for demagnetizing a previously saturated material) is called *coercivity*. It can be directly obtained by measuring the width of the hysteresis loop.

It might seem from the above that erasing a magnetized material requires the application of an external field H bringing the magnetization back to zero. This is not feasible in practice, however, since the coercivity of individual particles is not exactly the same. Instead, ac erasing (also called *degaussing*) is used. AC fields reduce the area of the hysteresis loop by randomly orienting the magnetization of the particles. Ideally, after applying an ac field, the material is located at the coordinate origin in the B-H plot. DC erasing is an alternative way of wiping the stored information. In this case, the whole

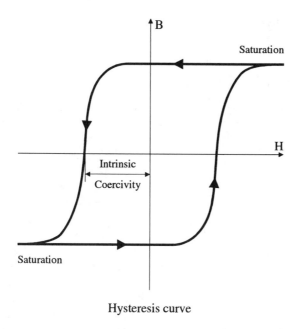

Hysteresis curve

Figure 2.1 Magnetization saturation and intrinsic coercivity can be obtained from the material's hysteresis curve. The magnetization of magnetic stripes, however, does not follow the curve, but remains near the B axis.

stripe is oriented in the same direction. A consequence of the erasing procedure is that magnetic stripes need not be restricted to the hysteresis loop. In fact, they are usually confined to the vertical B axis (Figure 2.1).

2.1.2 Magnetic Stripe Encoding

As mentioned above, N-S and S-N longitudinal magnetizations along the stripe are the only two possible states of the magnetic particles. Therefore, this medium is useful for storing digital information. The needles located in the same region, oriented with the same magnetic field, add up their magnetization, becoming a macroscopic magnetic *domain*. These domains are used for storing data bits. However, binary 0s and 1s are not associated to opposite magnetizations, but to magnetization *changes*. This encoding system is dictated by the reading procedure, as shown in the next section.

When two contiguous domains have opposite magnetizations, a sudden polarity reversal occurs on the intermediate border. This is called *flux reversal*. The magnetic stripe encoding system (Figure 2.2) produces flux reversals between every pair of contiguous bits. In other words, any bit, regardless of being 0 or 1, has magnetization opposite to its leading and trailing neighbors. The difference between binary 0s and 1s is that 0s keep

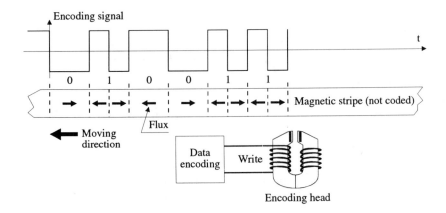

Figure 2.2 Encoding magnetic stripes with an F/2F system.

their orientation along their full length, while 1s have another flux reversal in the middle. Therefore, 0s are made of single domains while 1s are made of two domains each. The typical length of these domains is quite small; for example, the bit length in a standard track 2 (bit density 75 bpi) is just 1/75 = 0.0013 in, or 0.34 mm. A number of leading and trailing 0s are routinely included in the data tracks to improve reading reliability.

It easily follows from the above that this two-frequency encoding system for magnetic stripes, called *F/2F*, relies on accurate measurements of bit lengths, since length is the only difference between a binary 1 and two binary 0s. Bit length errors can make it difficult to decide whether a particular flux reversal is located between two bits or in the middle of a bit. These inaccuracies in the positions of flux reversals are called *jitter*. The magnetic stripe must be carefully positioned and displaced during the encoding procedure to minimize jitter.

2.1.3 Magnetic Stripe Reading

A well-known electromagnetic phenomenon relates magnetic field to electric current: a *variable* magnetic field induces an electric intensity in any close conductor. In our case the magnetic stripe is dragged over a steady reading head (a pickup coil). The variations in the magnetic field are produced by the flux reversals between consecutive bits and the intermediate flux reversals of binary 1s. Every flux reversal induces a current in the coil its sign being imposed by the magnetic domain orientation at both sides (Figure 2.3). At the same time, an electronic circuit in the reader determines the length of each domain. Since the electric signals are not produced by the magnetic domains themselves but by their variations, it becomes clear why schemes having continuous flux reversals such as F/2F, are used for encoding magnetic stripes. It is also apparent that the reliability of the system is limited by the shortcomings of the encoder, reader, and stripe, particularly

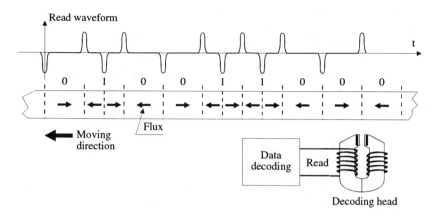

Figure 2.3 Reading F/2F-encoded magnetic stripes. Monopolar current pulses are induced in the decoding head by flux reversals.

bit length deviations. Cumulative jitters from the encoder, reader, and card defects and deformations may hinder the accurate reading of the stripe.

Accurate reading is also impaired by inadequate magnetization. Ideally, the external magnetic field saturates the domains upon encoding. In practice, the coercivity of the magnetic particles is not a single value; thus, the stripe zones may be partially magnetized by applying lower magnetic field strengths. The use of oversaturating magnetic fields is not advisable, since the magnetization of the zones *decreases* when the external encoding magnetic field is too high. The reason is that the field is so strong that it alters the previous and subsequent stripe areas (which, by definition of F/2F encoding, are magnetized in the opposite direction). On the other hand, complete degaussing (erasure) of the stripe may be difficult to achieve. A residual magnetization usually remains, producing spurious induced currents when being read.

Another potential problem comes from accidental stripe erasures produced by magnetic fields or electric devices. Even when the stored information is not deleted, partial erasures alter the reading reliability, since they result in apparent jitter. In this context, it is worth mentioning the extended belief, not quite technically assessed, that eel-skin wallets erase magnetic stripes.

2.1.4 High-Coercivity Stripes

The magnetic field required for magnetizing or erasing a stripe depends on the material coercivity. In the world of magnetic stripes, several *coercivities* are employed and often misused. The *intrinsic* coercivity, a characteristic of the material, is given by its hysteresis loop. The *effective* coercivity, a more practical parameter, is defined as the magnetic field required for the material to be saturated in operating conditions. Coercivity specifications given by manufacturers are often expressed as nominal values.

The traditional gamma ferric oxide stripes are encoded at 300 oersteds (Oe). In the past few years, there has been increasing interest in the use of high-coercivity materials in magnetic media, including cards' magnetic stripes. These materials, such as barium ferrite, require magnetic fields ranging from 2,000 to 4,000 Oe or more. The obvious advantage of high-coercivity materials is an enhanced magnetic immunity; that is, the magnetic damage from accidental exposure to magnetic fields is greatly reduced. The adaptation of encoding systems to these stripes is relatively easy. However, for high-coercivity stripes to be acceptable, it is crucial that reading equipment, especially in EPOS, remains unchanged. There have been some reports describing alterations in the reader response when using high-coercivity magnetic stripes. Some magnetic head manufacturers have warned that coercivities over 3,000 Oe may cause problems in equipment. Nevertheless, high coercivity seems to be the future of magnetic stripe cards, although the precise ranges have not been set.

2.1.5 Fraud in Financial Magnetic Stripe Cards

Financial cards are by far the main application of magnetic stripe cards. About one billion magnetic stripe cards have been issued worldwide in the last decade. This widely accepted "plastic money," however, has also produced new kinds of crime, mostly derived from security pitfalls of the magnetic media. For instance, three people in Spain obtained over $10 million by using forged magnetic stripe cards before being discovered in September 1993. In 1992, quite conservative estimates of card fraud in the U.S. were about $200 million. In the U.K., card fraud increased 100% from 1989 to 1990, and 25% again in 1991, reaching £150 million. These figures do not include credit losses (i.e., settlement failures). Conversely, France reported for the first time a 5% decrease in card fraud in 1991 (although transactions increased 15%). This decrease coincides with the implementation of chips in French financial cards.

The following paragraphs describe the four primary methods of magnetic stripe card fraud.

- *Theft.* Legal cards may be stolen and used in ATMs or EPOSs. Temporarily off-line ATMs may be used for finding out cards' PIN. Many cardholders modify their original card PINs, assigning numbers easier to remember (e.g., birthdays, repeated digits). Even worse, some users write down their PINs elsewhere. If the card is stolen with the entire wallet or purse, the thieves may find out the PIN in a few minutes.

- *Counterfeit.* Fraudulent cards may be prepared by reading another (e.g., stolen) legal card and encoding a piece of magnetic tape with the same sequence. The tape is then affixed on a credit card-sized piece of plastic (or on an actual credit card). PINs may be searched for with multiple copies of the same card.

- *Buffering.* To avoid reaching the card limit in ATM cash withdrawal, the original data may be read and stored elsewhere. Once the card is depleted, former data are recovered and encoded back onto the card.

- *Skimming.* Original encoded data may be altered, or additional data may be encoded in the stripe. This is used, for example, to increase the card's credit limit.

All the above methods, except the first one, are specific to magnetic stripe cards. It is not difficult for anybody with some technical skills to read and encode magnetic stripes using standard electronic equipment. Digital audio tape units, now common in consumer electronics, open new possibilities for low-cost magnetic stripe card fraud.

PINs alone may not be adequate for financial cards. As an example, let us mention an example of sophisticated fraud developed several years ago in Italy, and repeated in April 1993 in Connecticut. In the latter case, three men placed a forged ATM in a shopping center. More than 2,000 people attempted to use it. After inserting their cards and entering their PINs, the ATM displayed an "Out of Order" message and returned the cards. The swindlers removed the ATM two weeks later, and used the collected database of cards and PINs to prepare counterfeit cards. By the time it came to light, the thieves had obtained $58,000 from their victims' accounts.

2.1.6 Magnetic Stripe Security

Concerns about financial card security, especially in magnetic stripe cards, have led to the development of several security techniques for either avoiding more card fraud or making it difficult. All the techniques mentioned below are manufacturers' patents and/ or trademarks.

ValuGard from Rand McNally relies on the imperfections and irregularities of standard magnetic stripes. Although these alterations are within acceptable limits for the card to function properly, they are electronically measurable. The company claims that it is possible to obtain a *card fingerprint* whose parameters are encrypted and stored in separate tracks of the card. The system is completed with a special read head that allows the reading of these tracks along with regular data tracks.

XSec from XTec Inc. employs the natural jitter of the encoded data to produce a security *signature* of the card. Again, this signature is claimed to be unique for every card. Standard jitter tolerances are within 5% to 15% of the bit length. The XSec system measures jitter to a precision of 0.5% with digital techniques. The company states that their system works on standard cards with standard equipment, the only hardware modification being an XSec chip for jitter measurements that can be easily included in existing terminals.

Watermark Magnetics from Thorn EMI involves modifications in the structure of the magnetic medium. Watermark tapes contain blocks of ferric oxide needles oriented perpendicularly to the usual longitudinal orientation. Unique patterns are obtained when the stripes are encoded. These patterns are permanently fixed in the tape; that is, they cannot be magnetically erased. The patterns are used to build hexadecimal numbers for tagging the tapes. Eventually these tapes are applied to the cards using conventional laminating techniques. A track 0 contains the Watermark pattern; therefore, Watermark stripes are not usually placed in the same position as regular stripes, but slightly closer to the card edge, allowing tracks 1 to 3 to be placed in their standard positions. The system requires specific Watermark Magnetics readers to read the structural information included in the extra track (regular tracks are compatible with the existing magnetic systems). To improve security, the reading system is not based on the magnetic state of the stripe, but on a combined amplitude-modulated and frequency-modulated resonant circuit. According to the company, over 100,000 Watermark readers are currently being used throughout the world.

Another system modifying the regular magnetic stripe of the card is Imprint Magnetics from General Electric Company (GEC). GEC Imprint (GIM) cards contain several patches of high-coercivity magnetic material located in various positions around the card outside the stripe area. Earlier versions had seven patches, one in each of the four corners and three on the longitudinal card axis. Current models have five patches; two in the lower corners and three on the axis. This magnetic material has some built-in security features for avoiding cloning and data alteration.

2.1.7 Nonfinancial Magnetic Stripe Cards

Magnetic stripe cards are also employed in different fields other than the financial world. In most instances, the cards are used for ID purposes. For example, the French Santé-Pharma magnetic stripe cards are used for drug prescriptions in pharmacies. Nearly one million cards are expected to be in use by the end of 1993.

Public telephones in several countries use magnetic stripe cards. Semipublic phones, located in parlors, cafeterias, restaurants, and hotels, often accept regular credit cards, as do some public phones. Japan's NTT has sold over two billion magnetic prepaid phone cards over the last ten years. These thin (0.25 mm), colorful, high-quality printed cards are not strictly magnetic stripe cards, since a magnetic layer entirely covers the card's rear surface (this is called *magnetic wash*). More than 800,000 public phones in Japan are magnetic card phones. NTT has managed to create a widely accepted product, offering many versions that are even collected or used as informal gifts.

Watermark cards are used for public phones in several countries, including some areas of Ireland and Denmark. GIM phone cards are also used in these countries, as well as in the U.K. (Mercury Communications).

Within the limited capacity of magnetic stripes, some operators have managed to introduce several new card phone applications, such as short-code dialing and dialing a fixed number. The latter may be used by a sales manager as a business card for selected clients, or by parents providing their children with a cashless way to phone home.

Magnetic stripes are heavily used in public transportation as well. In this case, the paper or plastic substrate does not usually have the same size as that of standard credit cards. Technical Committee (TC) 224 of CEN (competent on machine-readable cards; see Chapter 7) has a working group devoted to *Thin Flexible Cards* (TFC). TFCs are defined as media (cards, badges, vouchers, tags, tickets, etc.) automatically readable by machines using different technologies, such as bar code, optical character recognition (OCR), and magnetic stripe. To date, only the first draft standard on this subject has been put into circulation by TC224. This draft covers magnetic stripe TFCs. The draft was rejected, chiefly as a result of pressure from U.S. manufacturers and standards' organizations. However, it is expected that a new, acceptable draft will be launched soon. TFC standardization would open new business areas to magnetic stripe manufacturers, especially in low-security environments, where price is usually the main argument for the implementation of a particular technology.

2.2 OPTICAL CARDS

Compared to magnetic stripe cards, optical cards are a newcomer. They are even newer than smart cards, since they became commercial at the beginning of the 1980s, although the underlying physics and technology have been known since the 1930s. The most representative optical card is LaserCard, a trademark of Drexler Technology Corp. Drexler has licensed most of the existing laser card writing/reading units worldwide, especially to Japanese and European companies. In 1989, Drexler reached an agreement with Canon (Japan), for Canon to be a second supplier of optical cards. Some other manufacturers have appeared since then in Canada and Japan.

Optical cards are usually associated with large storage capacity. Although this is essentially correct, it should be mentioned that there are also low-capacity, inexpensive optical cards. Indeed, optical prepaid cards (e.g., Landis and Gyr) for pay phones have been in use for a number of years in several countries, including Italy and the U.K. (BT). In these cards, the optical surface is reduced to a thin track similar to magnetic stripes. The surface contains a microscopic optical structure (hologram) stamped on the card. Surface reflections from a light source are measured under certain angles. The optical structure may be destroyed by applying heat. As the prepaid money is spent, a line of tiny melted marks is made in the stripe, irreversibly invalidating the area. Cards are thrown away when exhausted; obviously, they cannot be recharged. The manufacturing cost is about $0.30. The following sections focus on high-capacity optical cards.

2.2.1 Optical Card Standards

Optical card technology is quite recent; therefore, standards for these cards and associated devices are not yet official (as are most magnetic stripe standards). As happens in many other areas, including smart cards, manufacturers have provided *de facto* standards that are eventually "officialized" by international standards organizations following lengthy agreements between different manufacturers and administrations. Currently, several optical card manufacturers in Japan, Europe, and the U.S. follow the DELA standards (Figure

2.4), while the first ISO standards for optical cards, currently in draft international standard (DIS) form, are expected to be approved by 1994.

DELA is a group of American National Standards Institute (ANSI) draft standards for optical cards supported by the Drexler European Licensees Association (DELA). DELA standards specify the physical characteristics (part 1), the dimensions and locations of the optical stripe (part 2), the optical properties and characteristics (part 3), and the

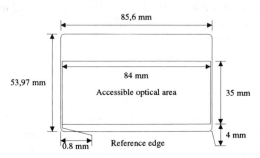

DELA standard

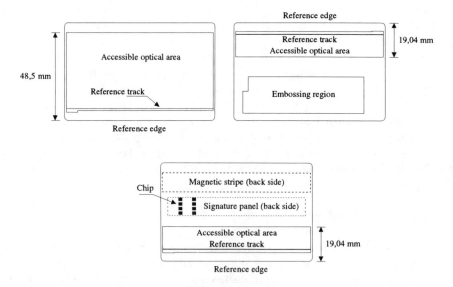

ISO standard

Figure 2.4 Optical cards according to DELA and ISO standards.

logical data structure (part 4) of optical cards. ISO applies general card standards for card material (ISO 7810), card dimensions (ISO 7813), and some physical characteristics (ISO 7816/1). Specific standards (drafts) for optical cards are ISO 11693 ("Optical Memory Cards") and ISO 11694 ("Optical Memory Cards—Linear Recording Method"). Unless otherwise stated, data given in these sections refer to "standard" optical cards. However, it is important to realize that standards themselves recognize the existence of different methods for writing and reading optical information. These methods are not usually compatible with each other.

2.2.2 Writing and Reading Optical Cards

Optical cards are usually operated with laser diodes. However, optical cards need not be, in principle, laser cards. Optical writing and reading may be achieved using other devices, such as light-emitting diodes (LED). Optical card drives of some manufacturers, like OMRON, employ a two-light source pickup: an LD is used for writing, while reading is carried out with an LED. The advantage of LDs is that, due to the unique properties of laser light (monochromaticity and coherence), its light may be focused onto extremely small spots. This in turn multiplies the bit density (i.e., the number of bits per surface unit). Moreover, light power in the spots may reach very high values, while LD power is relatively modest, since the power density is increased by the reduced spot size. ISO standards assume in their tests that LDs are used.

As mentioned in the first chapter, this high power density is used to burn tiny pits in the front optical surface of the card; the reflection properties of these pits are different from the former surface (Figure 2.5). In some optical card models, the original surface has high reflectivity, and the pits make visible a second, low-reflective, layer. (The opposite technique is also used in other optical storage media.) In other cases, the pits themselves have different reflectivity than their surrounding areas.

Bits are coded as high-reflectivity/low-reflectivity areas in the card. According to current standards proposals, the background reflectivity (i.e., the reflectivity of an unwritten region) shall be between 12% and 18%, or between 27% and 48%. Usual pit diameters are 5 μm or less, allowing the card to store several megabytes. ISO tests for optical cards specify a number of parameters of the light source: wavelength between 760 and 850 nm, writing power less than 10 mW, write beam pulse width 60 μs, read power 0.5 mW, and $1/e^2$ beam spot size 3 μm. (Some values are modified in different tests.)

Interestingly enough, ISO standards do not specify that pit reflectivity should be lower than background reflectivity. Instead, a contrast ratio is defined as the *relative* difference between these reflectivities (i.e., the reflectivity difference divided by the background reflectivity). Contrast shall be higher than 0.3. Incidentally, reading by reflection is not taken for granted either. In fact, ISO standards provide reference data for both reflection and transmission reading. Anyhow, reflection is the manufacturer's preferred technique at present. (Transmissive cards would require the card body to be transparent and to remain transparent throughout the card's life.)

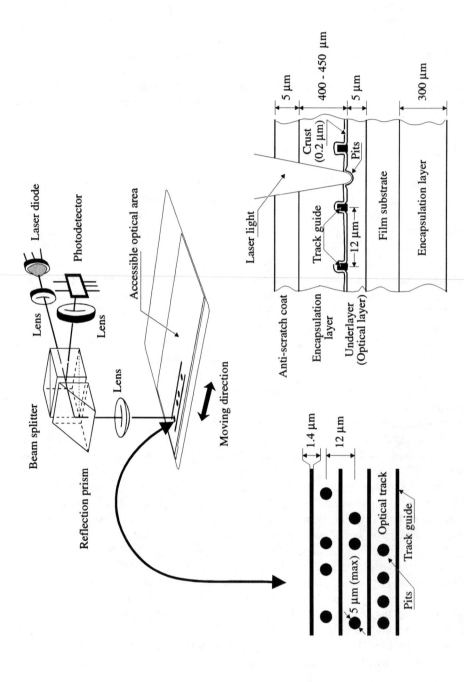

Figure 2.5 Writing/reading system in optical cards. Below right: the optical card section, showing the protective and active layers.

It is worth mentioning that some other card types use optical reading, but should not strictly be considered optical cards, since the writing process is not optical. For example, bar code and OCR cards are read by optical means. Permanent information may be stored in card-shaped devices and eventually read with LDs. These devices may be manufactured using the same techniques as audio compact disks (CD) and computer CD-ROMs (i.e., by molding the surface with a stamper). Again, these cards are not purely optical.

2.2.3 Formatting Optical Cards

The most common (and possibly the future standard) method of storing information in optical cards is called *linear recording*. In this system, digital data are stored in a linear x-y format. The optical surface is divided into longitudinal tracks; every track is filled with a linear array of holes (pits) containing the data bits. Optical card drives usually push forward and pull back the card longitudinally, while the laser head is fixed or scans the card laterally. (Other manufacturers, such as the Canadian company ORC, argue that linear recording is cumbersome and inaccurate. They claim that spinning the card and using circular tracks increases the storage to hundreds of megabytes while considerably reducing the access time. Polaroid has also filed a patent on an optical card with circular storage. No commercial products, to our knowledge, have yet been launched using this technology.)

The number of tracks is very large, typically over 2,500. (Note that optical cards may be combined with magnetic stripe, embossing, and/or chip. The card area reserved for optical use is different in each case, hence the storage capacity and number of tracks. A DELA optical card with no extra features has 2,571 tracks.) For the writing/reading operations to be successful, a highly accurate positioning of the laser head is required. To achieve this, preformatted lines called *track guides* are drawn on the card's optical surface. These guides have different (usually less) reflectivity than the background; each array of data bits is written between two track guides. ISO standards indicate that the contrast between the tracks and the track guides shall be higher than 0.3. Tracks are then divided into one or several sectors. Prior to use, other formatting information may be recorded: track addresses, sector addresses, error detection blocks, and clock synchronizations.

2.2.4 Error Correction in Optical Cards

Like any other optical storage medium, optical cards are affected by dust, fingerprints, and scratches on the outer, transparent surface. Manufacturers, being aware that card surfaces are far more exposed to the environment than any other optical storage, have managed to improve significantly the mechanical properties of these surfaces. Still, the bit error rate (BER) of optical cards is very high, from 0.001 to 0.0001. (The suggested figure in ISO standards is 0.0005).

According to standards, any anomaly in the optical surface greater than 2.5 μm is considered a defect. In addition, errors are produced during reading and/or writing. The most common errors in optical cards are called *drop-ins* and *drop-outs*. Drop-in is the incorrect detection of a bit not previously recorded. It usually comes from external defects reducing the reflectivity of the area. Drop-out is the failure to read a previously recorded bit. It may come from an incorrect recording of the area (e.g., a dirty outer surface reducing the laser power, thus producing defective pits), or from external causes increasing the reflectivity. Anyhow, such a huge BER is unacceptable for most digital storing applications. For example, storing text with a 0.001 BER would be equivalent to having, on average, a mistake in every text line. Only low-accuracy-demanding information, such as scanned image bit maps, can tolerate such a rate.

For this reason, optical card storage usually employs error correction strategies. Such a practice is so extensive that vendors specify the storage of their cards assuming the overhead of implementing error detection and correction (EDAC) methods. DELA cards use a (272, 190) cyclic code in which 82 bits for error correction are appended to every group of 190 data bits. This method guarantees recovery of up to 9 wrong bits per group. The actual storage capacity of the card is reduced by EDAC from 4.1 to 2.8 MB.

Error correction techniques are commonly associated with *interleaving*. In this context, interleaving is a procedure by which consecutive data are not consecutively stored in the card, but placed in different locations. This procedure avoids *error clustering*, i.e., the accumulation of errors in the same data sector due to a major defect on the optical surface (EDAC is only able to recover up to 9 bits out of 190). With this system, most sectors are successfully stored and retrieved. The use of EDAC and interleaving dramatically reduces BER. Technical specifications of current optical card drives give a typical BER figure of 10^{-12} (i.e., one bit per trillion).

Typically, the optical card drive writes the information when the card is moving in one direction and verifies the track contents when coming back; a track check mark may then be added. Reading is performed in both directions. Thus, reading speed is usually twice the writing speed. Writing rates of current drives are 30 to 100 kbps, and reading rates double these figures. This is about one-half the rate of a floppy disk. Reading the full contents of an optical card may take several minutes.

2.2.5 Optical Card Applications

Optical cards, being essentially nonsmart, high-capacity storage devices, are not well suited to financial applications. Basic data for financial cards can be stored in the few hundred bytes available in magnetic stripe cards. Optical cards are far more expensive; their immunity to the aggressive mechanical and chemical environmental wear-and-tear is not significantly improved (although they are immune to magnetic fields and static electricity, of course) and, above all, they are not erasable. However, the latter argument is partially overcome by a huge memory that allows it, in fact, to hold a complete audit trail of all data additions and updates throughout the card's life span.

Quite understandably, optical cards have found the right place in applications requiring vast memory storage. The health care sector has traditionally been, and still is, the main consumer of optical cards. Medical images such as x-ray radiographies, ultrasound scans, tomographies, and nuclear magnetic resonance pictures can be stored in these cards, along with the entire medical record of the cardholder. Medical data are not usually erased; instead, new data are appended to the record. This practice suits WORM storage of optical cards. From a practical point of view, it has been argued that patients do not need to (or should not) carry their medical records; moreover, cards are easily lost. Therefore, the same information must be stored elsewhere. Following this argument, health care optical cards do no better than centralized health data bases. However, if these regionwide or countrywide health data systems are not implemented, optical cards could give any physician instant access to all health data of patients, regardless of their origin. Elsewhere in this book, the advantages and disadvantages of health care optical cards as compared to smart cards are discussed.

Health care optical cards are being used in Europe (Netherlands, Italy, Spain, and France), Japan, and the U.S. Generally, these cards are not yet employed for regular patients, but for selected groups (e.g., chronic or high-risk patients, children, pregnant women) or patients undergoing specific therapies (e.g., nuclear medicine, eye surgery). High-capacity storage of optical cards is useful for follow-up of long-term patients. Moreover, some medical image archive systems based on optical cards have been proposed.

Besides to their use in health care, optical cards are used in several fields. For example, the deployment of over 500,000 troops for Desert Shield and Desert Storm operations in the Persian Gulf was helped by an optical card-based application with regards to the contents of SeaVan containers used for supplies. Every container had two associated optical cards: one inside along with the paper documentation, and another affixed to the container surface. The container traveled with its card mates from origin to destination by sea and land transport. At every checkpoint, laser card readers were installed, allowing rapid information on all contents, which in turn updated the databases of supplies. The same system has been proposed for the Restore Hope operation in Somalia.

2.2.6 Erasable Optical Cards

In the last few years, erasable, rewritable optical devices have been marketed as massive storage peripherals for computers. A 5.25-in optical removable disk, for example, may store over 1 GB (1,000 MB) of data. Card technologies are usually adaptations of peer technologies developed for computers. It seems reasonable to expect the arrival of commercial erasable optical cards in the near future. A number of technical solutions, from reversible amorphous-crystalline alloys to various nonlinear optical effects, have been proposed for erasable optical storage. However, looking at current optical disk technologies, only two possible solutions for erasable optical cards seem feasible in the short term: hybrid magnetic/optic storage and magneto-optical storage.

Hybrid magnetic/optic storage is not strictly optical. Tracks are drawn on the disk surface similar to the track guides described above. These guides, illuminated by LEDs or LDs, are used by *optical* sensors to locate a *magnetic* read/write head on the tracks. Data storage and retrieval are done by magnetic devices. The accurate positioning achieved by optical means allows a substantial increase in the disk storage capacity. For instance, a hybrid 3.5-in floppy disk stores up to 21 MB of data. In addition, since purely magnetic writing/reading technology is used, the same disk drive may be used for regular floppy disks. Similarly, hybrid magnetic/optic card drive units could manage current magnetic stripes as well as high-capacity storage cards.

Magneto-optical storage is becoming competitive in computer applications demanding high-capacity storage requirements. It is based on two phenomena called the *Faraday effect* (for light transmission) and the *magneto-optical Kerr effect* (for light reflection, not to be confused with another common nonlinear phenomenon called the *electro-optical Kerr effect*). Most magneto-optical devices employ the Kerr effect. This effect is based on changes produced by some magnetized materials on the *polarization* of incoming light. Light polarization is described by the orientation of its oscillating electric field in the plane perpendicular to the light propagation direction. If this orientation is constant, light is said to be linearly polarized. When a linearly polarized light beam impinges on a magneto-optical surface, its polarization may be modified by the surface magnetization. The polarization of the reflected light, therefore, may be rotated from the original polarization. Changes in light polarization are easily transformed into changes in light intensity by placing a polarizer in the reflected light path. Thus, light is used as a probe to find out the magnetic orientation on the surface. The information is stored by using two opposite magnetic orientations of the surface, as in magnetic stripes. However, these orientations are not longitudinal, but perpendicular to the surface.

Information recording is optical, too. Magnetic materials can be demagnetized by heating them above a certain temperature called the *Curie point*. Over this point, the material becomes paramagnetic; that is, the magnetic domains disappear. If a magnetic field is then applied and the material is allowed to cool down, it becomes magnetized again and is preferentially oriented according to the external magnetic field. In magneto-optical materials, data recording is achieved by heating microscopic zones of the surface with a focused laser diode. These heated areas are then oriented by a magnetic field placed close to the beam spot (in magneto-optical disks, the disk rotation brings the heated surface to the magnetic field). It is important to realize that no magnetic recording is done. The information is provided by laser pulses heating specific areas of the surface; nonheated areas are not modified by the magnetic field. The magnetic field is constant, and thus carries no information. In 1989, 3M unveiled a prototype of a plastic card containing a magneto-optical rewritable disk in the center, which was claimed to store up to 28 MB.

2.3 CHIP-BASED STORAGE CARDS

Chip-based cards with high storage capacity are at present the latest newcomer provided by card manufacturers. The Personal Computer Memory Card Industry Association (PCMCIA) has supported and standardized several products having the same dimensions as credit cards except thickness. These cardlike units contain microelectronic ICs, including memory chips and several kinds of memory managers (Figure 2.6). Three standard thicknesses are presently established: 3.3, 5.0, and 10.5 mm. The plastic body of these cards is covered with stainless steel panels producing rugged, reliable devices.

PCMCIA cards are mainly intended to be used in portable computers. Within this context, they are usually known as IC memory cards. IC memory cards are used as memory extensions in portable, notebook, and palmtop computers; even more importantly, IC memory cards may be used to transfer data from one portable computer to another or to a desktop personal computer, thus mimicking the role of floppy disks. This feature may be decisive in the design of smaller DOS computers. Those cards replacing floppy disks are called *PC cards* by the PCMCIA.

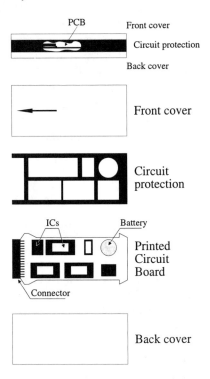

Figure 2.6 PCMCIA cross section and components. PCMCIA cards have an edge 2 × 34-pin connector. PCMCIA slots are becoming popular in portable computers.

Not surprisingly, the first standards for IC memory cards were launched in Japan. Japanese companies are almost the only manufacturers of these cards. A national standard was developed by JEIDA, a Japanese standards organization. Contacts with JEIDA began in 1989 to adopt or amend the Japanese standard in order to achieve an international standard. In 1990, it was agreed that version 4 of the JEIDA standard would be adopted worldwide.

PCMCIA standards include the definition of the slot for card insertion. Over 100,000 portable computers are estimated to be shipped with PCMCIA slots in 1993. Cards are provided with an edge connector containing 68 pins in two staggered rows of 34 pins each. It is worth mentioning that the same standard is used by other peripherals such as modems and radio-frequency transceivers.

PCMCIA memory cards support all kinds of permanent and volatile memory, such as dynamic and static RAM, EEPROM, and flash (see Chapter 4 for description). Card prices vary depending on the type and amount of memory. Prices are expected to decrease as new technologies like chip-on-board and multichip modules replace the existing technology. Current PCMCIA cards store up to 32 MB, and their price is about $400.

Compared to the above described cards and smart cards, PCMCIA cards are not, for the moment, a competitor looking for a share in the card markets. However, since memory prices are steadily declining, it is not impossible for these devices to become a serious competitor in a few years. Smart cards would still be the best choice in many areas where their unsurpassed security features are required. (Moreover, smart card memory is expected to reach 1 MB by the year 2000.) Optical cards, however, would have to face a presumably faster, erasable alternative mass-storage medium requiring no expensive peripherals for attaching to a computer. Should the price of PCMCIA cards fall below $20 by the end of the decade, as some experts predict, the optical card market may be seriously threatened.

2.4 CONCLUSIONS

In this chapter, the main nonsmart card technologies have been extensively revised. Advantages and disadvantages of every technology have been pointed out. With regard to market sectors, magnetic stripe cards are the preferred choice for financial applications; optical cards, to a lesser extent, are used in mass-memory applications, especially in health care. PCMCIA cards are currently classified as memory extensions for portable computers, rather than personal information dossiers (they are too expensive for that); therefore, they are not envisaged to be found in card applications for a while.

If a single word had to be chosen for defining each card technology, most people would associate magnetic stripe cards with price, optical cards with storage, and smart cards with security. Sensitive data are generated in many areas, and the financial and health care sectors are not exceptions. Therefore, although magnetic stripe cards and optical cards do not compete with each other, smart cards share markets with both of them. Hybrid cards containing two or the three systems (magnetic stripe, optical surface, chip) are well suited to a number of applications in several sectors. However, some technical problems may arise from the different codification of magnetic stripes and chips (7 bits and 8 bits per character, respectively).

The next chapter is an overview of chip card technology and applications, and it may be used to compare the performance of chip cards (both memory and smart cards) with the data storage cards described in this chapter. It is also an introduction to smart card concepts used in subsequent chapters.

Chapter 3
Chip Cards

At 7:30 in the morning, at the exact time she had programmed it the previous evening with her smart card, Iona B. Ming is awakened by the chime of her videophone. While dressing, she inserts her smart card into the same videophone slot for checking the latest stock market trends; the information is provided by a financial service after a remote checking of her subscription. Before leaving the building, she uses the card to switch the burglar alarm on, access the underground garage through the elevator, get into her car, and switch off the vehicle's blocking system. All these applications are stored in the personal area of her card.

Iona is the sales manager of a company whose premises are located in a smart building. The professional area of her smart card stores information concerning the security gates she may come through and building areas she is permitted to enter. Some of these gates give access to highly restricted areas. To get admittance, she has to insert the card in the door slot and repeat a sentence shown in a display, since the gates are activated by voice recognition. She prefers this biometric system to the fingerprint scanner she had to use in her last job.

Once in her office, she inserts the card into her desk phone to advise the phone system that calls to her personal number are to be addressed to that phone. Moreover, by entering a personal keyword, the phone repeats all the messages left for that number since the previous day. She then inserts the card into a slot of her desktop terminal. The company's mainframe computer carries out a user authentication allowing her to access her private files. Revising the health care area of her card, the computer also reminds her that she has a medical checkup for hypertension that afternoon. Later in the morning, she has a meeting in another room in the building. Because the agenda is quite long, she inserts her card in the meeting room phone to get her calls redirected to that location. At lunch time, she meets some clients in a nearby restaurant. The lunch bill is paid using one of the card's credit lines, in this case the company's line. Some commercial agreements have been achieved during the lunch. A draft document prepared on a portable computer is sent via modem to the company and to the clients' office. Since the document holds sensitive information, the transmission is enciphered using the card's built-in encryption algorithm.

In the afternoon, she undergoes her medical checkup. She has arrived a bit early, and has a soft drink while she is waiting. The drink is obtained from a vending machine using the prepaid area of the card. The physician finds her latest blood pressure data in the card, since she had her last check up during summer holidays in a different health care center (whose data are also in the card). A change in the treatment had been recommended. The physician agrees with the new therapy and issues an electronic drug prescription, which allows Iona to obtain her medication at the pharmacy for the next two months.

Back at home, she orders some goods from the supermarket, which are charged to her personal credit line. After dinner she relaxes for a while watching a coded TV channel whose subscription is stored in the card. Because the image quality is poor, she sends a message to the TV company requesting a new remote recording of the card decoding area. At the same time, she renews her subscription using the debit area of the smart card.

Iona is fictitious, but the story need not be. Current smart cards are able to perform every task described above. More importantly, the latest card models are able to perform multiple tasks by splitting the card memory into several independent areas whose access is restricted to single service providers. Iona's card may become a commercial product in two or three years.

This chapter provides a general overview of chip cards (also called *IC cards*). Two chip card families, chip memory cards and smart cards, are separately studied, along with some special card types, such as contactless cards, and related smart devices, such as smart keys and smart disks. Card development and evolution, early experiences, and basic concepts of performance and application areas are also included. This approach provides an overall knowledge of the cards' rich world, prior to delving into more technical matters in later chapters.

3.1 ORIGIN OF CHIP CARDS

The first implementation of microelectronic devices in plastic substrate is attributed to a Japanese inventor, Kunitaka Arimura, who filed his first patent concerning "a plastic card incorporating one or more integrated circuit chips for the generation of distinguishing signals" in 1970. The patent mainly focused on microcircuit embedding rather than functional features of the system. Moreover, the patent was filed with a scope restricted to Japan. For these reasons, Arimura's patents had reduced influence on eventual card development, except in Japan, where all manufactured cards are under license from the Arimura Technology Institute.

A few years later, in 1974, a renewed interest in smart cards arose in France. There, the journalist Roland Moreno rediscovered the issue and filed his first patent on "an independent electronic object with memory.'' In this case, more attention was paid to the functional aspects of the card, including the use of secret keywords, such as PIN, for access control of the card's stored data. In the same year, Moreno founded the *Societé Internationale pour l'Innovation* (Innovatron) with the purpose of developing the new technology and extending its patents worldwide. Currently, most chip card manufacturers are licensees of Innovatron. Many people consider 1974 to be the starting point of the smart card era.

3.1.1 First Chip Card Manufacturers

The first licensee of Innovatron was Honeywell Bull, a major French computer manufacturer. (Eventually, in 1985, Bull CP8 was created for the chip card and magnetic stripe card business.) Bull, in collaboration with Motorola, shipped the first chip card (without microprocessor) to Innovatron in 1976 and the first smart card (with microprocessor) in 1979. The very first CP8 smart card had two chips, one containing the memory and the other the microprocessor. This system was rather unreliable, since the connecting wires between the chips could be easily damaged by normal use. Even worse, the card security was jeopardized by the connecting bridge, because memory contents could be easily violated by tampering with the wires. Eventually, Bull developed a single chip card and filed a patent for it. This patent was successful, since almost all manufacturers of microchips for cards have taken licenses for it.

Other French companies or subsidiaries soon joined Bull as chip card manufacturers. By the beginning of the 1980s, the technology was mature enough to attract the interest of the French government along with the financial, health care, and telecommunications sectors. (French banks were more prone to improve security in financial transactions than their colleagues in other countries, because French ATMs, due to computer network regulations, usually operate off line.) It was time to verify the new product performance and economic viability under real conditions by launching a series of field tests.

3.1.2 Early Experiences

The most important trial in these early days was conducted by the French Bank Card Association, currently *Carte Bancaire*, between 1982 and 1984. A working group including *Carte Bleue* (Blue Card, related to VISA) and *Carte Verte* (Green Card, related to MasterCard), along with the Telecommunications Administration, was formed. The overall experience, called *IPSO*, included more than 100,000 cards and over 700 EPOSs. Several experiments were carried out in three French cities: Blois, Caën, and Lyon. Three chip card manufacturers, Bull, Schlumberger, and Philips, were selected for the experience.

Because one of the goals was to establish the best technology for smart cards, each manufacturer used a different technical approach. Bull employed 8-kb Motorola MC6805SC01 microprocessor-based CP8 cards in Blois (20,000 cards, 250 EPOSs);

Schlumberger distributed 4.6-kb wired logic cards in Lyon (50,000 cards, 200 EPOSs), and Philips used a two-chip card based on the 16-kb Intel 8021 microprocessor in Caën (50,000 cards, 250 EPOSs).

From a technical point of view, the results of the IPSO experience were excellent. The problems reported by the cardholders and retailers were negligible, and the overall opinion of the users was very positive. Upon evaluation of the competing technologies, *Carte Bancaire* selected the Bull CP8 smart card as the most suitable system for financial applications. Moreover, the use of a hybrid card (magnetic stripe and chip) was recommended to guarantee that the card would be compatible with the existing magnetic-based technology.

The IPSO experience, along with other tests, has ultimately resulted in France having the largest financial smart card market in the world. French banks had issued over 21 million smart cards by the end of 1992. Besides the banking system, the Schlumberger wired logic card was selected as the best product for pay phones. Indeed, the 256-bit F256 card, an offspring of the former card, is at present a de facto standard in public telephones. As for Philips, an agreement was signed between Philips and Bull in 1984, allowing Philips to manufacture CP8 cards under Bull's license.

Other experiences followed in France and other countries. For example, experiments with university cards started in 1983. Tests were done at different times in the universities of Paris, Lille, and Rome. These applications are discussed extensively in Chapter 8. Another major event in the card's history occurred in 1986. This was the appearance of the first standard for IC cards, ISO 7816/1. This event is perhaps the turning point between the early and current experiences in the smart card world.

3.1.3 Chip Cards for Public Phones

Yet another major event related to cards took place in 1986. That year, after several trials in reduced areas, the French telecommunication authorities decided to use prepaid chip cards for public pay phones. The French public phone network required by those days a major renewal. Public telegraph and telephone (PTT) authorities were concerned about the increasing vandalism and theft occurring in coin pay phones and their consequences in service quality and maintenance costs.

Chip cards were demonstrated to be a cost-effective solution. Although the investments and unit price were larger than those of more traditional systems, the difference was largely compensated for by the reduction in vandalism and thefts. Moreover, the overall quality of the service improved as a result of this reduction, since more phones were available to users for a longer time without failures. As a consequence, the use of public phones increased significantly in France in subsequent years.

The French example was followed by many other countries, mainly European ones (Figure 3.1). Today, more than 30 national PTTs employ chip cards for their public phone systems. In fact, prepaid phone cards are the largest application for chip cards. Perhaps three out of every four cards sold in the world are used in this area.

Figure 3.1(a) Public pay phone that accepts coins, chip cards, and magnetic stripe cards. (Courtesy of Telefónica)

3.2 CARD SECURITY

Chip cards, especially smart cards, are provided with a number of hardware and software security features. Software protection is based on data access control and the use of encryption techniques. Hardware protection is included in the IC during manufacturing. In this section, the fundamentals of encryption systems and their application to cards are reviewed, along with some details regarding access control. Hardware protection for chip cards is studied in the next section.

Cryptography, the study of secret writing and cipher systems, is a venerable science. People have used encoded messages for centuries. It was not until the advent of computers, however, that cryptography has been able to develop almost invulnerable encoding systems defying the most sophisticated counterfeiting techniques. One of the first computers ever built was used to decipher the German codes from the famous electromechanical ENIGMA cipher machine during World War II. Current computer encryption systems rely on algorithms whose average resolution time is measured in hundreds or thousands of years (or the age of the universe, in some cases).

3.2.1 PIN in Magnetic Stripe Cards

Magnetic stripe cards usually hold a PIN for the cardholder to prove his/her identity. An enciphered version of the PIN is stored in one of the card tracks. Since the card security

Figure 3.1(b) Colorful collection of telephone chip cards. (Courtesy of Telefónica)

relies on an external system (a networked computer or an off-line EPOS), it is the system's responsibility to allow the transaction to progress. The enciphered version of the PIN is read; the user is requested to enter the PIN, and the external system performs a number of operations using the PIN and one or several secret numbers carefully hidden in the system's memory. The result of such operations is then compared to the card's enciphered PIN. If both match, the transaction is permitted.

The weakest point of this scheme is interchange. ATMs from different financial companies and off-line EPOSs manufactured by others must share their enciphering keys for any system to manage someone else's cards. Encryption algorithms are usually one-way functions; that is, it is possible to obtain the result by knowing the PIN and the keys, but it is not possible to find out the PIN by knowing the keys and the result (which can be merely obtained by reading the card). Therefore, the PIN is relatively safe for on-line operations, as long as the system knows in advance which result it should expect. Off-line transactions, however, can only check whether the result matches the card's enciphered PIN. Unless additional protecting mechanisms are set, it might be possible to store the enciphered result of a new PIN on a forged card.

3.2.2 Message Encryption and Decryption

Encryption techniques are customarily based on secret words or *keys*. Many techniques are currently in use, depending on the purpose of the encryption process, which in turn determines the use and scope of secret keys.

In *symmetric* cryptosystems, there is one secret key, which is shared by the sender and the recipient of the message. The same key is used to encrypt and decrypt the message (Figure 3.2(a)). Confidentiality is guaranteed as long as the key is kept secret. The most well-known example of a symmetric system is DES.

In *asymmetric* cryptosystems, two keys are used. The first one, called the *private key*, is known only to the user. The second key, called the *public key*, is publicly known. Every user has a private and a public key. These keys are linked to each other: one is used for encryption and the other for decryption (Figure 3.2(b)). Several encryption strategies may be achieved with these systems (see below). The best known asymmetric system is RSA (after its creators, R. Rivest, A. Shamir, and L. Adleman).

Zero knowledge cryptosystems are based on one or several keys known only to a third party, the authority granting the communication or access rights. These systems are less suitable for messages, but are often used in the computer world for identification purposes. Neither the one demonstrating his/her identity nor the one verifying it needs to know the system's secret keys or encryption algorithms.

3.2.3 Secret Codes in Smart Cards

Smart card contents are usually protected by a number of secret codes. One or several encryption algorithms (typically DES) are also stored in protected memory areas. Secret

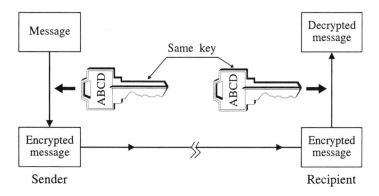

Figure 3.2(a) Symmetric cryptosystem: sender and recipient share the same key.

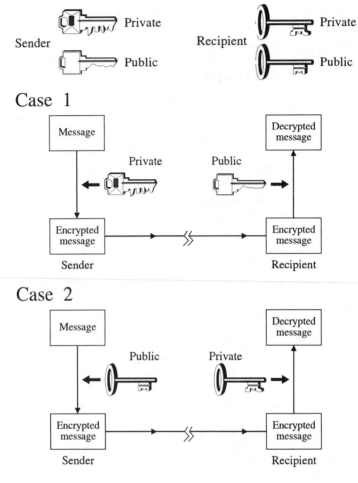

Figure 3.2(b) Asymmetric cryptosystem: in the first case, the sender uses his/her private key and the recipient decrypts the message with the sender's public key. In the second case, the sender uses the recipient's public key and the recipient decrypts the message with his/her private key.

keys for encryption algorithms are stored by the manufacturers or by selected issuers. The manufacturers also store some private information concerning personalization. This process, described in Chapter 7, allows cards of the same model to be split into unrelated families, thus avoiding security leaks coming from peer cards manipulated by unauthorized users. Personalization data are vital for card security; these are protected by one or several *manufacturer keys* and possibly by encryption processes.

When issuers design applications for any given customers, they include further personalization in the cards. Moreover, it is customary to reserve one or more *issuer keys* within the memory space for shielding areas where sensitive information is stored. Depending on the card model, issuer keys may be taken from the stock of regular secret codes, or be special keys prepared by the manufacturer. It is customary to have at least one special key in the card, which is usually owned by the issuer. This is called *master key*. Privileges of master key may include permission to perform some restricted commands, such as partial or total card erasing (except the manufacturer's area, of course), PIN reactivation, loading of electronic purses, or utilization of encryption/decryption facilities. Master keys are usually encrypted.

The remaining memory and secret codes are left for users. User/application memory (see next chapter) is divided into files. Each file may be protected by one or more secret codes for reading and/or writing processes. Depending again on the card model, one of the user's secret codes may have some privileges over the others. As a holdover of magnetic stripe cards' vocabulary, this code is usually called the PIN. (Actually, smart card PINs are not numbers, but alphanumeric strings.) PIN privileges include giving access to the entire application (i.e., to be the card's "gatekeeper") or being reactivated by a master key-protected command. (Note: reactivation is a process by which the card is brought back to life after consuming the allowed number of consecutive incorrect entries of a secret code. This does not mean erasing the code and issuing a new one; see Chapter 7 for details.)

Other user's secret codes may be employed for protecting partial aspects of the application. Logic functions are implemented in many cards for secret code handling, thus allowing combined protection of specific areas. For instance, writing permission on an area may be granted by secret codes #7 AND #12, while reading permission is granted by secret codes #3 OR #6.

The use of secret codes becomes more involved when several applications share the same card. Multiapplication cards from a single user can be managed much like the above. Multipurpose cards in open environments, which theoretically allow the user to select the applications (and the issuers) coming into the card, would require a strict control of data flow from/to the outside and within applications. These cards are currently under development, making use of the hierarchical file structure defined in ISO 7816/4.

Anyway, access to smart card memory is always controlled by the microprocessor, which is in charge of checking that all the permissions requested for reading or writing that particular memory area have been fulfilled. Above all, the ultimate decision of carrying out any transaction is adopted by the card itself, not by the system. On-line and off-line transactions are therefore functionally equivalent for a smart card.

3.2.4 Cryptography in Smart Cards

Smart cards use encryption processes to carry out several tasks. Many card models include DES as a built-in feature. Some manufacturers have developed other cryptosystems for telecommand, communications, or data handling (e.g., Bull's TELEPASS).

DES is a commercially available system sponsored by the U.S. National Institute of Standards and Technology (NIST) and the National Security Agency. The algorithm, based on a former IBM cryptosystem called Lucifer, provides 2^{56} possible combinations (checking all these combinations at a rate of 100,000 keys a second would take more than 22,000 years). Although it was launched in 1977, and some experts are concerned about its security nowadays, no reports (or crimes) have proven the ability to break DES. Every five years, NIST requests comments about maintaining DES as an encryption standard for another five years. The last request was in 1992; although more powerful cryptosystems (e.g., International Data Encryption Algorithm (IDEA)) have been proposed, it seems that DES will be approved for the next period. Enhanced security may be also achieved with DES itself by using *triple DES*: encrypt with key #1, decrypt with key #2, encrypt again with key #1. Triple DES increases the number of combinations up to 2^{112}.

Being a symmetric cryptosystem, DES keys are shared by both the sender and the recipient of the message (Figure 3.2(a)). One of them is the card and the other is an external system. In this way DES may be used for a number of services. *Access control* is achieved by entering one or several secret codes. Issuer's keys (e.g., the master key) are held by the system. Should the master key be required for any transaction, it might not be safe sending the actual key to the card, because the communication lines could have been tampered with. Instead, the master key is encrypted at the origin and the resulting string is sent. The card decrypts the string and compares it with its own copy. The master key is padded with random numbers to avoid repetitions in the encrypted string.

A similar process, called *challenge*, is used by the card to verify that the external system is authorized to work with it, or vice versa. For instance, the card challenges the system by generating a random number and sending an encrypted version to the external device. The system must decrypt the number and give the correct answer back to the card. This can only be achieved if the system holds the same keys as the card. The challenge may also be initiated by the system to verify the card.

Communications by modem or networks may be encrypted by the sender using a smart card and decrypted by the recipient with another smart card *of the same family*. (Encryption keys are varied every time a new batch of cards is prepared by the manufacturer.) Message *integrity* and *authentication* are achieved by computing a cryptographic checksum over the message using the shared encryption key.

Asymmetric cryptosystems are less commonly used by current cards. Although much slower than symmetric cryptosystems, these algorithms can perform sophisticated cryptographic processes; therefore, an increased use of such systems is expected in the near future. Several semiconductor manufacturers, such as Atmel and Philips, already include public-key encryption hardware in their chips. Algorithms may be implemented by the card's application designer; they need not be built in upon manufacturing. The NIST Datakey smart card, built on Hitachi's H8/310 microprocessor, implements an asymmetric cryptosystem. Cylink and Philips have both announced similar implementations.

Two linked keys, one public and one private, are used for encryption and decryption in these systems (Figure 3.2(b)). *Secured destination* is achieved by the sender using the recipient's public key to encrypt the message. This message can only be decrypted by using the associated private key. Therefore, only the recipient can decrypt the message. *Sender authentication* is performed by using the sender's private key for encryption. As the recipient receives the message, he/she decrypts it using the sender's public key. The recipient then knows that the message has been sent by the person whose public key has successfully decrypted it.

Asymmetric systems' keys are too long (e.g., 128 hexadecimal digits) for the user to memorize them. Should the private key be stored in a computer, protected by a password, the system would be vulnerable to password crackers. A much more secured system is achieved by using the memory of a smart card to store the key or an enciphered version of it. Switching roles, the smart card DES algorithm may be used for *message confidentiality* (i.e., messages decrypted by a specific recipient). This is achieved by choosing DES keys asymmetrically encrypted with the public key of the recipient. Once the keys are decrypted, they are shared only by the sender and the recipient. DES may then be used to send messages that cannot be decrypted by anybody else, even those people owning smart cards from the same batch. This procedure is similar to the secured destination described above; the advantage is that symmetric systems are much faster than asymmetric ones (e.g., Hitachi's microprocessor takes 20 sec to perform a 512-bit operation).

These strategies may be used to produce *digital signatures* (i.e., the electronic equivalent to handwritten signatures for authenticating documents). Digital signatures are appended to digested versions of messages.* Any message including a digital signature may be checked for authentication and integrity, as above, as well as for *nonrepudiation*. This is a procedure by which the recipient proves the identity of the sender to a third party. In asymmetric systems, this can be done by means of the sender's public key. The U.S. government has proposed a digital signature standard called DSS. Such a standard, if widely accepted, would allow real-time financial transactions and commercial agreements.

The public keys themselves may be questioned, especially if the sender and the recipient have never met. This is avoided with *public key certificates* containing the name of the key issuer, the public key, a validity period, and additional data from the user and his/her entity. These data are encrypted with the user's private key introducing a digital signature. In this way, the recipient may check at any time that the public key used to decrypt the message is the same as the key included in the message itself.

3.3 CHIPS FOR CARDS

When reading for the first time the technical characteristics of card chips, many people have the feeling that they are looking at an obsolete technology. A typical current smart card chip has an 8-bit microprocessor working at 5 MHz; the user memory is seldom

---

*Digital signatures are not usually linked to entire messages, but to a reduced version. This is called a *digest*.

higher than 8K. These characteristics could be found in the pioneer personal computers some 15 years ago. Since then, the clock frequency in PCs has increased up to 66 or even 100 MHz, and 32-bit microprocessors have become a common product (64-bit and 128-bit microprocessors now being available). The user memory is expressed in megabytes, not kilobytes.

3.3.1 Integration Scale in Microelectronics

The microelectronic industry has undergone an amazing evolution in the integration of active components (transistors) for preparing gates, the basic units of digital electronics. Beginning with small-scale integration (SSI) (less than 100 gates) through the development of medium- (MSI) and large-scale integration (LSI), the industry is at present comfortably situated in the very-large-scale integration (VLSI) range, making chips up to 100,000 gates. Most advanced circuits, like Intel 486 or Pentium, are leaping over this limit, placing themselves in a new integration range, sometimes called *ultra-large-scale integration* (ULSI) (Intel 486 has over 1,000,000 transistors; i.e., more than 250,000 gates).

At the same time, the design rule (i.e., the width of the silicon tracks from which the components are made) has been steadily decreasing. Ten years ago, the design rule was over 2 μm; at present, VLSI manufacturers are designing below 0.5 μm, probably in the 0.2- to 0.3-μm region. The design rule for card chips is about 1.0 to 1.5 μm. Again, it seems that the performance of card chips is well behind the state of the art of the microelectronic industry.

This is not the case, however; the manufacturers of card chips are among the world's leading semiconductor companies (see below). Chips for smart cards and, to a lesser extent, for memory cards, have unique features that avoid the use of leading-edge-scale integration:

- *Single Chip.* For the reasons stated above, all the microcircuit components—microprocessor, memory, input/output port—will be integrated in the same chip.
- *Memory.* Card chip memory, at least the user's memory, must be permanent; that is, it must store data for a long time without needing refreshing. This avoids the use of popular dynamic RAM (see Chapter 4). If user memory is also requested to be rewritable, the chip card memory becomes a technological challenge.
- *Security.* Card chips must be extremely rugged, not only for working properly under normal use, but also for avoiding security failures with improper use. This point deserves an explanation, which is presented in the next section.

3.3.2 Card Chip Security

When microelectronic manufacturers prepare a new microcircuit, it is sold with an accompanying data sheet or catalog, where the working conditions (e.g., voltage, frequency) are specified. Nobody wonders if a microcircuit designed for working at, say, 5V ±5% and 1.0 MHz ±10% fails at 10 MHz or behaves erratically with a 3V power supply.

This must not happen with smart card chips. Indeed, they have to work properly within specified conditions (usually 5V or 3V supply, 1 to 5 MHz); moreover, they have to be safe under any other conditions. This means that when the circuit is operated within other parameters, it may be destroyed, but under no circumstances may the stored information be read or altered. It must be also prepared for a power failure (card unplugging) at any time during its operation. The card should function properly after this. One should not expect this behavior in many digital electronic components. These factors make card chips unique in microelectronic design.

Wired logic chip memory cards are usually protected by the blowing of a fuse (physically or logically) once the required information is stored during manufacturing. Smart cards must be more versatile, especially the latest models designed for multifunction or multiapplication environments. In this case, the security requirements decisively affect the chip design and operation. Let us review some sophisticated fraudulent manipulations of smart cards and the corresponding countermeasures.

Power Consumption. Instruction sequences can be tracked by measuring the power consumption while the code is being executed. The smart card microprocessor may avoid this attack by generating erratic consumptions or by performing dummy operations in the meantime. This includes bit storage in dummy cells to avoid detection of physical memory locations.

Chip Extraction. Smart card chips should refuse to work when their encapsulation protection is removed. This avoids dangerous attacks using electronic microscopy (detecting currents in the chip) or microprobes. Countermeasures include light detectors and constraint monitoring. Permanent mechanical constraints are induced in the chip when embedding as a result of the hardening of the encapsulating material. Detecting the constraints on manufacturing, the chip may detect if it has been extracted from the card.

Low/High Voltage. A sudden change in the power supply voltage may cause the card to give access to forbidden memory areas, because it "thinks" the correct PIN has been entered. The microprocessor should be provided with a reference voltage for comparison with the actual power supply. If this is too high or too low, the card should refuse to work.

Partial Erasing. Although cards are protected against ultraviolet light and x-rays (see Chapter 4), it is theoretically possible to erase specific chunks of the memory by focusing high power beams. Card memory is scrambled to counter such practices, which could specifically erase vital information such as secret codes. Additionally, sentinel bits are randomly placed in the memory area. The microprocessor checks these bits from time to time, and stops working if they have been erased.

3.3.3 Card Chip Manufacturers

The section above shows that, regardless of their integration level and clock frequency, smart card chips are state-of-the-art electronic components. It is not surprising that only a few chip manufacturers in the world prepare chips for smart cards. There are about 200 manufacturers worldwide of smart cards and related equipment. However, unlike magnetic stripe cards, smart card manufacturers do not usually make their own chips, but get them from semiconductor suppliers. The following list of card chip manufacturers is believed to be correct at the beginning of 1993.

- Japan: Hitachi, NEC, Toshiba, Oki;
- U.S.: Texas Instruments, Atmel, Catalyst;
- Europe: SGS-Thomson (France), Philips (Netherlands), Siemens (Germany), Motorola (U.K.).[†]

The largest manufacturer of microprocessor smart card chips by that time was Motorola. The largest manufacturer of wired logic card chips was SGS-Thomson.

The market for chip cards is growing fast. The worldwide sales in 1991 were about 130 million units, jumping to nearly 200 million in 1992. Forecasts for 1993, as of this writing, point to 285 million units. Estimates for 1995 are quite diverse, but all the figures assume a steady increase of sales, perhaps doubling the 1993 amount. The share of smart cards in these overall figures is about 15%.

3.4 SMART CARDS AND SMART DEVICES

Smart cards, like any other plastic card, follow ISO and CEN standards both in physical dimensions and functional characteristics. These credit-card-sized smart cards are studied throughout the book. However, it is worth mentioning some smart card spin-offs designed for specific application areas for which the shape, size, or some functional aspects of standard cards are not suitable. Classified under the generic term *smart devices*, these less common smart units are covered here.

A few smart devices, such as reduced-size cards, are currently being standardized. Others are not yet fully developed or commercially established. Some of these devices are studied in Chapters 8 and 9, where smart card applications are reviewed.

3.4.1 Reduced-Size Cards

Cards smaller than typical credit cards have been proposed for a number of applications. Some of these cards, called *minicards* (Figure 3.3), are mainly designed for ticketing, especially in public transportation. As such, these cards are the size of a subway or bus paper ticket.

Some draft standards concerning minicards have been prepared by CEN. The exact dimensions have not been decided yet, chiefly because several countries want the card to have the precise dimensions of their current ticketing devices (e.g., the card width of the German proposal is 3 mm higher than French proposal, which matches the Paris

---

[†]Motorola is a well-known U.S. manufacturer; however, Motorola chips for smart cards are made in its manufacturing facility in East Kilbride, Scotland.

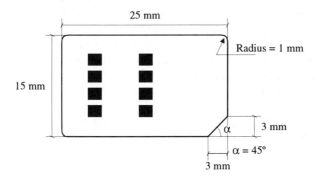

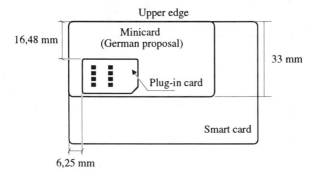

Figure 3.3 Plug-in card dimensions and contacts (top); plug-in card and minicard (German proposal) on top of a smart card matching the contacts (bottom).

subway ticketing machines; the chip position is also altered). Once an agreement is achieved, these cards would probably be provided with wired logic chips, since their scope does not require high security, and unit prices must be minimized.

Plug-in cards (Figure 3.3) are even smaller devices, the size of a postage stamp. These cards are not intended to be inserted and removed for every transaction, but to be permanently attached to another device, namely a mobile phone. Therefore, their size is just what is required to hold the chip contacts. Plug-in cards are smart cards. Standards should be ready in 1993. The chip of these cards is quite similar to those of regular smart cards, except that the power supply specification is 3V rather than the usual 5V. These cards are being developed as a component of the Global System for Mobile Communications (GSM) (see Section 9.2).

3.4.2 Smart Keys

Smart keys usually have an embedded microprocessor, much like smart cards. The physical shape has been changed simply to make its handling easier in several applications. Smart keys with no microprocessor are typically employed as magnetic keys for opening and closing gates of garages and parking lots. Real smart keys (i.e., with microprocessor have become popular in pay TV. In this case, the chip stores some crucial information linked to the required codes for descrambling the TV signal, along with payment supervision and remote control facilities.

3.4.3 Smart Disks

An offspring of Innovatron, smart disks or smart diskettes are devices designed as smart cards that can be handled by a computer with no extra peripherals. From the outside Innovatron smart disks look like any 3.5-in floppy disk (Figure 3.4). No disk is inside the plastic envelope, however—only memory and control chips, as well as a battery. A transducer emulates the magnetic field signals of standard magnetic media in such a way that the computer "thinks" that a regular disk has been inserted in the floppy disk drive However, unlike floppy disks, smart card disks can be protected like smart cards; the

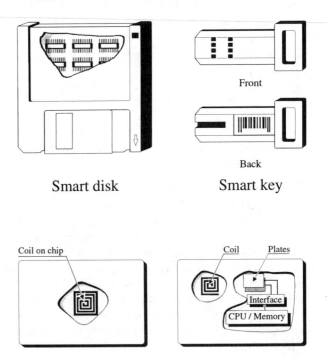

Smart disk   Smart key

Contactless cards

Figure 3.4 Smart devices.

information cannot be retrieved and the disk cannot be copied unless there is authorization. They can also be used as actual computers, allowing a peer-to-peer dialog with the PC.

Current smart disks have 1 to 3 MB of permanent memory; models having ten times as much have been announced. Some models hold a battery that is recharged by the spinning of the disk drive.

3.4.4 Contactless Cards

Contactless cards, first developed by the Arimura Institute in 1978, are chip cards in their own right. However, their appearance is different from the outside, since the microchip has no contacts; no direct electrical connection is established between the card chip and the interface device. Card dimensions are usually the same as those of ISO cards, except thickness, which varies from 0.76 mm (credit card standard) to about 3 mm. There is also a number of contactless *tokens* (keys, badges, etc.) with different shapes, some of them hardly identifiable as cards. Contactless cards may be classified under the criteria described below.

Power Supply. Besides the chip, the card may contain a battery for powering up the circuit. Otherwise, the card obtains its power from an external source. In the second case, the card has an embedded coil (Figure 3.4), which is inductively excited by an external electromagnetic field. Either method restricts card's functionality. Batteries must be periodically replaced and are affected by extreme temperatures more than silicon components are. Inductive coupling reduces the operation range and requires a relative orientation of the card and the electric field (e.g., the card and the field must be coplanar ±45 deg).

Range. The operation range is technically important, since it delimits the system's working conditions. Many contactless cards must be located at a small distance (a few millimeters) from their interface device. Others work at a distance of several centimeters (short range) or even meters (long range and ultralong range). The cards of the second group are called *slotless,* as opposed to the first cards, which are usually inserted into a slot, much like contact cards. Long-range (up to 2m) and ultralong-range (>2m) cards usually require batteries. Moreover, communication with these cards is usually more involved, since several cards may be simultaneously within the operation range of the device.

I/O, R/W. The cards may be read-only (R/O) or read-write (R/W). R/O cards, like optical bar codes, are employed for remote (i.e., nontouching) identification of people or goods. These cards are used where optical scanning is not feasible or is inappropriate. For example, subcutaneous implants of encapsulated contactless chips are used for identification of animals, such as dogs and horses. Long-range R/O contactless ID badges are useful for indoor security gates, since gate devices detect the cards while the bearers are still approaching them. R/W cards are closer to chip cards, sharing the same markets, although the lack of contacts results in some specific advantages and disadvantages as compared to contact-equipped cards.

Frequency. Cards operate in the low-frequency (LF), high-frequency (HF), and microwave (MW) spectral regions. Frequency is determined by national radio-frequency regulations and by the required data transfer rate. LF regulations usually allow enough power for the card to be powered by external induction. HF and MW cards are usually powered by batteries. As for data rate, LF carriers are very suitable for low data rates where transfer time is not important (e.g., ticketing in public transportation). At the other end of the scale, automatic, nonstop highway tolls are tested in cars running over 160 km/h (100 mi/h) using MW carriers. Data are transferred by inductive or capacitive coupling, which is achieved by embedding plates inside the card. Alternatively, the coil may be used for powering and communications. Data rates up to 19,200 bauds are achieved.

The coil is usually a separate component connected to the chip. Some card models (e.g., AT&T cards) include an additional interface chip. A *coil-on-chip* system has recently been presented; in this model, power and communications are included in the chip itself thus greatly simplifying embedding procedures.

The cost of contactless cards is quite variable, as can be easily deduced from the multiplicity of card models. Compared to contact chip cards, contactless cards are usually more expensive for the same chip performance, because the power system increases the price. As for security, contactless cards are traditionally considered less secure than their homologous surface-mounted contact cards, since it is easy to eavesdrop on radio communications. If sensitive information is handled, the use of cryptographic algorithms is mandatory in these cards. Nevertheless, contactless terminals (especially those for slotless cards) can be sealed, thus making vandalism more difficult.

Some typical applications in transport, where contactless cards' distinctive characteristics fit very well, have been already mentioned. The Greater Manchester Passenger Transport Executive (GMPTE) has recently ordered 500,000 contactless cards from GEC for train, tram, and bus stations.

3.5 CONCLUSIONS

Using chip cards to perform tasks and applications seems quite similar to using other cards from the user point of view. The innermost details of the transactions, however, are usually quite different. This chapter has presented an overview of these devices. The technical details can be found in the following chapters.

Security and versatility are probably the most noticeable characteristics of chip cards. However, a straight comparison of these card types is not a fair one, not even of their top models, without considering their relative prices. As a rule, any card issuer pays for security only if and when security matters, and forecasts of fraud losses or potential dangers make the investment in a new technology economically sound. Similarly, no issuer cares about versatility when the goal is a single-user, single-task application in which cards are thrown away after the expiry date.

Hybrid cards, especially smart cards with magnetic stripes, look like promising products for financial applications. Some issues have to be resolved before fully adapting these media. For example, 7-bit magnetic stripe coding, restricted to 128 ASCII characters, cannot support international alphabet letters such as the French ç, the German ß, or the Spanish ñ. Smart cards, working with 8-bit bytes, can support extended ASCII sets. An agreement is thus needed for these media to share the same information (e.g., embossed data).

The smart card market in the U.S. is quite modest. However, the expiry dates of initial U.S. patents on smart cards occur in 1993 and 1994, and this could stimulate the U.S. card industry.

Chapter 4
Anatomy of a Smart Card

In this chapter, we will take a fascinating trip through the microscopic world of card microelectronics. We will give you the ability to peer into the ICs included in a smart card and into their functional blocks. Some details on microcircuit manufacturing are also reviewed. ISO standards, as far as hardware is concerned, will be included here and there throughout the chapter.

Smart cards are the main subject of this book. However, it seems interesting to include here some references to non-ISO related devices sharing the same manufacturing technologies, but having different applications. Technologies of data banks, memory cartridges, and similar storage devices on the one hand and battery-powered chip cards on the other hand are mentioned below.

4.1 INSIDE A CARD

Chip cards from the outside can be easily distinguished from common credit cards by a dime-sized golden plate located near the edge. The plate is divided into eight areas (some cards, such as McCorquodale and Gemplus, have only six; see Section 4.6). These are the contacts employed by the microcircuit to communicate with the outer world. If the contacts were transparent, a dark, shiny, 1-mm^2 gadget could be seen behind them. This is the microcircuit. Looking inside (see Figure 4.1), several connected large and small rectangular blocks may be found:

- Memory areas;
- Central processing unit (CPU);
- Protection circuits;
- Reset circuit;
- Clock;
- Input-output area.

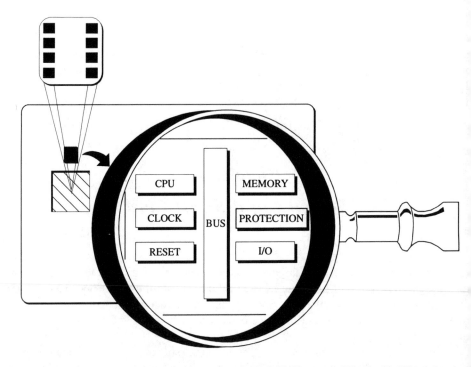

Figure 4.1 Inside a smart card, behind contacts, a microcircuit divided into several blocks with different functions may be found.

The specific areas found inside the chip depend on the card model. Memory cards have no CPU, whereas other cards may lack reset circuitry or clock.

4.2 MEMORY

The largest microcircuit areas are occupied by different kinds of memory. Cards must hold data, code, and other permanently stored information in order to perform their tasks. In standard desktop computers, data and instructions managed by CPUs are stored in electronic ICs, where they can be randomly accessed; under this form, data are compiled, modified, read, written, and moved. This data crunching is at the very heart of computing. Once the task is finished, however, intermediate results are no longer needed and must be erased to allow space for the next task. Hence, the internal memory of computers is erasable. Moreover, it is usually dynamic; that is, data are lost upon power removal. When the power is on, the memory must be refreshed every now and then (every few milliseconds, in fact) to keep data stored in their place.

Support for permanent data backup in computers is given by external peripherals, usually hard disks, floppy disks, or similar magnetic media. Fast, inexpensive dynamic

memory and magnetic permanent media make a perfect team for handling data in computers. It is worth mentioning that, in practice, magnetically stored code cannot be directly
executed by microprocessors (i.e., a magnetic stripe card could not store an executable
program, though it could store the program *code*); besides, the seek access time of hard
disks is measured in milliseconds whereas the access time of dynamic memory is measured
in nanoseconds, some million times faster.

Smart and memory cards usually need permanent or nonvolatile memory for most
applications and memory zones. Small chunks of volatile memory may also be included
as intermediate memory storage for direct code execution and scratch pad data handling
(Figure 4.2). The use of dynamic memory is not realistic for permanent storage, even in
battery-powered cards. Instead, nonvolatile IC technologies for internal card memory are
employed in the manufacturing process. Smart cards, memory cards, and other cardlike
storage devices share this technology. An important difference, however, arises from
storage capacity. Smart cards require at most a few kilobytes of storage memory. Some
IC memory cards, such as PCMCIA cards, require several megabytes. These devices are

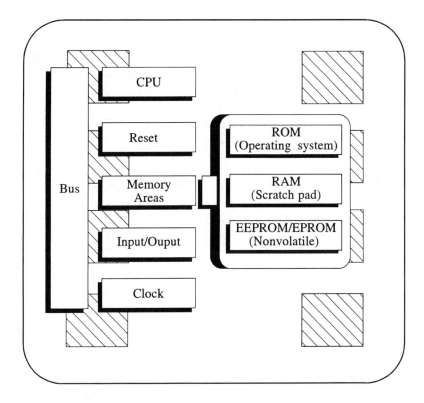

Figure 4.2 Main blocks and memory technologies found in a card chip.

used as nonerasable (read-only) data banks or even as high-density removable storage for smaller and smaller portable computers.

IC memory technologies, like most electronic systems, are based on silicon. Several silicon technologies are currently used in cards. Volatile Memory includes dynamic random access memory (DRAM) and static random access memory (SRAM). Nonvolatile Memory includes read-only memory (ROM) and erasable, programmable read-only memory (EPROM). The nonvolatile categories are actually a bunch of different technologies sharing nonvolatility and little else. Details are discussed in the following sections.

4.2.1 Volatile Memory

Dynamic and static RAM may be employed inside a card for several uses. Unless the card is battery powered, the contents of these types of memory are lost in the short or long term (usually in the short term). The difference between dynamic and static RAM is that static RAM need not be refreshed, allowing data storage with very low power consumption. Nevertheless, data are lost if power is removed (i.e., if the battery runs out). SRAM may be used in cards containing batteries to keep some relevant though noncritical data such as time and date.

DRAM is employed in cards as a working area (scratch pad) when the card is inserted into a reader (i.e., it has an external power supply). Cards use that volatile memory in a RAM stack where intermediate results of calculations or data encryption processes are stored. After finishing every step, data are erased and DRAM is used in new calculations. DRAM is preferred over SRAM for its simpler, more reliable design (a bit is made of a single metal oxide silicon transistor attached to a capacitor). SRAM features low voltage and power consumption, but its architecture (four transistors, two resistors per cell) reduces storage density and increases the cost-per-bit ratio.

Although RAM is usually associated with volatile memory, new technologies for achieving nonvolatile RAM are being developed. For example, ferroelectronic RAM (based on ferroelectric materials like lead zirconate titanate) might be a breakthrough in memory technologies by combining the performance of DRAM with the nonvolatility goal.

4.2.2 Nonvolatile Memory

Most memory zones in cards are based on nonvolatile memory. Data stored in this memory are not lost when power is removed (e.g., when the card is unplugged from the writing/reading unit). Storage, however, need not be permanent: in fact, many memory zones must be updated when the card is operating; other zones must always keep the same information (e.g., the card mask; see below). Several nonvolatile memory technologies may be found in cards to account for these different needs.

Permanent information can be stored in ROM. Either the information is recorded at the same time as the chip is created or is included in a further programming step. In the first case, the information (data, code, program, etc.) is included in the same photolithographic masking process used to manufacture the chip (hence the name *masked ROM*). Strictly speaking, this is the only ROM; memory created by other ROM technologies is written at least once. Masked ROM is an inexpensive, reliable, and high-density technology. Its major drawback comes from its own irreversibility: code errors and revisions imply costly modifications in the manufacturing chain.

The above situation is avoided by the use of write-once, read-many technologies. *Programmable ROMs* (PROM) allow customer programming by blowing specific fuses in the assembled chip. Again, the memory is permanent; once the information is written, it remains in the chip forever. A further step in flexibility (and a new letter in the acronym) is offered by EPROMs. In this case, the PROM may be erased by an external action, usually ultraviolet light exposure. This memory is easily identified in a computer mother board by its small transparent windows on the top of the chip. A major advance in nonvolatile technologies notwithstanding, EPROMs and PROMs are functionally identical in a chip card. For one thing, it is quite difficult to expose an embedded chip to ultraviolet radiation without destroying the card! The use of EPROMs in cards derives from other reasons, mainly reliability and simplicity (one transistor technology).

Finally, let us look at *electrically erasable, programmable ROM* (EEPROM). A two-transistor technology, EEPROM provides nonvolatile memory that is erasable and rewritable by electric signals. EEPROM may be used as RAM. Though its higher cost precludes its application in desktop computers, it is a perfect candidate for accomplishing most memory requirements in IC cards. A minor problem of EEPROMs is that erasing and writing operations usually require higher voltage than reading. ISO standards include a 21V power supply for these operations, though current cards often disregard this facility. The regular power supply (5V) is used instead, its voltage being internally increased as needed.

Flash memory is a simpler EEPROM technology (one dual gate transistor per cell), and is an alternative to classical EEPROMs. It features higher density, lower cost, and greater reliability. Besides, writing and erasing can be obtained at lower voltages than standard EEPROM. Its drawback is that single-bit erasure is not possible; flash memory must be block-erased. Hence, this memory may be used in memory zones where the information is modified as a whole; it cannot be employed when the updating of a single piece of data is required.

Memory complexity affects the size of the memory cells as well. Using a ROM cell as area unit, EPROM and EEPROM cells would cover two and six units, respectively. This is not as bad as SRAM, with sixteen units.

4.2.3 User/Application Memory

Several kinds of memory are used in a single IC card. From the issuer or user point of view, however, the most important (perhaps the *only* important) memory is the user/

application memory (UAM). UAM is EPROM or EEPROM that holds the specific information on every application. The information is usually a data set including user data, issuer data, and operations (transactions) performed by the card. In some applications, UAM may also contain executable functions (EXEC functions). Code is included in UAM, for example, when the standard ROM program (the mask; see next section) is not able to perform some operations, or simply when the issuer wants to take advantage of this option for security or speed. UAM size in current cards varies from 1K to 16K (some manufacturers are developing 64K UAMs).

UAM is protected by the microprocessor, which filters data flow, manages data storage and reading, and runs the preprogrammed executable functions, if any. A number of cards have UAM divided into several zones. *Memory zones* are in turn divided into files and records and are protected by special hardware. A typical partition is given below (Figure 4.3).

The *Manufacturer zone* includes microcircuit and/or card ID data, which are stored during manufacture and hardware-protected against further access.

In the *Secret zone* the data cannot be accessed from the outside. Only the microprocessor can take advantage of them. This zone holds, for example, secret codes such as the issuer key and the user PIN. Protection is provided via hardware, as in the previous case, or by means of an internal program.

The *Status zone* contains access attempts to the card, either through user PIN or through issuer key. Other secret codes may also be included. Attempts are sequentially stored, allowing the card to decide its self-blocking or self-destruction according to preprogrammed criteria. Following the issuer instructions, for example, the card may self-block after three consecutive wrong user PINs or may "commit suicide" after a single wrong issuer key.

Older IC cards required the separation of *free access data zones* and *protected data zones* (e.g., by PIN or issuer key). At present, many cards permit the definition of every file, either free or protected by any key combination. Therefore, free and confidential zones are currently found in the same memory zone. Definition of file attributes is customarily performed by the issuer and protected by the issuer key.

The *Transaction zone* contains most variable data (e.g., commercial transactions, hence the name). Data format, files, and record structure depend on the application. Typically, a secret code is required to access the zone. New card models allow different protection for reading and writing in the same file. For example, some data may be freely read, but permission is required to modify them. This feature is quite interesting in a number of instances (e.g., in electronic purses). Actually, there is no difference between transaction, free, and confidential zones. They are usually separated for historical reasons, since old cards had a fixed memory arrangement where these zones were predefined.

4.3 CPU AND OPERATING SYSTEM

Microcircuits of current smart cards are almost complete computer systems without keyboard and display. In fact, some non-ISO active cards such as super smart cards include

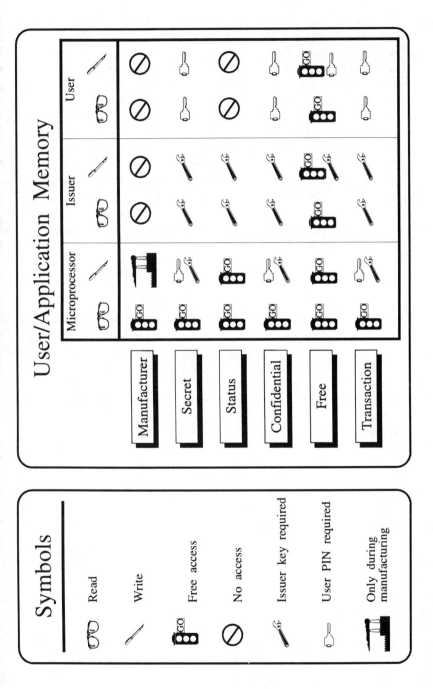

Figure 4.3 Typical zones of user/application memory.

keyboard, display, and battery inside the same card-sized device. The core of the card microcircuit is the microprocessor, usually called CPU. This CPU is able to execute an instruction set that ultimately defines the capabilities of the card. The instruction set is permanently wired into the card. Card chip manufacturers (see Section 3.3.3) use only a few architectures in smart card CPUs: H8/310 (Hitachi), 627xx (Oki), ST8 (Thomson), 8051 (Intel), and 6805 (Motorola). All of them employ 8-bit instructions and have a 16-bit data bus. Quite recently, Gemplus has introduced a reduced instruction set computer (RISC) processor for smart cards. Higher level functions are also permanently stored in the card memory, indicating to the CPU what to do, when, and how to do it. These functions could be considered the smart card operating system (SCOS). The SCOS allows the CPU to manage the UAM according to external commands the user invokes from an interface device. When a card is provided with a microprocessor, it always takes care of memory management and data security by itself. Any external access to card memory or functions is performed through the CPU. The SCOS is also used to define EXEC functions eventually stored in the UAM.

4.3.1 Card Mask

From the outside, card behavior is greatly determined by its SCOS. Different SCOSs applied to the same CPU results in cards with different capabilities, while the opposite situation, providing that CPUs of similar performance are used, may remain unnoticed. In the cards' world, the SCOS is traditionally known as the card *mask*.

The CPU and SCOS together make quite a powerful team. These cards are, in practice, independent computing systems. Programmed logic allows the card to make its own decisions concerning access to stored data (reading and writing), no-answer condition in uncertain situations, or self-blocking. In summary, smart cards are characterized by:

- *High Security.* Data access is thoroughly controlled by the CPU, and is only permitted when predefined conditions are met.
- *High Flexibility.* Data management may be altered depending on external requirements, thus allowing specific tailoring of the application.
- *Multiple Services.* Several applications (services) may share the same card. The CPU controls each application by itself or through EXEC functions. The applications may be independent or related and may be prepared by the same issuer or by different ones.

The SCOS is stored in ROM, a safe place to avoid eventual modifications. (The SCOS is sometimes called *standard ROM program.*) ROM is manufactured or prepared at the same time as the chip itself (see above). It can only be accessed and used by the card CPU. Being a constant part of the microcircuit for every smart card, card masks are usually identified by their ROM design. ROM size typically varies from 2K to 16K. Some cards employ EEPROM for the SCOS zone; these are usually used for the design and development of new functions and applications. They also offer higher security against electronic scanning microscopy, since EEPROM information is erased by electron beams. In most cases these cards are not commercially available. The highest flexibility in commercial cards is currently demonstrated by several manufacturers who have developed selectable SCOSs (different operating systems for the same card).

Besides ROM, the CPU employs other kinds of memory for different uses. Most important for CPU internal data handling is a volatile RAM called *RAM stack*. RAM size in current smart cards varies from 128 to 768 bytes. Intermediate results and encryption processes are temporarily stored in this memory. The memory is freed afterwards for the next task. The contents of this memory are lost when power is removed.

4.3.2 Wired Logic and Microprocessors

Many cards lack a microprocessor and many applications are nicely accomplished by not-so-smart cards. When designing an application where cards are involved, the first question to ask is how smart the cards need to be. IC cards are divided into three fundamental categories, ultimately depending on the way data are protected from fraudulent access. A sorted list for increasing IQ might be (1) dumb cards, (2) wired logic cards, and (3) smart cards.

Dumb cards have a memory circuit and are provided with reading and writing functions, but lack access control. Communications with external peripherals are usually synchronous. Advanced models of these cards are equipped with EEPROM (rewritable) memory ranging from 256 bytes to tens of kilobytes. Moreover, many data cartridges and memory banks should be included in this category, since they have no control over their stored data.

The second group, wired logic cards, features an access control unit, but card capabilities are limited to some prerecorded functions. Several types, described below, can be found, depending on the way access control is achieved.

Memory in *EPROM cards* is split into two or more zones, according to memory addresses. Data reading is allowed in every zone; however, one of the zones (read-only) does not allow writing. Protection of this zone is achieved by blowing an internal metallic or logic fuse. The issuer stores his/her data in the protectable zone and blows the fuse, creating some logic states (specific voltages) in the protection circuit gate. This action precludes any further writing and addressing of the zone. However, the circuit allows reading orders. These cards are chiefly employed in public telephone services or for ID purposes.

A certain device (e.g., a diode array) inside *programmable logic array (PLA) cards* is programmed with an access logic. The PLA compares a keyed access code with an internal code recorded in a memory zone. Access is allowed when matching is found. Some memory zones (e.g., where the code is stored) are restricted. Several applications may share the card, each one having its own PLA. For example, a memory zone may contain the issuer key and the user PIN. A logic may be defined in the PLA in such a way that the zone can never be rewritten, but can be read when the issuer key is introduced.

Similarly, another zone may be written via PIN, whereas reading is reserved for the issuer key.

Some other cards (*hybrid cards*) combine both protection systems. An area of the memory is protected by a fuse, whereas other zones are free or protected by PLAs. In these cards, the fuse-protected zone is usually employed to store user and issuer codes and application ID, while the PLA zone--programmed with all possible access combinations--is used for transactions. Memory in these cards may be EPROM or EEPROM.

The third group, smart cards, includes a microprocessor in the chip. The presence of the microprocessor opens new possibilities for memory management, as mentioned above. New cards allow a floppy-disk-like memory management, including directories, files, and records. The memory may contain data and/or executable code (EXEC functions). Moreover, the microprocessor allows asynchronous communication between the card and its interface device (writing/reading unit), increasing the system security.

4.4 OTHER CIRCUITS

In our journey around the card chip, several other circuits may also be seen. Besides metallic fuses for data protection (see previous section), the card may have *protection circuits* to avoid electric damage of card parts or counterfeiting. For example, it may be protected against voltage fluctuations in power supply or signals beyond the ranges allowed by the ISO standards. Moreover, the card requires extra circuits for three basic tasks: reset, synchronization, and communications.

4.4.1 Reset Circuit and ATR

Any computing system performs a reset operation when switched on. Through reset, the computer comes to life and realizes its own electronic existence. In cards, this operation is performed through an internal specific reset signal, triggered by an external command from the interface device. The reset signal may be either the same signal sent by the external command or a new signal generated by an internal reset circuit. In the second case, the external reset asks the internal reset circuit to generate the signal and to set up the different devices included in the card.

The most important fact in reset operations is that the command, either internal or external, also produces a specific answer, called *answer to reset* (ATR), which is sent back to the interface device. ATR is defined by a standard protocol (ISO 7816/3). It includes enough information identifying the card type and sometimes the card model and the application (Hello, I'm a standard card manufactured by ZZZ, I have a microprocessor, my working frequency is XXX, etc.). Any ISO card, therefore, can be properly identified by any reader, regardless of its brand and application. This feature is most useful for the external system in order to decide whether the card belongs to an application or not;

furthermore, the same writing/reading unit may be simultaneously used for several applications and services using cards from different manufacturers.

4.4.2 Clock and Synchronization Circuits

ATRs, as well as any other dialog between the card and the interface device, require signal synchronization. Timing signals are used to synchronize the card's internal operations and communications. These timing signals may come from an external clock provided by the interface device. The card is directly driven by the clock or through internal timing and buffer circuits (buffers are needed to avoid delays within the microcircuit devices).

Alternatively, the card may be provided with an internal clock. The internal clock frequency need not be the same as that employed in reset. In fact, the ATR signal provides the specific clock frequency of the card. This information may be used to select the frequency for eventual communications. The usual frequency of current cards ranges from 5 to 14 MHz.

4.4.3 Communication Circuits

Communications to and from the card are performed by an input/output (I/O) port, which makes use of one of the contacts (i.e., a bidirectional bitwise I/O port). The port may work in synchronous or asynchronous mode. There is some spurious electrical resistance in the circuit for signal flow from the card to the outside and vice versa. Indeed, the electrical continuity is performed by the interface device contacts pressing on the golden card contacts. Dirtiness in contacts produces ohmic resistance. To avoid signal degradation and electrical noise, the I/O port may include an internal amplifier.

4.5 DESIGN AND MANUFACTURING: AN EXAMPLE

There are no substantial differences in the techniques employed to manufacture IC cards compared to any other general-purpose microelectronic ICs, except for hardware protections and sensors discussed in the previous chapter. Detailed descriptions of IC manufacturing processes are beyond the scope of this book. Instead, we will describe the design steps of a specific card and will browse through hardware manufacturing.

4.5.1 Chip Design

Let us design a simple card for prepaid public telephone calls. First, we must define card capabilities and performance. In this case, the following characteristics are needed.

- It should allow storage of data related to the phone company (issuer), charge unit price, card serial number, and so forth.

- The above information must be protected; that is, it may not be altered after being recorded by the issuer.
- Data access should be controlled.
- A memory zone is needed to store credit (number of allowable call units) and used units. This zone, obviously, must be accessed for reading and writing.
- Finally, there must be a predefined working logic. In this case, a limited number of instructions is required: reset, bitwise reading and writing, and bit addressing.

The next step is a block (functional) design based on the above characteristics. Figure 4.4 shows the block diagram of our card. The blocks are:

- An EPROM consisting of 256 one-bit words. Words are addressed by a binary counter controlling row and column decoders. Our memory is thus addressed as a 16×16 matrix, where every element is accessed by its row and column coordinates.
- A small instruction decoder which generates card control signals. In our case, the required signals are writing and reading bit operations, counter increments, and reset.

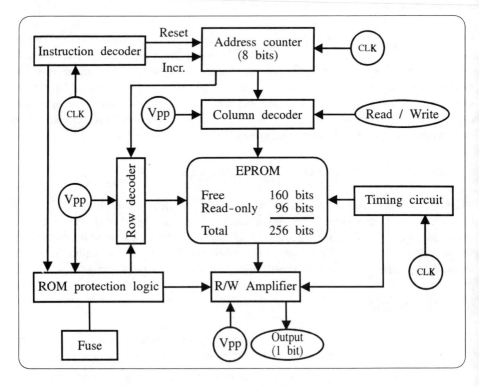

Figure 4.4 Electronic components of a PLA memory card.

- Two memory zones are defined inside the memory. The first zone has 160 read/write bits, whereas the second zone has 96 read-only bits. A protection block is added for detection and inhibition of writing operations in the protected zone.
- A timing circuit that produces two signals. Both are used to adapt the voltage levels of memory cells before reading.
- A writing/reading amplifier to send data from the card to outside, and to route EPROM programming voltage (i.e., voltage required to record data in selected memory positions).

System design should also include connections between blocks and power supply. As a result, the designer should prepare:

- An electrical diagram for every block;
- A description of internal and external electrical signals, including purpose and electrical characteristics;
- The system logic (truth tables), including simulations of logic behavior for every desired operation;
- Chronograms (signals versus time) for every global working mode (reset, writing, etc.) and, where necessary, those chronograms will be combined to show synchronism;
- The electrical diagram of the whole system (ground and power lines, communication buses, and so on).

4.5.2 Chip Manufacturing

It is now time to translate all these drawings and diagrams into electronic components. Masks for myriads of transistors, diodes, resistors, and the like are carefully prepared using computer-aided design (CAD) packages. Layouts 100 to 1,000 times larger than actual size are miniaturized onto a silicon wafer. New masks are added up, producing multiple layers of different materials (p-type silicon, n-type silicon, metal, oxides). Many circuits are simultaneously prepared on the same wafer. Circuits are individually tested before further manufacturing.

Manufacturing of card circuits is quite similar to other microelectronic fabrication, though a single smart card circuit includes functional blocks corresponding to several chips in other electronic systems (i.e., microprocessor, coprocessor, several kinds of memory, input/output circuit, etc.). Processing steps like oxidation, photolithography, etching, diffusion, sputtering, chemical vapor deposition, ion implantation, and epitaxy are similarly used. Perhaps the main difference is the overall manufacturing ruggedness of card circuits. Ruggedness is needed to accomplish quite strict ISO standards concerning environmental, chemical, and electric aggression. Electronic ruggedness is also required to avoid unexpected behaviors when the chip is tested outside specifications.

In the final steps, microcircuits are usually covered with a passivating silica layer, and pads for connections to external contacts (using metallic wires) are obtained. The wafer is then cut into separate microcircuit dice (Figure 4.5). The microcircuit is then ready to be attached to the contacts and embedded in the card body.

4.6 CONTACTS AND EMBEDDING

Contacts are the physical link between the microcircuit and the outer world. From the card's point of view, the outer world is merely an interface device that communicates with other computing systems.

4.6.1 Contact Manufacturing and Location

Contacts are made of copper coated with other metals or alloys to improve its electrical and mechanical properties. The coating used to be a thin gold film; at present, silver

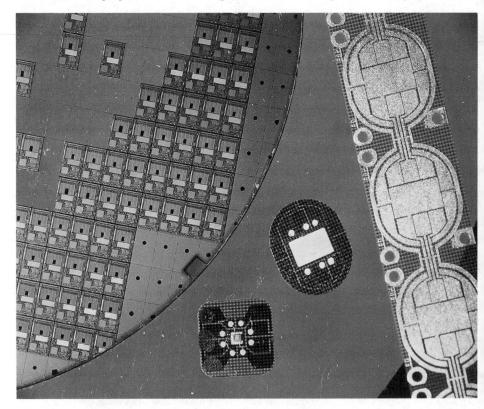

Figure 4.5 Silicon wafer for smart cards with some separate microcircuit dice (left), two microcircuits attached to the contacts (middle), and stripe of contacts (right). (Courtesy Fábrica Nacional de Moneda y Timbre)

palladium alloys are preferred because of the fragility of gold films. The contact module may be made on a glass fiber base, like a double-sided printed circuit board (Figure 4.6). The microcircuit is mounted on the other side of the board, where it is protected from the environment. Alternatively, contacts may be stamped out of a continuous metallic strip (Figure 4.5) like a photographic film. This system can be easily integrated on the assembly line. A similar solution is based on the use of single metallic elements mounted on a ceramic or plastic support, which eventually protects the microcircuit. Microcircuit and contacts are electrically connected by extremely thin gold or aluminum wires. These wires are bonded (Figure 4.7) to microcircuit pads and contacts using ultrasonic waves (ultrasonic wedge bonding) or heat and pressure (thermal compression wire bonding).

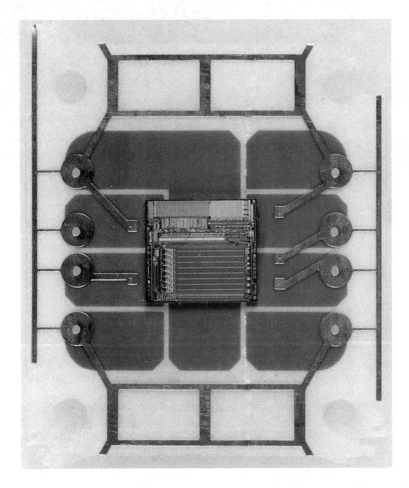

Figure 4.6 Contacts attached to a smart card using metallic strips. The chip and the contacts are located at opposite sides of a printed circuit board. The circuit board has been made transparent to allow viewing of both sides. (Courtesy of Schlumberger Technologies)

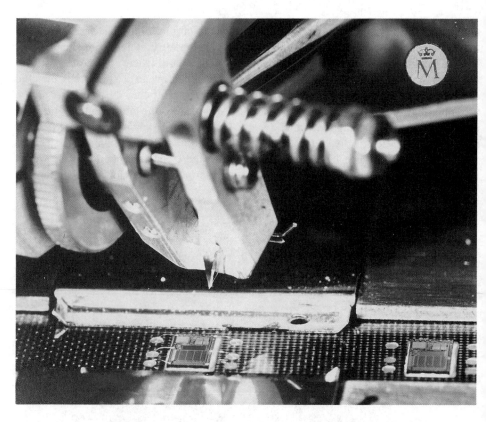

Figure 4.7 Wire bonding system for smart card chips. (Courtesy of Fábrica Nacional de Moneda y Timbre)

The number (eight), arrangement (2×4 landscape), minimum size (2×1.7 mm), notation (C1 to C8), and function of contacts are defined by parts 2 and 3 of ISO 7816. Figure 4.8 shows standard contacts C1 to C8. No directives are given, however, concerning *maximum* size or geometrical shape. The maximum size is ultimately restricted by the distance between adjacent contacts. Freedom in geometry, on the other hand, has become a challenge for manufacturers, who make use of it to identify a specific shape with their products or models. Therefore, it is quite common to find IC cards with flamboyant contact shapes, which nevertheless strictly meet ISO regulations.

Contacts may be located on the front or back of the card. In either case, dimensions and distances refer to the left and upper edges of the corresponding side. The current contact position derives from a previous de facto standard developed in France at the beginning of the card age. This standard was provisionally accepted until 1991. The main difference between French and ISO standards arises from the contact location on the card. The French standard placed the contacts near the upper card edge (Figure 4.8). This location revealed several mechanical problems and, even worse, electrical interference

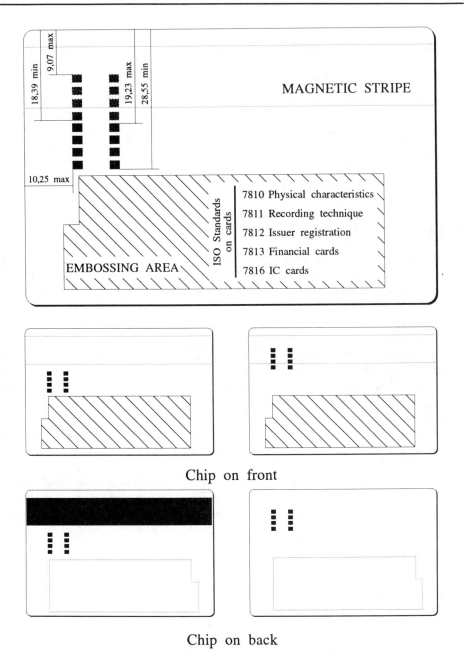

Figure 4.8 Location of contacts and dimensions according to ISO and old French standard along with embossing area and magnetic stripe (top). There are four possible contact locations in the card, front and back (bottom). Note that French standard does not allow a magnetic stripe when the chip is on the card back.

with an eventual magnetic stripe included on the same card (contacts overlap the magnetic stripe located on the other side). The new standard moves the contacts toward a position closer to the longitudinal card axis, while keeping the distance to the left card edge. Quite wisely, the displacement is the same as the length of the contact frame; that is, a card on which both contact sets were placed would show two contiguous rectangles of the same size. In this way, interface devices may easily be provided with two contact rows, each having eight equidistant interconnected leads servicing both old and new cards (Figure 4.8). A table in the appendix summarizes dimension limits for distances from normalized rectangular contacts (i.e., minimum-size contacts) to left and upper card edges. Old and present standards are included.

4.6.2 Contact Function

Let us study each contact separately. C4 and C8 are not defined yet. Their use is not permitted in the standard, however, because they are reserved for assignment in eventual parts or revisions of ISO 7816. Cards from some manufacturers have only six contacts, since unused C4 and C8 contacts are not provided. The function of the remaining contacts is defined in parts 2 and 3 of the above standard. Some of them are optional; others must always be present.

$C1$ is used for power supply input (V_{CC}) from the interface device. Its name is V_{CC}. Voltage must be +5V ± 0.25V (i.e., 5 positive volts ± 5%). Its use by the card is optional unless the card has internal reset circuits; in that case, its use is mandatory. The V_{CC} value was selected to allow the use of transistor-transistor logic technology, which was formerly employed in card microcircuits. Currently, logic circuits use other technologies (MOS, CMOS, etc.), which do not need such voltage, but can manage with it. The power supply of plug-in cards is 3V (i.e., not the ISO 7816 standard; a draft CEN standard for plug-in cards includes this specification).

$C2$ is called RST and is used by the interface device to send reset signals to the card microcircuit. RST signals are used by themselves or combined with internal reset circuits (optional use). In the second case, as mentioned above, the use of V_{CC} is mandatory, since the RST voltage level is referenced to V_{CC}. RST signals are made up of several parts, described in ISO 7816/3.

$C3$ is called *clock* or *CLK*, and timing signals are sent to the card through it. Its use is obviously optional, since the card may have its own internal clock. In this case, an initial frequency is used for reset and ATR operations. ATR includes clock frequency, which will be employed in further communications. The initial frequency depends on whether synchronous or asynchronous communications are used. The second frequency in asynchronous communications may not be lower than 1 MHz. Clock voltage levels and the relationship between both frequencies are defined in ISO 7816/3.

$C5$ is used as a reference voltage and is called *ground* or *GND*. It is mandatory for any card. The reference voltage must be the same as the interface ground. Since the remaining voltage levels are referenced to ground, its value is considered 0V.

C6 is optionally used to program (record) or erase the internal nonvolatile memory. It is usually known as V_{PP}. When used, the voltage V_{PP} has two levels. The lower voltage is called the *idle state*; it must be maintained by the interface device until the other voltage level (*active state*) is required. Again, details on voltage levels and timing of these signals are specified in ISO 7816/3.

C7 performs communication to and from the card. Quite reasonably, it is called *I/O*. Data flow depends on the mode: reception mode for input and transmission mode for output. Two states (voltage levels) are used by the card and the interface device to indicate whether they are ready to talk (transmit) or listen (receive). If nobody has anything to say, both ends adopt the reception mode and the line is maintained at the high state. When one of the ends wants to send any information to the other end, it goes to the low state and becomes the transmitter. ISO standards specify that both ends shall not be in transmit mode during operation. Synchronous and asynchronous communications are allowed. ISO standards include a communication protocol for asynchronous, half-duplex, bidirectional communications.

4.6.3 Chip Card Body

The microcircuit, already bonded to contacts, is encapsulated in ceramic or epoxy material and is embedded in the card body. Embedding techniques are usually those defined and patented by Arimura, one of the pioneers of the smart card, in the 1970s. The card body is made of a plastic material. Several plastics, such as PVC, polyvinyl chloride acetate (PVCA), polyethylene terephthalate (PET), and acrylic butadiene styrene (ABS) are used in current cards. For example, PET is used in Japanese phone cards, while ABS is employed in many German and French cards.

Standards for chip card dimensions are the same as those for ID and financial cards. ISO standards 7810 and 7813 describe the physical parameters of these cards. To increase further the compatibility with other cards, IC cards, specifically smart cards, may include the same elements as ID and financial cards (e.g., embossing and magnetic stripe). For the same reason, recording techniques on the stripe, location of elements, and issuer ID are identical for all cards. (Note: a problem still unresolved is the use of international alphabetic characters, which are supported by smart cards but cannot be included in magnetic stripes if ASCII characters are used.) Specifications for these elements are given in the above standards, as well as in ISO 7811 (five parts) and ISO 7812. In summary, ISO standards concerning smart cards are those prepared for all kinds of cards (7810 through 7813) and one standard specifically prepared for chip cards (7816).

Besides magnetic stripe and embossing, a chip card may include the same paraphernalia as other cards have: signatures, pictures, holograms, logos, acronyms, drawings, messages, and so on. Printing is usually done by offset or silk-screening. Quite often, especially in greatly extended applications like telephone cards, the card body is used for sponsors' publicity. The result may be a colorful card, where marketing or artistic realizations are combined with former applications. Many people have been captivated by the aesthetic aspects of these realizations. As a consequence, a new market of card collectors has arisen.

4.7 CONCLUSIONS

Smart card chips contain a microprocessor, several kinds of memory, and other circuits for reset, synchronization, and communications. All these circuits are included in the same chip. The user/applications memory is used for storing data and executable code. Memory areas are protected with different keys. Data flow is controlled by the microprocessor.

Our tour inside a smart card has finished. In this chapter, we have learned how cards are manufactured and quite a few functional details of the microcircuit. It is time to put our cards to work. To do this, we have to learn their language and addressing strategies. This is the subject of the next chapter.

Chapter 5
The Language of Smart Cards

As we saw in the previous chapter, a smart card is, in practice, an independent computing system lacking a display and keyboard. Such a microcomputer can be programmed (i.e., instructed to perform computing tasks on its own). Alternatively, it may be used as a slave system commanded by another computer. In a typical application, however, this slavery is not absolute, since the card usually has preprogrammed instructions from its former master(s) that ultimately decide which instructions are to be performed and which are to be simply ignored or, even worse, trigger hara kiri–style self-destruction mechanisms within the card, protecting its valuable data with its life.

The presence of a microprocessor in the card opens up a variety of different ways of designing specific features. We will restrict ourselves here to the most usual card development sequence: manufacturer, issuer, user. Some alternatives will be mentioned throughout the chapter. For example, the generic term *user* implies a single user or a group of users. The group, in turn, may or may not be made up of persons sharing the same access privileges; indeed, some applications distinguish between card owner and holder, while others are designed to keep in mind a generic (single or multiple) user.

In this chapter, we will learn how to manage a smart card from another computer via a writing/reading unit (WRU). This computer may be used to instruct the card itself, using the WRU as an intermediate step that merely removes the headers and trailers of the messages coming to and from the card (like a modem); alternatively, the computer may instruct the WRU to manage the card off line, thus making it an independent system. In either case, the WRU/card dialog begins with an identification message sent by the card after it is requested by a reset pulse from the WRU. Once the card is properly identified by its ATR, bidirectional communication starts. We will learn to translate ATRs in order to allow our application to identify the card. The structure of eventual messages to and from the card will be studied afterwards.

The whole book, and especially this chapter, may be read at two levels. A reader interested in smart card performance and applications need not worry about parity bits, direct conventions, and As and Zs that plague the first half of the chapter. This information is necessary, however, to fully understand the behavior of the cards or to design hardware for these devices.

Before going any further, there is one final point. At this time, the draft of the fourth part of ISO 7816 is soon to become a part of the ISO standards. It will most probably be approved with no major changes, even though it is not official yet. Because the sections on 7816/4 deal with software and communications, it will be discussed in paragraphs marked with a bar alongside it to distinguish between what is not ISO standard from what is (though it may well be so before publication). Most of the 7816/4 directives are intended to increase the possibilities of card management; the cards complying with 7816/3 are a subset of such directives. Therefore, while a current card may be less flexible than those to be designed under the 7816/4 standard, it is still completely operational.

5.1 INSTRUCTION SET AND SMART CARD OPERATING SYSTEM

As for any other microprocessor, card micros have tailored instruction sets determining the microprocessor capabilities. Most of the inner details remain unnoticed by the user, as long as the card adheres to standards. As mentioned above, cards are managed from the outside through external software either from a computer that uses the WRU/card as a peripheral, or from the WRU itself. Therefore, we need not worry about detailed sets unless we want to introduce executable code into the card. On the other hand, specific information on card instruction sets is seldom available to issuers (not to mention users), so EXEC functions cannot usually be employed, unless the manufacturer allows the issuer to know about the set.

Most cards are controlled using higher level commands which define their permitted operations. These commands made of instructions from the instruction set are the SCOS. Smart card manufacturers use different (often registered) names and acronyms for the card operating system, since it is the most distinctive feature of a smart card. (Remember that there are only a few manufacturers of chips for cards.) It should be noted that a manufacturer may prepare apparently different card types using the same chip (hence the same instruction set) by modifying the SCOS. The SCOS is stored in ROM memory; it is often referred as the card *mask*.

SCOS commands include orders to open, read, write, or erase files, just like any other operating system. The SCOS also features other specialized commands such as access control to records through keys or PINs, message certification, and communication with the outer world. Moreover, the SCOS may be used to develop applications. Again, this feature is used chiefly by manufacturers, but is seldom available to issuers or users. For example, encryption and decryption data algorithms may be developed as SCOS applications and included in ROM or UAM memory.

5.2 ANSWER TO RESET

WRUs are provided with a detection mechanism to ascertain whether a card has been introduced and properly positioned under the contacts. Once the card is positioned, the WRU powers up the device and sends a reset (RST) signal through C2 contact. The card uses that signal to reset itself or trigger an internal reset sequence upon receiving RST. In either case, after a while the card sends through its I/O port a string of bytes (ATR) whose frequency and binary value allow WRU to find out whether the card is synchronous or asynchronous, as well as some of the parameters needed to start the conversation (Figure 5.1). Most smart cards are asynchronous; unless otherwise stated, the following paragraphs assume asynchronous cards. Differences in ATR concerning the presence of an internal clock in the card are discussed below.

Using ATR parameters, the WRU may ask the card about any specific protocol for further communication. The card may answer by sending another string called *protocol type selection* (PTS), which contains the requested information. If the card does not respond, the WRU assumes that the card is happy with the former parameters and protocol, so these are used for communications.

Card ATR sequences may contain up to 33 characters (Table 5.1). Each character consists of 10 consecutive bits: a start bit, b_s, eight bits (b_a through b_h) of information, and a final parity bit, b_i. Bits b_a to b_h are called the *data byte*. Within this byte, bits are numbered b_1 to b_8, b_1 being the least significant bit (LSB), and b_8 being the most significant bit (MSB). Bit b_a is not necessarily b_1 (see below). The high and low voltage levels are called Z and A, respectively. The high level need not be logic level 1. Prior to a character

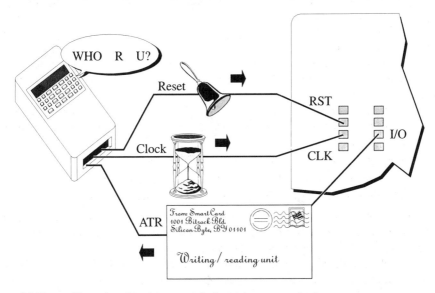

Figure 5.1 The card is awakened by the external device to start communication.

Table 5.1
ATR Characters

Name	Number	Function	Presence
TS	1	Initial character	Mandatory
T0	1	Format character	Mandatory
TA_i, TB_i, TC_i, TD_i	≤ 15	Interface characters	Optional
T1, T2, . . . , TK	≤ 15	Historical characters	Optional
TCK	1	Check character	Conditional

transmission, the I/O line must be at Z (i.e., high) state. Bit b_s is always A (low). After sending a character, the line goes to Z-state and waits at least the time corresponding to two bits (see below). Then the I/O line is ready to send the next character.

5.2.1 First ATR Character, Elementary Time Unit

The first character of ATR is called *TS*. It is of paramount importance, since it contains information on logic conventions and transmission rate. For this very first character, while the transmission rate is not yet established, the card must accept a frequency of between 1 and 5 MHz.

The elementary time unit (etu) is defined as the time required for the transmission of a bit in I/O operations. If the card has an internal clock, the initial etu is 1/9,600 sec. If not, the initial etu is $372/f_i$, where f_i is the frequency provided by the interface device (usually the WRU) on the clock.

The first four bits of TS are always AZZA. That is, after sending $b_s = A$, the first three bits of data byte—b_a, b_b, b_c—are ZZA. This leads to an alternative procedure of measuring the initial etu, defined as one-third of the time elapsed between the two leading edges of the first and fourth bits (i.e., the As). Note that the I/O line is initially at Z-state. Therefore, the sequence is (Z) AZZA, leaving two falling edges separated by 3 etu. This procedure (Figure 5.2) is recommended by ISO 7816/3, thus allowing some tolerance in card etu, since the actual etu is taken from the card response, not from external parameters.

The next three bits—b_d, b_e, b_f—are either AAA or ZZZ. These bits define the transmission convention for this and all the following characters.

- ZZZ—*Direct convention*: b_a is b_1 (LSB comes first) and logic 1 is Z.
- AAA—*Inverse convention*: b_a is b_8 (MSB comes first) and logic 1 is A.

The last three bits—b_g, b_h, b_i—are always AAZ. They are used for checking character parity. Parity bit b_i is adjusted to have an even number of logic 1s in the character. Note that this rule has different meanings depending on the adopted convention.

According to the above notation, the TS character is either (Z) A ZZA ZZZ AAZ (direct convention) or (Z) A ZZA AAA AAZ (inverse convention). Data bytes are 110 111 00 (direct, LSB first) and 001 111 11 (inverse, MSB first), respectively. Their values

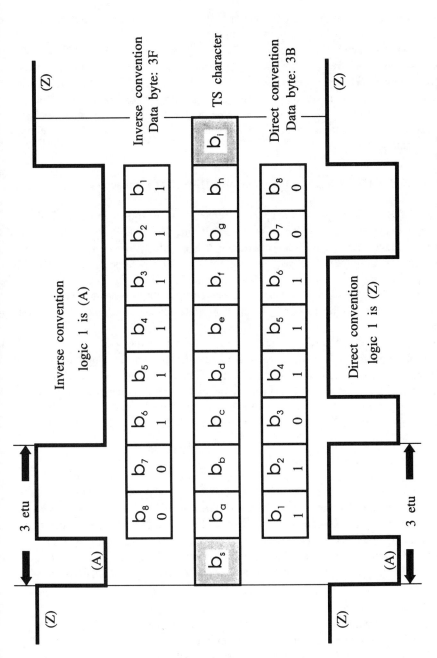

Figure 5.2 The first byte of the ATR establishes the basic rules needed to initiate a conversation between a smart card and an external device.

in hexadecimal notation are 3B (dec 59) and 3F (dec 63). These are the only expected values for TS in asynchronous communication.

A last comment concerning etu. WRU designers often employ 3.57 MHz as the clock frequency (the frequency must be between 1 and 5 MHz, as mentioned in the previous chapter). This frequency has two advantages: first, 3.57-MHz quartz oscillators are quite common and inexpensive; second, substituting this value for f_i in the above formula yields an etu of 1/9,600 sec, the same as that obtained in internal clock cards. This feature simplifies hardware design, since only one frequency is used for both internal and external clock cards.

5.2.2 Second ATR Character, Interface and Historical Characters

Following TS, ATR may contain up to 32 characters, as shown in Table 5.1. In this discussion, character names will also be used to define their data bytes. The second ATR character is called *T0* or the *format character*. It is mandatory and gives information on the presence and number of subsequent (optional) ATR characters. To do this, data byte T0 is split into two nibbles (i.e., two 4-bit groups). The most significant nibble (MSN) (bits b_5 to b_8) is called Y_1 and indicates the presence or absence of interface characters. The least significant nibble (LSN) is called K and indicates the number of historical characters, if any.

The way the information is coded in these nibbles is quite different (Figure 5.3). K is simply a binary number (0 to 15) that can be directly interpreted as the number of historical characters. Y_1 is used bitwise, the presence of a logic 1 in each bit being a flag to denote the presence of a specific character in the subsequent data stream: $b_5 = 1$ denotes the presence of TA_1; $b_6 = 1$ denotes the presence of TB_1; $b_7 = 1$ denotes the presence of TC_1; and $b_8 = 1$ denotes the presence of TD_1.

5.2.3 Extra Interface Characters

Code is more involved than that, since several groups (TA through TD) may be sent. Bytes TA, TB, and TC are called *protocol parameters*, the most relevant ones being discussed below. TD_1 is again split into two nibbles. The MSN of TD_1 is called Y_2, its function being the same as Y_1 applied to bytes TA_2, TB_2, TC_2, and TD_2. Similarly, the MSN of TD_n announces the eventual presence of bytes TA_{n+1}, TB_{n+1}, TC_{n+1}, and TD_{n+1}. The LSN of any TD byte is called T and contains the protocol type for subsequent transmission:

- $T = 0$—asynchronous half-duplex character transmission;
- $T = 1$—asynchronous half-duplex block transmission;
- $T = 2, 3$—reserved for future full-duplex protocols;
- $T = 4$—reserved for enhanced asynchronous half-duplex;
- $T = 5$ to 13—reserved for future use;

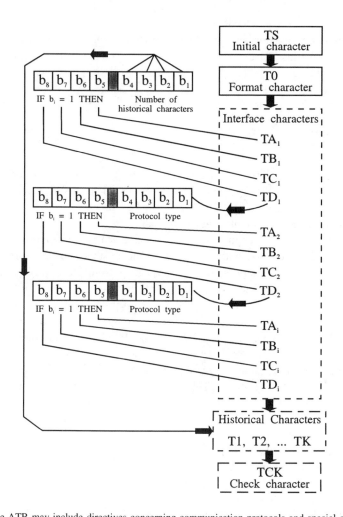

igure 5.3 The ATR may include directives concerning communication protocols and special card features.

- T = 14—protocols not adapted to ISO standards;
- T = 15—reserved for extensions.

Let us summarize the above conventions with an example. Imagine that T0 = F8 ex (i.e., 1111 1000 binary). The MSN is 1111; this means that bytes TA_1, TB_1, TC_1, and 'D$_1$ will be sent. LSN is 1000 (= 8 decimal); therefore, the eventual string will contain historical characters. Once the above interface characters, TA_1 through TD_1, are read, /e look at TD_1, whose value is 40 hex (i.e., 0100 0000 binary). The TD_1 MSN indicates nat only TC_2 is sent. The TD_1 LSN shows that our T protocol is 0, asynchronous half-uplex transmission of single characters. Our protocol parameters are dictated by bytes 'A$_1$, TB_1, TC_1, and TC_2. The protocol type would be T = 0 as established by TD_1. The string of protocol parameters ends when the corresponding TD byte is not sent (hence b8 = 0 in the previous TD byte). If TD_1 is not sent (i.e., $b_8 = 0$ in Y_1), then T = 0 i assumed by default.

5.2.4 Global Interface Bytes

Among all possible TA, TB, TC bytes allowed by the above convention, ISO 7816/. defines only bytes TA_1, TB_1, TC_1, and TB_2. These are called *global interface bytes*, use to define transmission parameters F, D, I, P, and N for the working etu (i.e., the etu employed in subsequent communication).

F is the clock rate conversion factor to be used instead of predetermined 372 numbe of initial etu. It is associated with f_s, a new frequency that substitutes for f_i. D is the adjustment factor for working etu. It is a power of 2 from 16 to 1/64 (i.e., from 2^4 to 2^{-6}). The working etu is defined as $(1/D) \times (F/f_s)$ for external clock cards, and $(1/D)$? $(1/9,600)$ for internal clock cards. I is the maximum programming current at VPP (see previous chapter). The current is expressed in milliamps. P is the maximum programming voltage at VPP (see previous chapter). The voltage is expressed in volts. N is the extr. guard time. There is a minimum delay between characters defined as 12 etu. This is the minimum time from the leading edge of one character to the leading edge of the nex character. Each character consumes 10 etu from b_s to b_i, hence leaving a 2-etu gap betwee characters. I/O must be at Z-state for these 2 etu, as mentioned above. Should the car need more time for *receiving* characters, N is used for its specification. The delay betwee characters is guaranteed to be at least $12 + N$ etu. No extra guard time is employed fo *sending* characters from the card. N may vary from 0 to 254. If $N = 255$, then the guard time is the same for sending and receiving characters. In this case, the guard time is 1 etu for T = 0 protocol (i.e., no extra guard time) and is reduced to 11 etu for T = protocol.

Default values of these parameters are $F = 372$, $D = 1$, $I = 50$, $P = 5$, and $N = 0$ Again, to save space in these bytes, parameters are not transmitted as such, but by usin a conversion table set out in 7816/3. We will mention here the most relevant relationship More information can be found in the Appendix.

For TA_1, MSN encodes FI. This nibble can be related to F and f_s through a table LSN encodes DI, which is related to D through a second table. For TB_1, b_8 is alway zero. b_7 and b_6 encode II, again related to I through a table. b_5 to b_1 define $PI1$, which i P voltage when $PI2$ is not present (see below). $PI1$ varying from 5 to 25 is the value o P in volts. If $PI1$ is zero, VPP is not connected; the card generates an internal programmin voltage from V_{CC} (see Chapter 4). TC_1 encodes N over the whole data byte. TB_2 encode $PI2$ over the whole data byte. If $PI2$ is present, $PI1$ should be ignored. $PI2$ values var from 50 to 250 and express P values in tenths of volts.

5.2.5 Historical Characters

Historical characters have been traditionally used by manufacturers to specify information such as IC, memory size, ROM mask version, SCOS version, memory areas, and number of failed accesses of their cards. ISO 7816/3 does not include any restriction to these characters, except for the maximum number, 15.

ISO 7816/4 does include several recommendations concerning historical characters. These recommendations are linked to the presence of a specific ATR file in the card. Such an ATR file is also defined in 7816/4; it is discussed below. Three fields are defined within the historical bytes: category (mandatory, 1 byte), objects (optional, variable length), and status (conditional, 3 bytes). If historical bytes comply with this standard, the MSN of category byte is 0, 1, or 8; the LSN is always 0. Objects are encoded using the TLV (tag, length, value) format described for ASN.1 (Abstract Syntax Notation One, a formal notation for specifying the data that cross the interface between the Presentation and Application layers defined in OSI) objects, a standard coding system. Information in these objects includes country code, manufacturer and chip model, issuer ID number, and card capabilities. The status consists of a 1-byte life status and bytes SW1 and SW2. The meaning of these bytes is explained below.

5.2.6 TCK Character, End of ATR

TCK is a check character, which must be the last character of ATR in all cases, except when T = 0 is the only protocol type employed by the card; then TCK is not sent. The value of a TCK data byte shall be such that an XOR logical operation performed with all bytes from TS to TCK would be zero.

5.3 PROTOCOL TYPE SELECTION

Once the ATR is correctly received, the interface device (usually the WRU) and the card are ready to communicate with each other, providing that only one protocol type has been sent. When the card sends more than one protocol and does not specify the one to be used (this is done with byte TA_2), the WRU may request a protocol type selection (PTS). PTS may also be used to modify transmission parameter values (*FI, D, N*) within the same protocol.

The WRU must use the first protocol sent by the card. Protocol T = 0 is preferred, and so it must be sent in the first place when the card supports it. If the WRU "feels right" about that protocol (or any one sent first), it may use it for further communication. If not, the WRU sends a PTS request to the card. It is important to note that PTS is decided by the WRU, not by the card.

The PTS request and card response as well as TA_2 contents are specified in the last revision of ISO 7816/3 (October 1992); details are beyond the scope of this general description. The approach is to grant sophisticated WRUs efficient communication with premier card models and, at the same time, allow a less clever partner to communicate with a much cleverer one. For example, if the card supports several protocols and the WRU does not support PTS nor the default protocol, the WRU may reset the card again to switch it to a specific mode. On the other hand, protocol T = 0 is widely accepted both by cards and by WRUs. It is established that any card supporting T = 0 must send it as the first option, thus allowing the WRU to use it by default with no further exchange.

5.4 PROTOCOL TYPE T = 0

Asynchronous half-duplex character transmission (T = 0) is the most common communication protocol in smart cards. It is the only protocol fully described in ISO˙7816/3; protocol T = 1 is foreseen as being included as a further addition to this part. Most cards and WRUs support protocol T = 0. The T = 0 protocol definition includes a new specific interface parameter, TC_2, which is called the *work waiting time*. It is the maximum delay allowed between characters during the communication. The TC_2 data byte, called *WI*, encodes the waiting time in the full byte. Waiting time is defined as $960 \times D \times WI$ etu. The *WI* default value is 10.

5.4.1 Command Structure

Commands are always started by the interface device. Any command includes a 5-byte header, which tells the card the task to be performed. Bytes are called *CLA*, *INS*, *P1*, *P2*, and *P3* (Figure 5.4). CLA is the instruction class. Any value is allowed except FF hex, which is reserved for PTS. INS is the instruction code within the instruction class. The LSB of valid instruction codes is always 0. The MSN cannot be 6 or 9. (This is simply a wise way to avoid conflicts with already existing internal manufacturers' codes.) P1 and P2 are a reference address that completes INS. P3 is the number of data bytes to be transferred. This includes data transfer from card to WRU or vice versa, depending on the instruction. P3 = 0 has a different meaning for incoming and outgoing messages. In outgoing messages (i.e., data coming from the card to the WRU), a 256-byte data transfer is requested. In incoming messages, no data are sent.

5.4.2 Procedure Byte

After sending the header, the interface device waits for an answer from the card. This is called the *procedure byte* (Table 5.2). This may be either ACK or SW1. If the card anticipates that a procedure byte will be sent, it may also, in the meantime, send a NULL (60 hex) byte to reset the working waiting time. All ACK bits except the LSB are either equal or complementary to INS bits. ACK LSB is used to control VPP. The card requests

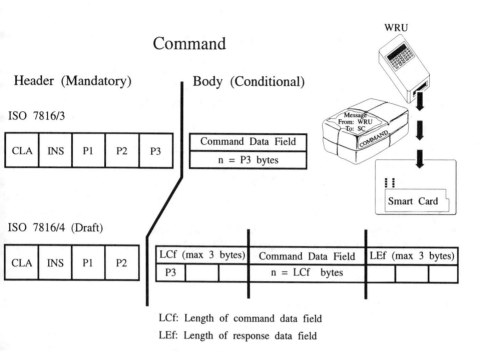

LCf: Length of command data field

LEf: Length of response data field

Figure 5.4 Structure of commands according to ISO 7816/3 and 7816/4.

Table 5.2
Procedure Bytes Sent by the Card in Protocol T = 0

Byte	Value	LSB	VPP	Further Actions
ACK	INS	0	Idle	All remaining data bytes are transferred
	INS + 1	1	Active	All remaining data bytes are transferred
	$\overline{INS}$	1	Idle	Next data byte is transferred
	$\overline{INS} = \overline{1}$	0	Active	Next data byte is transferred
SW1	6X or 9X except 60	N/A	Idle	Card sends SW2
NULL	60	N/A	No change	Wait for new procedure byte

Note: N/A = not applicable

VPP at the active voltage by adding 1 to the INS byte and VPP at the idle voltage by setting its value remain unmodified. (Note that the INS LSB is always zero.) When the card sends an SW1 byte, it simply means that a new SW2 byte will be sent to complete the command.

Note that the LSB for active VPP is not always 1, since ACK may be complementary to INS. The rule is that VPP is set at the idle state when XORing ACK with INS gives either 00 or FF hex. VPP is set at the active state when XORing gives either 01 or FE hex.

The byte couple SW1-SW2 is used by the card as an end sequence where card status is included. Following previous manufacturer conventions, several SW1 bytes have been defined and may be interpreted regardless of the application. Most of these SW1 bytes are hexadecimal *sixties*: 6E hex means that the card does not support that instruction class; the same goes for 6D hex for the instruction code; 6B hex indicates incorrect reference; 67 hex incorrect length; and so on. Only one *ninety* code is defined: 90 hex followed by 00 in SW2 means normal ending.

As can be seen in the above paragraphs, the interface device dictates what to do and the card chooses how to do it. Data transfer is governed by procedure bytes sent by the card. When requested, the card may include a data body in the response (Figure 5.5) before the mandatory status trailer. ACK or NULL bytes may be sent, or the process may be finished with an SW1-SW2 sequence. The card may even refuse to respond, thus aborting the command.

5.4.3 Communications Protocol in 7816/4

ISO 7816/4 includes several clauses regarding protocols for communications. The 5 byte header specified in the 7816/3 standard is maintained, but byte P3 (the last header

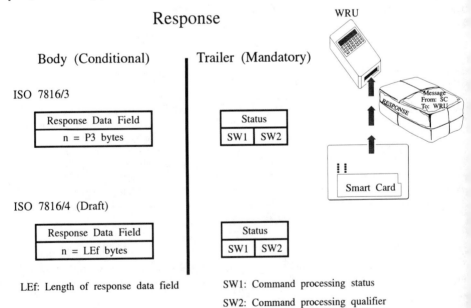

Figure 5.5 Structure of a card response to an external command.

byte) is now considered a part of the body message. Four command/response types are considered, depending on the origin and destination of the data stream.

1. The command does not require the sending or receiving of data.
2. The command includes data sent by the interface device to the card.
3. The command does not send data but requires the card to send data back in the response.
4. The command sends data and also requires data from the card.

Note that case 4 is not considered in 7816/3; in fact, it is impossible to send and receive data in the same command using the 5-byte header system proposed in that part.

Message structure in 7816/4 (Figure 5.6) is defined in terms of application protocol data units (APDU). APDUs contain either a command or a response message. The old P3 data byte becomes a data length field, whose size may be either 1 byte (short) or 3 bytes (extended). The default option is short field, allowing old cards to work under the new standard; new cards, however, may use extended data length fields, overcoming the 7816/3 limitation in data transfer (256 bytes).

APDU structure for commands depends on the data flow mentioned above. Indeed, every case has a different structure:

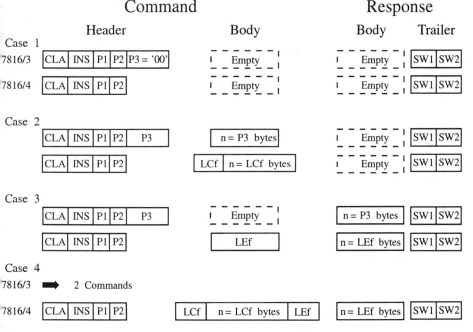

Figure 5.6 ISO 7816/4 foresees four command cases, depending on data flow direction. Case 4 (data in and data out) is adapted to 7816/3 by issuing two commands, one sending data to the card and one requesting data from the card.

- Case 1 (no data sent, no data expected): CLA INS P1 P2;
- Case 2 (data sent, no data expected): CLA INS P1 P2 LCfield Data field;
- Case 3 (no data sent, data expected): CLA INS P1 P2 LEfield;
- Case 4 (data sent, data expected): CLA INS P1 P2 LCfield Data field LEfield.

where LC and LE are the lengths of command data field and expected data response, respectively. Both LC and LE sizes may be either 1 or 3 bytes. In extended (i.e., 3 bytes) data field lengths, the first byte is always 00, whereas the second and third bytes declare data length. With this convention, data lengths are restricted to 65,536 bytes. The APDU structure for card response consists of a conditional data field (when requested by the command) and a mandatory 2-byte trailer (our old friends SW1 and SW2). If the command is rejected, an error condition is coded on trailer bytes.

5.4.4 Other Protocols

Protocol T = 0 is at present well established as the most common protocol for asynchronous communications with smart cards. The next standardized protocol will presumably be T = 1. Of course, development of the T = 0 protocol should continue. Protocols for synchronous communications are much less developed. To the best of our knowledge, no synchronous standard has been proposed yet.

ISO 7816/4 also includes some 12 tables with coding conventions for bytes CLA, INS, SW1, and SW2. The most relevant codes are indicated in the appendix. Some of these are used in the example in the following chapter. It is worth mentioning that ISO 7816/4 goes beyond the T = 0 protocol. Although T = 0 is the only defined protocol to date, part 4 includes several annexes where T = 0 is merely one possible protocol. T = 0 APDUs become TPDUs by assigning P3 = 00. Thus, case 1 above (CLA INS P1 P2) becomes CLA INS P1 P2 00. Case 4 is solved by splitting the command into two separate commands under certain conditions. Transportation of APDUs under the T = 1 protocol is also defined in 7816/4 annexes.

5.5 MEMORY STRUCTURE

In the previous chapter, we studied the different kinds of memory that may be found in a smart card. We will review here the logical structure of such kinds of memory. The size and functionality of the memory may vary from card to card. Generally, ROM memory containing the SCOS and several manufacturer codes cannot be accessed by issuers or by users. Let us concentrate, therefore, on the RAM and EEPROM memory (Figure 5.7).

5.5.1 Structure of RAM

This memory is employed chiefly to store intermediate results of the microprocessor. Moreover, it is used to handle ready-to-use information required by the microprocessor and so it usually has several predefined zones:

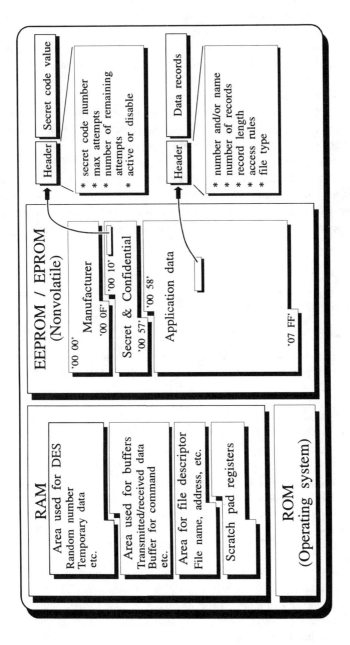

Figure 5.7 Memory structure in a card with no memory hierarchy. Most current cards follow this structure.

- *Scratch pad registers* have the same function as the usual microprocessor registers, such as holding numerical results, addresses, pointers, and the like. Scratch pad register length may be 1 byte or longer.
- *Built-in data encryption* usually has a dedicated RAM zone where data such as intermediate data, cryptographic parameters, and random numbers are stored and handled.
- *Buffer area* may be used to store command parameters (5-byte headers, for example). Additionally, data transmission and reception may use separate buffers; the transmission buffer may include a counter, whereas the reception buffer may store sequentially the last byte(s) received through the I/O port.
- *File data zone* stores the name and parameters of the working file when using files in the card. The microprocessor uses this zone to keep the address of the file within the user/application memory, as well as its size, record number, record lengths, and, most importantly, the addresses in the secret zone where the protection rules of that specific file are stored. These protection rules may in turn be temporarily stored in RAM.

5.5.2 Structure of Nonvolatile Memory

Nonvolatile memory is either EPROM or EEPROM (i.e., nonrewritable or rewritable). In any case, the most important part of this memory is the UAM. The UAM is structured according to one of the following formats.

- Memory is divided into several zones, whose size may be constant or variable. Every zone may hold one or several data files. Zones are separated according to their functionality, data type and/or protection level.
  - ISO 7816/4 describes a hierarchical file structure (similar to UNIX or DOS trees), though zones are also accepted for historical reasons (most current cards use zones) and for technological reasons (many cards cannot be hierarchically structured). Three file categories are considered: master files, dedicated files, and elementary files. Each card has a single master file (the *root*); paths are defined to access other files. There will be more discussion of this later.

In either case, the card must be formatted to define suitable areas. Some recent card models allow reformatting; other classic models are preformatted by the manufacturer. Let us assume for the following discussion that a single-byte format is used. Memory is divided into a finite number of elements, every one associated with an address. With the above condition, the maximum number of addresses is obviously the storage capacity of the card expressed in bytes.

5.5.3 Memory Zones

Memory zones are prepared by grouping several addresses, thus obtaining the corresponding memory chunk. Each zone may be split into different files, which in turn are made up of one or several records, each one having one or several bytes.

Let us introduce some file-related concepts using an example. We use a smart card whose UAM stores 2K. The first address is 00 00 and the last address is 07 FF hex. We want to define three zones: manufacturer zone, confidential zone, and application zone. (Note: the manufacturer zone will probably have been defined at manufacture; in fact, 2K cards seldom have 2K free.)

The manufacturer zone covers the first 16 bytes (i.e., from 00 00 to 00 0F hex). These addresses are organized into two 8-byte records; the first record (00 00 to 00 07) holds an ASCII-coded version of a card serial number, and the second (00 08 to 00 0F) holds other manufacturer data such as chip model and SCOS version. (Note: when files are made up of single records, both terms are often interchanged in smart card jargon.) Access to these records is free for reading, but writing is not allowed. (Therefore, our card has separate permission controls for reading and writing.) To read these bytes, we can use a pointer to the first address, 00 00, and send a command for sequential reading of 16 bytes. Alternatively, we may use record access by sending the corresponding command to read the first record and then the second record. In either case, the microprocessor has previously checked that no permission is required to read this zone.

The confidential zone in our example is located next to the manufacturer zone and covers 72 bytes, from 00 10 to 00 57 hex. We want to put here some secret access codes such as master key (issuer key), PIN, and a couple of confidential codes to allow partial access to other areas. We also include some space for data used in encryption/decryption processes, according to the built-in encipherment algorithm of our card (typically DES, described in Chapter 3; the encryption system gives an 8-byte result from an 8-byte secret number and an 8-byte input message; about 10^{18} combinations are possible). DES data are coded in a file containing one 8-byte record, located in the uppermost addresses of the zone (00 50 to 00 57 hex). The codes are stored in separate files, each file containing two 8-byte records. The second 8-byte record of each code holds the code itself (an enciphered version), whereas the first 8-byte record stores the specific handling parameters of that code, such as maximum number of permitted accesses, maximum number of consecutive wrong attempts to access, and whether the code may be modified by the user and/or the issuer.

Let us store the master key in hexadecimal addresses 00 10 to 00 1F, the PIN in 00 20 to 00 2F hex, and the other codes beginning at 00 30 and 00 40. When the user is instructed to enter his/her PIN, for example, the keyed-in alphanumeric string is compared to the hex number stored in 00 28 to 00 2F (after decryption, if necessary). The microprocessor has previously read the bytes 00 20 to 00 27 to decide what to do if the keyword is wrong, or the number of accesses is exceeded, or any other special situation. Once the keyword is accepted, the card allows access (for reading and/or writing) to those files that the user has proved he/she has the right to open.

The largest UAM area, from 00 58 to 07 FF hex, is dedicated in our example to application data. Older smart cards used to have predefined subzones with fixed access restrictions; in those cards, access to data was free or governed by different restrictions depending on subzone addresses. At present, each file has an associated field where access control is described. Every file consists of a header and a body for data. The header has a fixed length and structure (defined by the manufacturer unless new ISO standards are followed). Among other parameters, a header may contain the file name, number of records, size of data body, and protection for reading, writing, and/or erasing. Records within the file usually have the same length, although different record lengths are permitted. File access is allowed by the microprocessor after checking the header and working out that the required passwords have been previously validated.

5.5.4 Hierarchical Memory Structure

As mentioned above, ISO 7816/4 proposes a hierarchical file structure (Figure 5.8). The mandatory *root* is called *master file* (MF). The role of subdirectories is carried out by optional *dedicated files* (DF). Data are stored mainly in *elementary files* (EF). EFs may not be parents of DFs or other EFs. File control information is stored in the files or in the file's parents. Files are referenced by a 2-byte identifier. Paths to specific files are made by linking the identifiers of their parents, grandparents, and so forth, down to MF. MF identifier is always 3F 00 hex. DFs may also be referenced by unique file names.

Four EF types are defined:

- *Public EF*: free access;
- *Application control EF*: read protected; stores control information of the application;
- *Internal secret EF*: external access is always avoided;
- *Working EF*: to store application data.

EF structure may be one of the following.

- *Linear fixed*: several records of the same length;
- *Linear variable*: several records of different lengths;
- *Cyclic*: records of the same length in a ring;
- *Transparent*: sequence of bytes.

Several methods are also defined to reference data within files. Two basic systems are considered: byte reference and record reference. Byte reference (strictly speaking, data unit reference) uses a specific declaration of the byte address in two bytes. The first byte of the file is always 00 00. Record reference is done either by record number or by record identifier. Both are stored in single bytes, the main difference being that

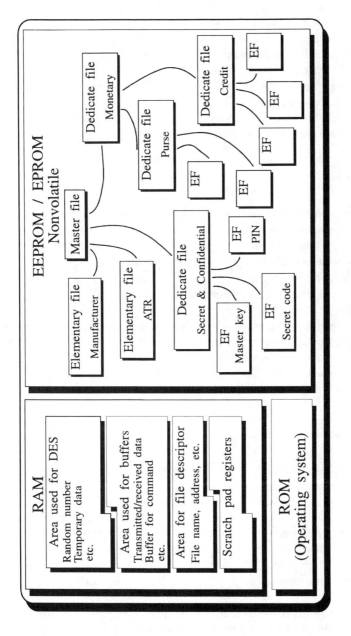

Figure 5.8 Hierarchical memory structure proposed by ISO 7816/4. ROM and RAM areas remain unmodified.

the record number is internally used by the card, while the record identifier is used from the outside. One important feature included in these reference systems is a predefined sequence: by definition, given a record whose number is N, the number of previous and subsequent records are $N - 1$ and $N + 1$; on the other hand, given a record whose identifier is ID, the previous and next records are those logically closest in lower and higher memory locations *with the same ID*.

Several special EF files are foreseen. The ATR file would store ATR information. Its default file identifier is 2F 01 hex. DIR files (default file identifier 2F 00 hex) are also considered. The structure of both ATR and DIR files is transparent. The presence of these files is revealed in the historical bytes.

5.6 SECURITY

Security is one of the main issues in smart cards. Every possible precaution has been taken to avoid fraudulent access to stored data. Memory is accessed through the microprocessor, which is continuously monitoring that every security requirement has been carried out, and permission to read, write, erase, and/or modify data is granted. The card may require identification, not only from card users, but even from the interface device with which it is trying to communicate. Mechanisms for temporal or permanent self-blocking of specific areas are provided. These mechanisms may be triggered by exceeding the number of consecutive wrong passwords or exceeding the number of permitted accesses, or simply by card invalidation from the application itself (expiry date, lost cards, etc.). The main concepts concerning security were reviewed in Chapter 3; these concepts will be applied here to actual cards. ISO 7816/4 is again mentioned, since it declares, for the first time, a standard security architecture for cards.

5.6.1 Cryptographic Algorithms

Most cards feature a cryptographic algorithm, usually wired into the microprocessor mask. In most instances, the algorithm currently implemented is DES. It employs two 64-bit numbers and gives a 64-bit result. For example, one of the numbers is typically an input message, and the other is a hidden cryptographic key. The mixing of these two numbers according to DES rules results in a third number R, the result. The algorithm is reversible; that is if R is mixed with the cryptographic key, the former input message is obtained. Cryptographic keys are written into card memory, and that memory area becomes read-protected; only the microprocessor may access those keys in order to perform its calculations.

Other proprietary cryptographic algorithms may involve more parameters. For example, Bull's TELEPASS gives a 96-bit result from a 96-bit cryptographic key, a 16-bit address, a 32-bit data field stored at this address, and a 48-bit external keyword.

Cryptographic keys are used to encrypt passwords, data, and messages. For example, sensitive data are not stored in card memory as such, but enciphered through a key. Issuers may use some algorithms to store specific encrypted information in selected addresses of the card; the constancy of such information may be checked afterwards. On the other hand, a smart card may be used on line for cryptographic data transmission to remote users, thus securing the communication. Issuer keys such as the master key, and sometimes PINs, are routinely encrypted, too. Therefore, even under the unlikely possibility of fraudulent access to a PIN, the obtained string is useless as a keyword.

5.6.2 Keys

Keys, keywords, or passwords are alphanumeric strings introduced into the cards from an external input. Keys are classified according to the generic holder of the information: manufacturer, issuer, external device, or user. The manufacturer may introduce security mechanisms into the card, including keywords, to avoid access to special memory zones. There is also a personalization key to be used at the beginning of card life cycle. This key is a card ID to allow applications to recognize their cards.

The issuer usually owns one or several issuer keys that protect his/her information or critical parts of the applications. Issuer keys may be used directly by the issuer, or preprogrammed in the application. An issuer key to recover blocked cards (e.g., by exceeding number of wrong user PINs) or to recycle (or refill) outdated cards is routinely included. Privileges to erase a PIN or create a new one may also be assigned to issuer keys. Users may have one or several PINs to access different memory zones or different applications in the case of multipurpose cards. There may be a primary PIN with higher access privileges than secondary PINs, thus distinguishing, for example, between card owner and holder.

A typical card may allow 8 to 16 keys, or as many as the applications need. For example, the information data sheet of one medium-level smart card specifies one manufacturer key, one personalization key, one primary issuer key, four secondary issuer keys, and four user keys. Of course, applications need not use all of them.

5.6.3 Key Functions

Keys may be used for a number of internal and external card tasks. Besides the common issuer key or user PIN request (Figure 5.9) to execute commands or allow access to data areas, four possible uses are worth mentioning: authentication, certification, telewriting, and invalidation. Note that the list loosely matches the tasks performed by symmetric cryptosystems, as described in Chapter 3, though the terms are not necessarily the same.

Authentication. A process by which the card recognizes the WRU, remote server, or interface unit with which it is trying to communicate. A message is sent from the card to the interface device. The device encrypts it using a key K, and returns the encrypted

Key presentation

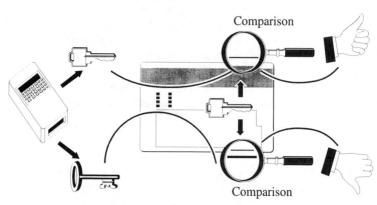

Figure 5.9(a) Steps followed in a key presentation to authenticate a user or issuer: direct key presentation, usually employed for user PINs.

message to the card. The card decrypts the message with its own key and compares it to the former string. If both messages match, the card learns that the external device holds the same key K as the one it has. Alternatively, the card may encrypt the message in advance, and the device must decrypt it and give the result back to the card. Note that, in this context, authentication and challenge are equivalent.

Certification. A process to check whether a data item is stored at a specific location in the card. It is used to identify cards within the scope of a certain application. The device asks the card to perform a calculation (e.g., encryption) on data located at a specific address using an internal card key K. The result is sent to the interface device, which analyzes the calculation and verifies that K matches the key stored in its own memory. Again, this is a challenge process, though in this case the card is challenged by the external device.

Telewriting. A process allowing an issuer to write protected information into the card while it is being handled by a user. The issuer prepares a message consisting of the desired information, address, and field reference. The message is encrypted using a key K. The encrypted message is introduced into the card by the application (after reading ATR, for example). The card decrypts the message using the same key K (an issuer key) and checks that the address and the reference match some previously stored data. The message is then accepted and stored.

Invalidation. An issuer may invalidate an outdated (stolen, lost) card. Providers of specific services in multifunction cards may invalidate their own services, with the card being still usable otherwise. Upon request of invalidation, the card sends a message to the external device. To authenticate the issuer or provider, the device encrypts the message using the invalidation key. The message is then decrypted by the card and compared to

Encrypted key presentation

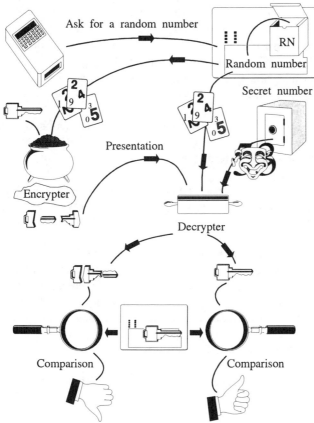

Figure 5.9(b) Steps followed in a key presentation to authenticate a user or issuer: presentation with encryption/decryption intermediate processes, usually employed for issuer authentication.

the former one. If a match is found, the invalidation procedure is executed. This mechanism is independent of automatic card blocking for such reasons as fraudulent access and exceeding PIN trials.

5.6.4 Security in ISO 7816/4

Security issues in 7816/4 are divided into two parts: card security and message security. The first part involves the actions and structures designed to protect the information stored in cards. Ultimately, a security architecture is defined for this purpose. The second part focuses on the protection of messages to and from the card. This involves encryption, checks for data integrity, and data concealment. The card security architecture consists of security status, security attributes, and security mechanisms.

Status is the current security state of the card, indicating the permitted actions and data restrictions. It is modified by the presentation of user and issuer keywords, and by device authentication. Security status may be global, file-oriented, or command-oriented. Global security status is modified by MF-related passwords; file-oriented security status is modified by DF-related keywords, and command-oriented status is used during the completion of an authentication command.

The security *attributes* of a file define the permitted actions and procedures. File attributes depend on the category (MF, DF, EF). Within EFs, attributes depend on the type of file. File control information of the file itself or of its parents may contain optional parameters.

Security *mechanisms* for presentation and invocation are defined. The presentation checks data sent to the card (e.g., user PINs or issuer keys); the invocation involves the use of a command containing encrypted data. The command is executed after checking that data are consistent with a hidden key.

Secure messaging is designed to protect data flow to and from the card. Data are sent and received in cryptographic form. ASN.1 encoding rules are recommended. Message format, cryptographic algorithm (including operation mode), and cryptographic keys are selected either implicitly or explicitly using identifiers.

Most items related to enciphering and cryptography in 7816/4 follow the general rules given above, though they are more thoroughly detailed. The use and scope of concealed objects is described. The idea is to include a hidden message in a data string by adding a cryptographic key. Once the key is decrypted, the hidden message is interpreted by XORing selected bytes of the string with the key. No padding is therefore needed.

5.7 CONCLUSIONS

In this chapter, the most important issues relating to data structure and communications with cards have been reviewed. State-of-the-art features and foreseen extensions announced in ISO 7816/4 have been extensively, though not exhaustively, studied. After reading the chapter, however, one may have the feeling that too many rules have been squeezed into such a tiny subject. This is not the case; actually, cards may come along using just a handful of the above standards. The existence of a general framework that rules most of the situations an issuer developing applications may deal with is quite useful nonetheless. When standards are tightly observed, compatibility between alien systems is guaranteed. In the next chapter, we will apply our recently acquired knowledge to the development of software modules for performing the most common tasks a well-behaved card is supposed to do. Leaving theory aside, we will delve into the world of real programming.

Chapter 6
Programming a Smart Card

It is time to prepare our own set of functions to allow the external world to communicate with cards. By the end of this chapter, the basic functions required for preparing an application for smart cards and applying those functions to a specific card model will have been presented. Smart cards are put to work by means of applications prepared by issuers. Cards are instructed by applications to perform precise duties. They have to be personalized, learning both who their owners are and what tasks they are supposed to do.

6.1 SOFTWARE FUNCTIONS

When designing an application, the issuer must take into account the main issues stated in the above lines. The software package will contain at least three groups of functions, each having precise responsibilities:

- *Format.* Functions for formatting the card, defining its internal structure, data areas, data protection mechanisms, and the necessary details of the application. These functions are to be used when the card is issued. Optionally, recovery functions to be used throughout the active life of the card are included in this group.
- *Identification.* Functions for identifying the card's owner. These include functions to create and modify PINs, as well as controls against fraudulent access. A card may have several users; multifunction cards may be employed by different users for different tasks. The holder of the card may be the same as the owner, or may be just restricted to some areas of the card. Finally, the issuer (or the manufacturer) may have reserved some areas that can only be accessed by means of a master key (MK).
- *Management.* Functions for handling the user transactions. Both this group and the previous one must be resident in the external device that drives the card (usually a computer or a WRU). The management group includes functions for opening,

reading, writing, modifying, and erasing data files according to the restriction and protection controls present in the above functions.

This chapter provides examples of the functions needed by an external computer to manage a smart card. From a logical point of view, these functions are classified in levels, according to their use and scope. High-level functions are hardware-independent; that is, they may be used with any computer and smart card. Lower-level functions are sometimes dependent either on the computer, the smart card, or both.

Trying to be as general as possible, we developed the examples below on a PC-compatible computer, using the general-purpose communication functions of an RS-232 serial port. The functions are written in the ANSI C language to improve portability. For the same reason, our WRU will be the simplest one, merely devoted to handling the messages coming to and from the card; smarter WRUs, which may even be employed as independent units, require upload/download functions to program the unit at the beginning of the session and to bring back accumulated data at the end.

The card chosen for the example is a GUTI GC2, a fictitious card, which exemplifies fairly well the current performance of a medium-high-level smart card. The WRU is a GUTI ULE2. Both WRU and card adhere tightly to ISO standards, specifically ISO 7816/3. In an attempt to demonstrate card dependence in a nutshell, the chapter finishes with a program designed to analyze ATRs from ISO cards.

The WRU is installed as a peripheral of a personal computer using a serial port. We will review the main features of this peripheral. The most interesting characteristics of the smart card will also be described. Initially, some descriptions may look too detailed for such a subject. Keep in mind, however, that this information may be applied, with few changes, to many current cards and WRUs.

6.2 WRITING/READING UNIT

A WRU is the typical interface device that links the card to external devices. As mentioned several times throughout the book, WRUs range from simple communication links between the card and an external computer to complete computing systems that manage the cards on their own. The best WRU for an application need not be the most expensive nor the most complete; the choice ultimately depends on several factors, the most important being whether the application will run on line or off line, whether off-line situations in an on-line application are foreseen and supported, and, finally, whether we need our system to be portable or not.

Commercial WRUs are offered as internal units (just a card-sized slot in the front panel of the computer) or external units, which look like a pocket calculator (Figure 6.1), often including keyboard, display, and a second serial port to be connected to a printer (Figure 6.2). Some models allow simultaneous insertion of two cards; these models are specially useful in applications where one of the cards is used as a hardware key to control the operations performed by the other cards. At the same time, it may be used to summarize the transactions carried out by the WRU.

Figure 6.1 External WRU for smart cards (courtesy of Philips).

Even the simplest WRU is supposed to perform several tasks concerning card handling. In addition to communications, WRU duties include several basic functions that allow the card to work properly. Many WRUs perform these functions upon request from the external system, while other, more sophisticated WRUs are able to manage the card by themselves.

- *Card Detection.* The WRU must detect the presence of the card when it is introduced and when it is removed (and determine whether the object that has been introduced *is* a chip card or not). A WRU should not allow, for example, the substitution of a card by another before closing the transactions and requesting removal of the former card.
- V_{CC} *Supply.* This voltage must be supplied upon card insertion to start the card's internal routines.
- *Clock.* The WRU must supply clock signals if needed. This depends on the card type: synchronous or asynchronous, with or without internal clock.
- *Reset.* Reset signals should be provided as needed. In particular, as soon as the card is inserted, the WRU must connect the clock and send a reset pulse to request the ATR from the card. This task may be accomplished by the WRU itself with no external actions. In this way, most anomalous situations are solved with a mere

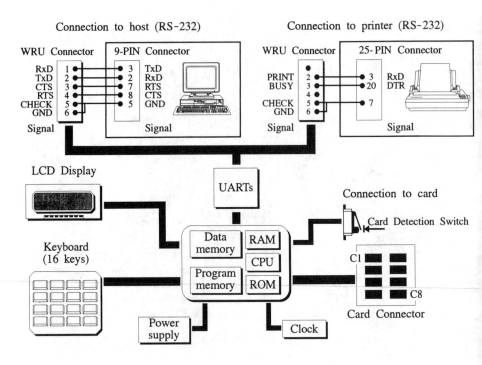

Figure 6.2 Typical WRU.

"No ATR received" message from the WRU to the external computer. Anomalous situations include improper card insertion (e.g., cards inserted upside down or back to front, or cards without chip), nonstandard (or unsuitable) cards, and malfunctioning and defective cards. To avoid rejections arising from minor problems, such as dirty contacts, WRUs repeat the reset procedure several times prior to rejecting the card. Another anomalous situation the WRU must handle is the unexpected removal of the card when the communication is still active (i.e., when the current procedure has not yet finished).

- V_{PP} *Supply.* V_{PP} must be supplied *if and when* requested by the card. In the previous chapter, we studied the convention employed by cards to solicit V_{PP} depending on the instructions and the card hardware. Note that this service requires the WRU to analyze the card answers to external orders to see whether V_{PP} has been requested or not.

- *Electrical Protection.* The card is protected against static charges. Yet improper voltages (such as spikes) may damage the microcircuit. These voltages must be filtered out by the WRU.

- *Protocols.* The WRU must support at least one communication protocol, usually $T = 0$. This should include the corresponding translation of serial port messages to the card protocol and vice versa.

Many WRUs include extra features, namely, ATR recognition or multiple start/reset routines. ATR recognition allows WRUs to adapt automatically their communication parameters to those suggested or imposed by the card. Multiple routines may be used to attempt connection to different card types (e.g., synchronous and asynchronous cards). Our quite simple fictitious reader, for example, attempts a synchronous protocol several times, and then it performs the routine for asynchronous cards. Since the clock frequency for synchronous protocols is only a few tens of kilohertz, asynchronous cards remain silent during synchronous attempts, waiting for a frequency of between 1 and 5 MHz.

An important point derived from this section is that the computer interfaced to the WRU must expect incoming messages from both the card and the WRU itself.

6.3 GUTI GC2 SMART CARD

Our fictitious GUTI GC2 is an ISO 7816 smart card equipped with an 8-bit microprocessor operating up to 5 MHz. The memory is divided into several areas:

- RAM—128 bytes;
- ROM—4,096 bytes;
- EEPROM—2,048 bytes.

The card implements a DES encryption/decryption algorithm. DES operations are performed in the scratch pad (RAM) memory. The minimum execution time for executing one instruction at the maximum frequency is about 1 μs (DES algorithms on 8 bytes typically take some 150 ms). The microprocessor employs 100 instructions. The programming voltage V_{PP} is obtained out of V_{CC}; therefore, this card uses only five contacts: VCC C1, RST C2, CLK C3, GND C5, and I/O C7. (See Chapter 4 for more details on memory areas and contacts.)

ISO environmental requirements (e.g., mechanical, electromagnetic, X-ray) are fulfilled or surpassed by the card. An interesting feature is that the user/application memory is of the EEPROM type (not EPROM as in older models). This allows multiple erasing and rewriting of UAM; in fact, the card includes an instruction for global erasing, returning the card to its initial (as manufactured) state.

6.3.1 EEPROM Structure

Rewritable UAM of GC2 (Figure 6.3) is divided into three parts:

- An area for secret codes and the MK (usually the issuer key). This area uses the first 160 bytes of UAM to store 16 secret codes, including the MK and the PIN.
- An area for data files next to the previous area, covering most of UAM.
- A fabrication area to store the card serial number. This area uses the last 9 bytes of UAM.

104

Organization of EEPROM

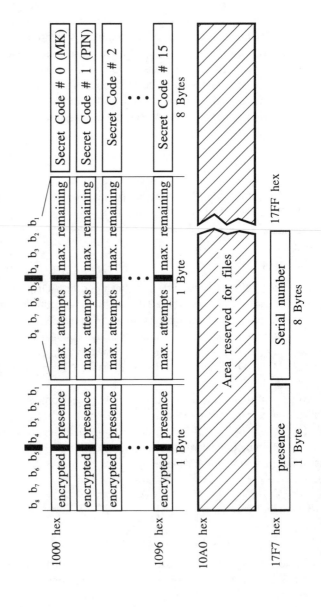

Figure 6.3 Areas of GC2 EEPROM memory.

The first secret code (code #0 or SK0) is the MK, and the second secret code (code #1 or SK1) is the PIN. The remaining codes are numbered SK2 through SK15. MK and PIN have several privileges, which are chiefly related to card blocking (see Section 6.5.6). All the secret codes, including MK and PIN, have 10 bytes with the same structure.

- The first byte indicates whether the code has been written (byte = xxxx xxx0) or not (byte = xxxx xxx1).
- If the code has been written, then the least significant bit of the upper nibble indicates whether the code is encrypted (byte = xxx0 xxx0) or not (byte = xxx1 xxx0). Otherwise, the bit is meaningless. The card implements a built-in DES algorithm, which is used for encryption. The remaining bits of the upper nibble may be used for indicating code encryption with other algorithms (implemented in EXEC functions, for example). The remaining bits of the lower nibble are reserved for future use (RFU).
- The second byte is also split into two nibbles. The upper nibble contains the maximum number of consecutive incorrect attempts permitted for the code (1 to 15). If the number is zero, then the number is unlimited. The lower nibble controls the current number of incorrect attempts. When the secret code is created, both nibbles have the same value. The lower nibble is decreased by one each time a wrong code is entered. If the correct code is entered, the nibble is reset to the maximum number.
- The remaining 8 bytes contain the secret code.

The area reserved for the manufacturer at the end of the data area consists of 1 presence byte, as above, and 8 bytes for the serial number. All the bytes in these areas (actually, all EEPROM bytes) are initially set to FF hex.

EEPROM addresses are located at 1000 hex. Therefore, the address of the MK-present byte is precisely 1000 hex. The address of the PIN-present byte is 100A hex, and so on. The final byte of the last secret code is at 109F hex, and the first byte of the data area is at 10A0 hex. The last byte of the data area is at 17F6 hex, and the remaining addresses, from 17F7 hex to 17FF hex are reserved for the manufacturer. A simple hexadecimal subtraction gives 757 hex, or 1,879 bytes, remaining for data.

6.3.2 Answer to Reset

GC2 ATR consists of the following bytes (Figure 6.4): 3F, F9, 11, 20, 04, 40, FF, xx, yy, zz, ww, 47, 43, 32, 90, 00. Let us analyze the information contained here. Refer to the previous chapters for detailed explanation of byte meanings.

- 3F is the TS byte, indicating that this card employs inverse convention.
- F9 is the T0 byte. The first nibble F hex announces that TA_1, TB_1, TC_1, and TD_1 follow. The second nibble 9 hex indicates that 9 historical characters are included.
- 11: TA_1 establishes a transfer rate of 9,600 bps and a clock frequency of 3.57 MHz.
- 20: TB_1 shows that no programming voltage V_{PP} is required and limits the maximum programming current to 50 mA.

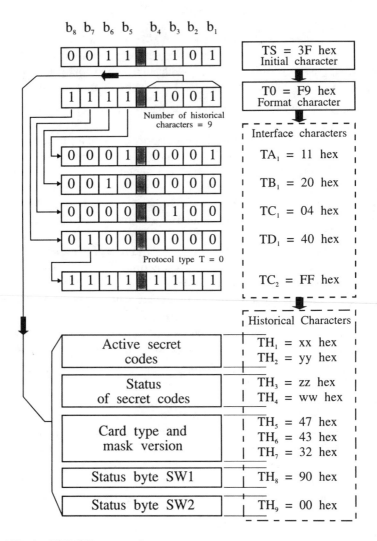

b$_8$ b$_7$ b$_6$ b$_5$ b$_4$ b$_3$ b$_2$ b$_1$

| 0 | 0 | 1 | 1 | | 1 | 1 | 0 | 1 |

TS = 3F hex
Initial character

| 1 | 1 | 1 | 1 | | 1 | 0 | 0 | 1 |

T0 = F9 hex
Format character

Number of historical
characters = 9

Interface characters

| 0 | 0 | 0 | 1 | | 0 | 0 | 0 | 1 | TA$_1$ = 11 hex

| 0 | 0 | 1 | 0 | | 0 | 0 | 0 | 0 | TB$_1$ = 20 hex

| 0 | 0 | 0 | 0 | | 0 | 1 | 0 | 0 | TC$_1$ = 04 hex

| 0 | 1 | 0 | 0 | | 0 | 0 | 0 | 0 | TD$_1$ = 40 hex

Protocol type T = 0

| 1 | 1 | 1 | 1 | | 1 | 1 | 1 | 1 | TC$_2$ = FF hex

Historical Characters

Active secret codes	TH$_1$ = xx hex TH$_2$ = yy hex
Status of secret codes	TH$_3$ = zz hex TH$_4$ = ww hex
Card type and mask version	TH$_5$ = 47 hex TH$_6$ = 43 hex TH$_7$ = 32 hex
Status byte SW1	TH$_8$ = 90 hex
Status byte SW2	TH$_9$ = 00 hex

Figure 6.4 ATR of a GUTI GC2 smart card.

- 04: TC$_1$ asks for an extra guard time of 4 etu.
- 40: TD$_1$ announces that protocol T = 0 is to be used. Regarding the second set of interface bytes, only TC$_2$ will be sent.
- FF: TC$_2$ (as defined in ISO standards for T = 0) establishes that the maximum waiting time between two consecutive characters is 25.5 sec. This is the last interface byte; the following bytes are historical.
- xx, yy: these 16 bits are associated with the 16 secret codes. Every bit = 1 announces that its corresponding secret code is active. For example, if xx = 72 hex, the secret

codes #9, 12, 13, and 14 (SK9, SK12, SK13, and SK14) are active. Similarly, if yy = 0F hex, the MK, PIN, SK2, and SK3 are active.

- zz, ww: again, these 16 bits are associated with the 16 secret codes, indicating which code, if any, has reached the permitted number of consecutive wrong attempts. For instance, if zz = 00 hex and ww = 04 hex, SK2 has reached its limit of attempts. If ww = xxxx xxx1 bin (MK out of limits), the card cannot be used. If ww = xxxx xx10 bin (PIN blocked), the card only accepts the reactivation command through the MK.
- 47, 43, 32 are ASCII characters G, C, and 2, indicating card type and mask version.
- 90, 00 are status bytes.

Note that the only declared protocol is T = 0; therefore, TCK has not been sent. The historical bytes chosen in this card are quite useful for rejecting disabled cards as soon as the ATR is received. For example, any reader would reject a card whose MK is blocked; only special WRUs in which card reactivation is permitted would accept a card whose PIN is blocked.

6.3.3 File Types

Files within the GUTI GC2 consist of records. These records are all of the same length. Only one file may be handled at a time. Three types of files may be created.

- *Regular files* 00 hex. These files are protected by any group of secret codes, including MK and/or PIN.
- *Purse files* 01 hex. A purse is a special kind of file prepared for financial transactions, containing four records: balance, transaction number, transaction date, and credit limit (see Section 6.3.6).
- *Read-only files* 02 hex. These files are created and written once through specific instructions (therefore, they are actually WORM files). After creation, the files cannot be rewritten or erased, except if the whole card is erased.

All the files are located at the same level: no hierarchical structure is allowed. Records are accessed by positioning a pointer on the file and specifying a record number. Records may have up to 240 bytes.

6.3.4 Access Rules

Access to files is separately controlled for reading and writing. The file header (see below) contains access-rules bytes split into nibbles (Figure 6.5). Within each byte, the MSN controls access for reading, and the LSN controls access for writing. Each bit of any nibble activates a different protection.

- $b_1 = 1$: the file is protected by a secret code SKa.
- $b_2 = 1$: the file is protected by a second secret code SKb.

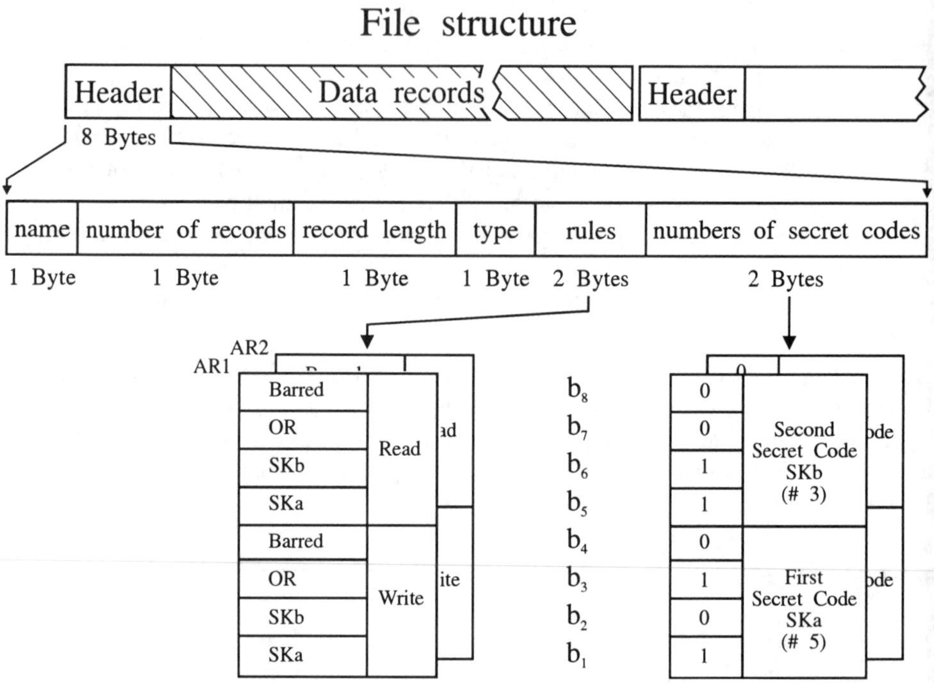

File structure

Figure 6.5 Structure of a file, a file header, and an access-rules byte.

- $b_3 = 1$: OR bit. The file is protected by SKa OR SKb. If b_3 is set, b_2 and b_1 are meaningless.
- $b_4 = 1$: the file is blocked for reading and/or writing. This bit is also used in WORM files for labeling the file as read-only.

SKa and SKb are secret codes, including MK and PIN. Any combination is allowed. For example, if MSN = 0011 bin (3 hex), reading access to the file requires the use of two SKs. If MSN = 0000 bin and LSN = 01xx bin (4, 5, 6, or 7 hex), reading is free but writing requires the use of one secret code (either SKa or SKb). Any access-rules byte 1xxx 1xxx bin avoids reading/writing of the file.

As mentioned above, b_4 bits are also employed in WORM files (02 hex type). When a WORM file is created, the access-rules byte is set to 1xxx 0xxx (write-only). When it is written, the byte changes to 0xxx 1xxx (read-only). With this access-rules byte, the file cannot be rewritten, but it can be read (providing the requested SKs are presented). As in regular files, if the byte is 1xxx 1xxx, the file is blocked for reading and writing. The remaining bits work in the same way as in regular files, though permissions for writing are not active, of course.

Two access-rules bytes are included in the header of every file. Therefore, any file may be protected by zero to four secret codes. b_4 bits of the second-byte nibbles are meaningless.

6.3.5 File Header

Every file is made of an 8-byte header and an arbitrary number of identical records. The header includes six fields.

- byte 1: file name. Any hexadecimal number but FF may be used.
- byte 2: number of records contained in the file.
- byte 3: record length. The file size excluding the header may be calculated as the byte 2 times the byte 3.
- byte 4: file type. In this card, it must be either 00 hex (ordinary), 01 hex (purse), or 02 hex (read-only file).
- bytes 5, 6: access rules. The nibbles of these bytes are used as flags to establish different protections.
- bytes 7, 8: secret codes. The nibbles of bytes 7 and 8 contain the numbers of the secret codes (0 to 15 hex) employed in the access rules of bytes 5 and 6, respectively. If byte 6 is 00 hex, byte 8 is meaningless. If byte 5 is 00 hex (i.e., free access), both bytes 7 and 8 are meaningless, since byte 5 is used before byte 6 for access rules.

6.3.6 Purse Files

Purse files have the same header structure, but the file content is slightly different. Any purse file must have one 2-byte and three 3-byte *records*. The records always contain the same information: balance, transaction number (two bytes, containing authorization number, service provider ID, and so on), transaction date, and credit limit for that purse. Debit instructions are governed by the first access-rules byte, while credit instructions are governed by the second. An extra byte next to the transaction number is used for controlling the access rules applying in each case (therefore, purse files have actually four records of the same length). This structure allows the purses to be used as electronic cash.

Moreover, the contents of purse files are protected by a *mirror* memory outside the UAM. The mirror consists of a copy of the last accessed purse and the name of that purse file. Any operation performed in the purse is copied in the mirror memory. When the card is inserted, it checks the contents of the mirror, and compares them with the contents of the corresponding purse. By duplicating the information, the card may reconstruct the data even in anomalous situations, such as premature card removal. The card software eventually restores the potentially damaged data. Since only one file is opened at any time, the mirror always has updated information on the last purse file used, precisely the one whose data may be damaged.

6.3.7 Card Instructions

Instructions accepted by GC2 cards are summarized in Tables 6.1 to 6.5. The instructions belong to cases 1, 2, and 3 of transmission protocol T = 0, as defined in ISO 7816/3

Table 6.1
File and Record Commands

Name	Case	INS	P1	P2	P3	Data
MakeFile	2	A0	File name 00 to FE	Number of records*	05	Record length Two bytes for access rules Two bytes for secret codes
MakeWORM	2	A6	File name 00 to FE	Number of records*	05	Record length Two bytes for access rules Two bytes for secret codes
SelectFile	1	A4	File name	00	00	
WriteRecord	2	D2	00	Record number†	Number of bytes‡	String to be written
WriteWORM	2	D6	00	Record number	Number of bytes	String to be written
ReadRecord	3	B2	00	Record Number†	Number of bytes‡	String to be read

*A file may contain up to 255 records.
†Record #0 in functions WriteRecord and ReadRecord, means writing and reading in RAM, respectively.
‡A record may contain up to 240 bytes. RAM "records" are limited to 8 bytes.

Table 6.2
Electronic Purse Commands

Name	Case	INS	P1	P2	P3	Data
MakePurse	2	A2	File name 00 to FE	00	0A	Transaction date (3 bytes) Credit limit (3 bytes) Two bytes for access rules Two bytes for secret codes
Loan	2	50	00	00	03	Loan amount (3 bytes)
Payment	2	52	00	00	03	Payment amount (3 bytes)
PurseInfo	3	54	00	00	08	Remaining balance (3 bytes) Transaction number (2 bytes) Transaction date (3 bytes)

(Figure 6.6). Extensions suggested in 7816/4 are not supported by this card. Therefore instructions may carry no data (case 1), may carry data from the WRU to the card (case 2), or may carry data from the card to the WRU (case 3); bidirectional data flow (case 4) is not permitted. From a functional point of view, GC2 instructions may be divided into five categories.

- Related to *files* (e.g., create, read, write);
- Related to *purses* (e.g., credit, debit);
- Related to *keys* (e.g., write, change, present);

Table 6.3

Keys/PIN Management

Name	Case	INS	P1	P2	P3	Data
SetSK	2	22	Max attempts[*]	Secret code number[†] 00 to 0F or 10 to 1F[‡]	08	Secret code
VerifySK	2	20	00	Secret code number[†] 00 to 0F	08	Secret code
ModifySK	2	24	00	Secret code number[†] 00 to 0F	08	New secret code
ReactKeys	1	26	00	00	00	

[*]Number of consecutive incorrect entry attempts allowed before disabling (infinity if P1 = 00).
[†]The secret code #00 is called the master key of the card and the secret code #01 is called the PIN code of the card.
[‡]The first nibble of the number indicates whether the secret code is encrypted (xxx0) or not (xxx1).

Table 6.4

Enciphering Functions

Name	Case	INS	P1	P2	P3	Data
Encrypt	1	E0	Destination[*]	Source[*]	00	
Decrypt	1	E2	Destination[*]	Source[*]	00	
Random	1	E4	00	00	00	
Challenge	1	E6	00	00	00	
ChallengeAns	2	E8	00	00	08	The answer to challenge

[*]If 0, data is stored in or read from RAM, or else data is stored in or read from EEPROM (P1, P2 indicating record numbers of the file currently selected).

Table 6.5

Special Functions

Name	Case	INS	P1	P2	P3	Data
ReadSerialNo	3	BA	00	00	08	Serial Number
WipeOutCard	1	02	00	00	00	
EraseFile	1	04	Number of records	Number of bytes	00	
CrunchCard	1	06	00	00	00	
ReportSK	3	28	Secret code number	00	02	1st byte MSN: SK encrypted 1st byte LSN: SK active 2nd byte: max and remaining attempts

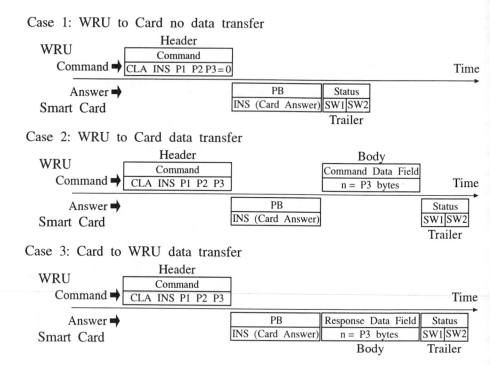

Figure 6.6 Data flow in the three allowed cases of transmission protocol T = 0.

- Related to data *enciphering* (e.g., encrypt, decrypt, random generation);
- *Special* instructions (e.g., read manufacturer's serial number, status of secret codes, erase card).

Tables 6.1 to 6.5 follow this order. The instructions have the classic format CLA INS P1 P2 P3 (P3 = L, the length of data sent or expected; see Chapter 5). CLA is not included in the tables, since GUTI cards always use CLA = 0A hex. The execution of many commands requires the previous presentation of one or several secret codes; besides those specifically requested by the application program, many restrictions arise simply from common sense: for example, the MK cannot be read, nor can it be modified if the old MK is not previously introduced.

6.3.8 Return Codes

Status bytes SW1 and SW2 are used by the card to indicate the fate of the executed commands; when any problem precludes execution, a complaint message is sent in these bytes. The messages loosely follow ISO 7816/4 conventions. When any problem is found, SW1 byte is 6x hex, where x is any hex digit except 0. The hexadecimal values of possible answers are:

- 90 00: command executed OK.
- 62 81: returned data may be corrupted.
- 62 82: the end of the file has been reached before the end of reading.
- 62 84: selected file is not valid.
- 65 01: memory failure. There have been problems in writing or reading the EEPROM. Other hardware problems may also bring about this error.
- 67 00: the command length is not correct.
- 68 00: the requested function is not supported by the card.
- 69 00: unknown command. The instruction is not recognized; most probably it is a problem of erroneous typing, protocol violation, or incorrect format. Some instructions included in the T = 0 description included in the ISO 7816/4 draft are not known by this card.
- 6A 00: bytes P1 and/or P2 are incorrect.
- 6A 80: the parameters in the data field are incorrect.
- 6A 82: file not found.
- 6A 83: record not found.
- 6A 84: there is insufficient memory space in record or file.
- 6A 87: the P3 value is not consistent with P1 and P2 values.
- 6A 88: referenced data not found.
- 6C xx: incorrect P3 length.
- 6D xx: wrong instruction code.
- 6E xx: the instruction class is not supported by this card.
- 6F xx: generic error. An error has been detected, but a precise diagnosis cannot be given.

.4 COMMUNICATIONS

The computer will be connected to the WRU through a serial port; messages for the card and for the WRU itself must be made distinguishable, since both are sent through the same port.

.4.1 WRU Communication Conventions

All the commands come from the computer. The transmission protocol for the serial port of GUTI ULE2 is 19,200 bauds, 8 data bits, 1 stop bit, no parity. The format of the communication packages is:

| STX | Number of bytes | Message | ETX | LRC |

LRC is an XOR of all Message characters (i.e., a check sum). The unit answers use the same format, including in the Message body 1 byte indicating the status of the WRU and the card type (the GUTI ULE2 WRU recognizes several types of GUTI cards, as well a generic synchronous and asynchronous cards). The format is the same regardless c whether the command destination is the WRU or the card. The WRU finds out the messag destination by checking the first two bytes of the message (message header; see below. If the command is for the card, the WRU removes the package headers and trailer, send the command to the card, and waits for the card answer. Once the answer is receivec the WRU prepares the corresponding communication package and sends it back to th computer.

Besides the commands addressed to the card, there exist some commands for th WRU itself. These are identified by their message headers. The most important are Powe On ("ON" header) and Power Off ("OF" header), which are needed to insert (i.e., rese and withdraw the card from the unit.

Commands for the card must be headed by "IN" or "OU" for input and outpt commands, respectively (i.e., for commands sending data to or from the card). Thus, th structure CLA INS P1 P2 P3 becomes "IN" CLA INS P1 P2 P3 for cases 1 and 2, an "OU" CLA INS P1 P2 P3 for case 3 instructions.

6.4.2 Serial Communications

In the example below, we will use standard RS-232 serial communication functions t send the commands. The listings of such functions are beyond the scope of this book; if yo need further information on this issue, please consult any book on serial communications i C. Listing 6.1 is the header file *ser_port.h*, which contains the preprocessor constant and function prototypes of the serial communication functions employed by the WRl and card functions shown below. All listings discussed in this chapter may be found i Appendix B.

The serial port is accessed through function *TxRxMessage()* for commands comin to and from the card and through several auxiliary functions for commands addressed t the WRU. Listings 6.2 and 6.3 are *wru_guti.h* and *wru_guti.c*, the header file and sourc code for managing the WRU.

The source code *wru_guti.c* contains several functions. However, the card functior mentioned in the next paragraph call only one of these functions, *TxRxMessage()*. Thi is intended to be a general-purpose transmission function, which handles all possibl communication features between the computer and the WRU. The other functions ar used internally by the general function.

6.5 CARD FUNCTIONS

The preceding and several subsequent functions use type definitions which deserve a explanation. We routinely use **enum** types to define the different return values of function: For example, the type **t_err_tx**, which is heavily used above, is defined as

```
typedef enum { ERROR_TX,
               OK_TX
             } t_err_tx;
```

he use of **enum** types has the advantage of limiting the number of permitted return alues from the functions while behaving as **int** values otherwise. By using the default alue assignment of these types, a sequential list of **int** values is obtained. The types also elp to enhance the readability of the listings, since symbolic names are used to represent nteger values. **enum** types are used instead of separate constants to stress the clustering f these constants. The use of a different WRU and/or card model may require the nodification of some of these groups (e.g., increasing or decreasing the number of options).

Management of smart card commands is done in file *card_cmd.c*, which contains s many functions as commands accepted by the card (and a few extra functions; see elow). The prototypes of these functions are stored in *card_cmd.h*. Wherever possible, unctions use symbolic names mimicking the names of the card instructions. The type eclaration for error management is stored in a separate file named *sc_tools.h*.

.5.1 *#includes*, *#defines*, **typedefs, and Function Prototypes**

isting 6.4 is the header file *sc_tools.h*, which must be *#include*d at the beginning of the ile *card_cmd.h*. *sc_tools.h* holds all the required type definitions and a couple of function rototypes whose code is developed in Listing 6.5, *sc_tools.c*. The most interesting code ragment in *sc_tools.h* is the **typedef** defining the **enum** type **t_error_card**. This type is sed in the card functions of *card_cmd.c*; therefore, the return value of these functions nay eventually be used to detect errors and problems arising either from communications r from the card itself. Error analysis depends on the answer received from the WRU/card ystem. This task is performed by the function *CardErrorAnalysis( )* from file *sc_tools.c*.)ccasionally, the error analysis also depends on the specific instruction; this feature has ot been implemented here. The other function of *sc_tools.c*, *FillMessage( )*, merely fills p the first five bytes of every instruction (i.e., CLA, INS, P1, P2, P3). *sc_tools.h* also ontains the sentence *#include wru_guti.h* to access the WRU and the serial port (as ru_guti.h, in turn, *#include*s *ser_port.h*). Looking at the modularity and structure of the iles, several levels may be found:

- *Level 0*. Low-level files that take care of serial communications: *ser_port.c* (not shown here) and *ser_port.h*;
- *Level 1*. Intermediate-level files that control low level files, using the WRU resources: *wru_guti.h* and *wru_guti.c*;
- *Level 2*. Functions managing card instructions, data flow, and error conditions. The complete set of GC2 instructions is shown below in *card_cmd.h* and *card_cmd.c*. These files employ several subordinate functions and type definitions stored in *sc_tools.h* and *sc_tools.c*. Strictly speaking, these two files should be considered at level 1.5;

- *Level 3.* (Coming soon). Executable programs relying on the above functions. Two examples are given in this chapter: one using the card functions and the other using level 1 and level 0 files to get information from the ATR.

6.5.2 Header File *card_cmd.h*

Listing 6.6 is the header file of the main group of functions, *card_cmd.h*. It is basically made up of: a group of *#define* preprocessor directives that mostly assign names to all the instruction-field lengths and the prototypes of the functions coded in *card_cmd.c*. These prototypes include comments for the parameters used by every function.

6.5.3 File *card_cmd.c*

The file *card_cmd.c*, shown in the following sections, has been separated into several listings. The listings follow the same order as the instructions in Tables 6.1 to 6.5. The complete file can be obtained by joining these listings. Then the following two lines should be added at the beginning.

```
#include <mem.h>      /* From the standard library */
#include "card_cmd.h"
```

There are several overall rules that may be seen throughout the whole file. The return value is obtained from function *CardErrorAnalysis()*. Communications through the serial port are managed by one single function named *TxRxMessage()*, as mentioned above. This function may work either in transmission mode or in reception mode by calling two auxiliary functions named *MesToSc()* and *MesFromSc()* (see *wru_guti.c*). Errors in communications are returned by *TxRxMessage()* and stored in **error**. This variable is sent to *CardErrorAnalysis()*, together with the WRU status and the card answer. In this card, the function may decide quite accurately the kind of error that has occurred. The information might be completed by knowing the instruction involved in the command (e.g., through an **enum**-type constant sent as the fourth parameter in the function call). This rather involved procedure becomes necessary in several current cards whose answers are very limited, avoiding a proper error identification unless the answers are complemented by other data.

6.5.4 *card_cmd.c*: Functions Related to Files

Functions included in Listing 6.7 are used to create, open, read from, and write to files. Two creation functions (*MakeFile()* and *MakeWORM()*) are used, since read-only files employ a different instruction and some specific parameters.

memset() is a function of the standard library, defined in *mem.h* and *string.h*. It is sed here to fill up the string used for card response with zeros.

To begin working with a file, the first thing to do is to create it, specifying the umber of records and their size. Moreover, file creation implies giving a unique name) that file. Since the file name is only 1 byte long, this rule limits in practice the number f files to 256 (actually, to 255, since FF hex is not permitted as a file name). The number f records in a file is also limited to 255. Records within the file are consecutively umbered starting from 1. Record #0 has a special meaning related to RAM memory, as hown below.

Access rules, specified in the nibbles of two **char**s, are also included while creating ie file. Any file may use from zero to four secret codes (also specified in two **char**s). he same code may be used for reading and writing protection. Regular files customarily se only one access-rules byte, protecting reading and writing either with one or two ecret codes. Most sensitive data may be additionally protected by two extra secret codes. lost often, file protection is done through MK and/or PIN. In this card, MK and PIN re simply the secret codes #0 and #1; no specific instructions are used for creating files rotected by these codes. If needed, these instructions may be easily implemented as eparate functions of the same listing.

Once the file is created, it has to be opened with *SelectFile()*. A pointer is positioned t the beginning of the file with this command. In the meantime, the card closes any reviously opened file, looks at the codes protecting the newly opened file and checks vhether these codes have been previously introduced or not.

Read and/or write commands of the file records may follow. The access will not be permitted until the security rules have been fulfilled. *WriteRecord()* and *ReadRecord()* pecify the record number where the operation is performed. If the record number is zero, he operation is not performed in the file, but in RAM memory (warning: the record ength is limited to 8 bytes in this case, regardless of the actual record length in the file). This feature is useful for enciphering commands (see Section 6.5.7).

In WORM files, *WriteWORM()* may be used as long as the file has unwritten ecords. Once all the records have been written, the file becomes read-only. Typically, hese files are written by the issuer during the personalization process, thus being read-only for the user.

i.5.5 *card_cmd.c*: Functions Related to Purse Files

_isting 6.8 contains the files concerning financial transactions with purse files. The creation of a purse file is done through the function *MakePurse()*, which assumes a file type 01. Besides the access rules and required secret codes, the function sets the credit limit and he transaction date upon file creation. (The number of records and their length are determined by the purse structure.) The purse functions allow credit and debit operations hrough functions *Loan()* and *Payment()*. The set of functions is completed with *Purse-*

Info(), a useful function for finding out the transaction number, the remaining balance and the transaction date.

6.5.6 *card_cmd.c*: Functions Related to Secret Codes, PIN, and MK

The functions of Listing 6.9 are responsible for the management of secret codes. Function for writing, changing, and entering the MK, the PIN, or any other secret codes are shown The first time a secret code is written, its presence flag is activated. Further modification of any secret code require the previous presentation of the former one. No secret cod may be read, erased, or modified without meeting this requirement. In this context, th MK has no preferences over other secret codes. (However, the MK irreversibly block the entire card when the number of wrong consecutive presentations is reached.)

PIN is merely considered the secret code #1. Again, no privileges are assigned t this code, with the exception that when the card is blocked by PIN, the only availabl instruction is the card command RECOVER (see *ReactKeys()* below) upon presentatio of the MK. The remaining secret codes can also be recovered, but they do not block th card, only the files protected by them.

The above issue notwithstanding, the PIN and the MK (which usually becomes th issuer key) are usually used much more than any other secret code. For this reason separate sets of functions for PIN (*SetPIN()*, *VerifyPIN()*, and *ModifyPIN()*) and MI (*SetMasterKey()*, *VerifyMasterKey()*, and *ModifyMasterKey()*) are employed, making us of the same command as the other secret codes and of the parameters defined for PIN and MKs, respectively.

Besides the functions mentioned above, the reactivation function *ReactKeys()* i included. This function permits new PIN (and any other SK except MK) trials afte reaching the maximum number of consecutive wrong attempts of secret code presentations For security reasons, however, the scope of this function is quite limited. For example suppose that our PIN accepts up to three consecutive wrong trials. Once three wron; PINs have been introduced in a row, the files protected by PIN become barred (and th card is blocked). Using *ReactKeys()* (after introducing the MK; otherwise, the functio does not work at all), three new attempts are allowed. This is the only action of thi function. In other words, the function does not erase or change the PIN; if the user ha forgotten his/her PIN, the files protected by PIN remain unavailable (though the card i unblocked). Since selective erasing is not permitted when the protecting code is no known, the only way to reuse the card is to perform a complete erasure, causing all store data (at least, all data protected by PIN) to be lost.

6.5.7 *card_cmd.c*: Functions Related to Data Enciphering

Encryption and decryption processes are driven by the functions presented in Listing 6.10 The DES algorithm is prestored in the card and can be accessed for several uses.

Encrypt() encrypts 8-byte data using the first 8 bytes of the record specified as the second parameter of the function call (a file must be previously opened). The result is stored in another record (first parameter). If the instruction is repeated (or linked with *ReadRecord()* and *WriteRecord()* using record #0), the next 8 bytes are encrypted. This procedure may be repeated until the end of the record is reached. The last group of bytes in the record is automatically padded with zeros if necessary. Either the first or the second function parameter (or both) may be zero, indicating that the data origin and/or destination is RAM memory. *Decrypt()* performs the opposite operations.

Random() generates an 8-byte random number and stores it in RAM memory. *Challenge()* generates a random number, encrypts it and stores the result in RAM memory. This result may then be taken by the external system and brought back to the smart card after decryption, using *ChallengeAns()*. This is used for authentication of the external system. Typically, the card may be self-blocked through an EXEC function, the challenge being necessary for the card to accept the system. (Note that the card cannot generate commands; therefore, it must wait for the external system to initiate the challenge, though it is the external system which is actually challenged.) Card certification may be performed with the above functions by asking the card to decrypt a previously encrypted random number.

5.8 *card_cmd.c*: Special Functions

The final set of card functions, the so-called *special functions*, is presented in Listing 5.11. These are functions whose action is irreversible, or functions applying to the whole card. All these functions require MK. *EraseFile()* also requires the secret codes specified for write protection in that file.

ReadSerialNo() allows reading of the card serial number located at the manufacturing area of EEPROM. This is not, of course, the only manufacturing area in the card; most of it, including SCOS, is permanently stored in ROM. This card has the ability to allow permanent writing in EEPROM, which may be used by the issuer to distinguish between different applications. In this card, the number is previously stored by the issuer or manufacturer. Other cards allow eventual writing of this number.

WipeOutCard() erases the entire card (the UAM) except the manufacturing area. This instruction is used for recycling cards after the expiry date or for reusing the card when the user has forgotten the PIN or any other relevant secret code. Note that cards blocked by MK attempts cannot be erased, since MK is mandatory for performing this operation.

EraseFile() erases the contents of the selected file and its structure. This instruction requires, besides the MK, the writing protection codes of the file. The instruction is usually followed by *CrunchCard()*, which shifts the remaining files located in upper memory addresses, thus "filling the hole" in the UAM memory. Although it is not mandatory, this practice is recommended, since UAM files are sequentially stored, because the SCOS

lacks a DOS-style file allocation table (FAT) for managing fragmented files. Usin
CrunchCard(), the unused UAM memory is kept as a single block.

The last function, *ReportSK()*, is used to indicate whether the SK is set, whether i
is encrypted, and its maximum and remaining attempts. The card answer is merely a cop
of the SK's first two bytes; the function extracts the information from the byte nibbles
If the maximum number of attempts is zero, the number of wrong trials is infinity (an
the number of remaining attempts is meaningless). If the remaining number of attempt
is zero and the maximum number of attempts is not zero, the files protected by that secre
code are blocked. If the secret code is the PIN or any other SK, then the card may b
reactivated (see Section 6.5.6). If the code is the MK, the card is irreversibly blocked.

6.6 TEST PROGRAM FOR SMART CARDS

kike.c (Listing 6.12) is a small program to test the functions shown above. It accepts
string of alphanumeric characters (each character being a command) and sequentiall
executes the instructions. In this way, any conceivable string may be tried. Being a tes
program, the commands are intentionally associated with single card instructions. In actua
applications, however, single high-level instructions should often perform several car
commands. For instance, *Random()* is useless as a single instruction, since the result i
stored in the card's RAM memory, a further *ReadRecord()* instruction being necessar
for the external device to receive the random number.

To avoid long listings, most parameters required for the function calls have bee
#defined. If the program is run as it is, the source code would have to be modified ever
time we want to use a different file, protection scheme, or access rules, among others
This is not so bad, however, since current PCs (386s and higher) can compile the whol
source code in less than 30 sec. Besides, this design allows tight control over parameter
coming back and forth. The reader, in any case, may easily add a few lines at the beginnin
for the program to ask for the required information, thus avoiding recompilation. A muc
better solution is to store such information in a separate text file which may be read b
the program when running.

We are using a file (named 27 hex in this example), which is a regular file additionall
protected by secret codes other than PIN and MK. The file has one record containing 1
bytes. (Of course, the reader may modify any of these values.) The additional protectin
codes are SK2 and SK3. Other secret codes may be used as long as they are previousl
defined. Two access-rules bytes are *#defined*, since the file needs both of them at th
same time (remember that all files use 2 bytes). To use these codes, keywords for MK
PIN, and secret codes 2 and 3 have been prepared, as well as a wrong keyword to tes
the attempts' countdown. Some extra constants have also been defined to allow testin
of other commands.

Looking at the nibbles of the access-rules bytes, the first byte AR1 prevents fil
reading by PIN, while file writing is protected by both PIN and MK. AR2 protects readin
by SK2 *or* SK3, while writing is protected by SK2 *and* SK3.

The program includes the function *DisplayCardError()*, which translates the messages coming from *CardErrorAnalysis()* into human-readable sentences. Note that some ambiguous card messages cannot be completely solved by *CardErrorAnalysis()*. In these cases, the function displays all the possible error sources. The abilities of *CardErrorAnalysis()* would improve by tracking previously issued commands when an error arises. This modification of the function can be left as an exercise for inquisitive readers.

.7 ATR ANALYSIS

Software examples finish with *lookatr.c*, a program for extracting as much information as possible from ATR. One possible application of this program would be to identify card brands and models by comparing card ATRs and previously known responses from selected cards. Keep in mind, however, that the ATR does not provide unique identification of manufacturers; on the other hand, different card models from the same manufacturer usually (but not necessarily) give different ATRs. To achieve such card identification from ATR, one has to restrict the card families involved in the recognition; in fact, different users of this program would probably have to modify the set of cards, depending on the country and the scope of their candidates (communications, financial, health care, etc.). The program analyzes any hexadecimal string as an ATR; therefore, it can be tested without using smart cards or a WRU.

The program makes use of level 1 and level 0 files described above. Two level 2 files (Listings 6.13 and 6.14) are specifically defined for ATR recognition: *atr_iso.h* and *atr_iso.c*. The header file is used to define constants and types of variables employed by the source file. *atr_iso.c*, the workhorse of the package, contains the functions for learning the ATR information. The results are displayed by auxiliary functions located in the main file, *look_atr.c* (Listing 6.15). The main program merely resets the serial port and the WRU and calls the functions contained in the above files.

.8 CONCLUSIONS

The software presented in this chapter has been designed using a layered approach whereby high-level functions call upon lower-level functions to undertake the actual tasks. The advantage of this approach is that high-level functions relate to the activities to be performed, while the low-level functions relate to the detailed card operations. Moreover, high-level functions are device-independent, while low-level functions depend on the smart card model, the WRU, or both. In the next chapter, we will assume the issuer's point of view to design applications based on the above functions. We will analyze the application requirements and will study different ways of meeting such requirements within the card environment. For this task, our newly gained experience in card programming will prove to be most useful.

Chapter 7
Designing Smart Card Applications

In the last part of this book, especially in this chapter, the role of issuer will be adopted. At present, the issuer role as the single link between the card manufacturer and the card user is being replaced by two sequential roles: the issuer and the card personalizer. Moreover, the concept of a single "issuer" is currently being questioned as multifunction cards become popular. Multifunction cards lead to a new concept of issuer as an overall manager of card applications, who is less involved in specific details of single applications. Problems derived from multifunction cards will be reviewed in the second part of this chapter.

Prior to this, we will follow the steps of a smart card from its manufacture through its personalization process, until it is ready to perform the duties it has been assigned to carry out. For this part, the simple manufacturer—issuer—user sequence employed throughout the book will still be assumed. With this sequence, a simple application will be designed using an example. Additionally, some concepts concerning card memory structure and management will be revisited to show a few tricks for improving the performance of our applications.

7.1 CARD TRAINING: AN EXAMPLE

A new card has been manufactured. Just delivered from the production line, the card is only aware of its own electronic existence and little else. The manufacturer has made it and many, many more from the same set of masks; very few hardware differences are introduced in the first production stages. However, the cards are supplied to different issuers. It is advisable, and often necessary, to prepare different sets of cards for different issuers, or even for different applications of the same issuer.

7.1.1 Card Setup: Batch Cards and Parent Cards

Before the card is sent to the issuer, it is usually prepersonalized by the manufacturer. The primary aim of this stage is security. Some permanent data are stored in every card in the batch, providing a unique identification code to all of the cards belonging to each batch. The information includes the manufacturer key, which, in principle, should be different for every batch.

The information assigned to the batch is generated by a software package. For security reasons, the package is customarily controlled by another smart card. Each batch is produced by a different card, usually called the *batch card* (Figure 7.1). Some manufacturers deliver unlocked batch cards to selected issuers (developers of multimillion card applications), but these batch cards are usually kept by the manufacturers.

In a further step, the personalization process of the card continues under the guidance of a *parent card* (Figure 7.2). This step is performed either by the manufacturer or by the issuer. A card batch may use several parent cards, thus producing separate subgroups of cards sharing the same manufacturer "seal" (Figure 7.3). The information provided by parent cards is mainly related to encryption algorithms. Each parent card gives a unique set of secret directives for random number generation and/or encryption/decryption processes. Cards spawned from different parents are unable to communicate with each other using enciphered information. This feature is useful, for example, when cards are employed for secure communications; only the cards belonging to the same application would be able to decrypt the information encrypted by one of its brothers or sisters.[*] It is time to leave. Our card is wrapped up with many of its siblings and sent to the premises of its new master, where it will learn specific abilities, thus becoming qualified for a job.

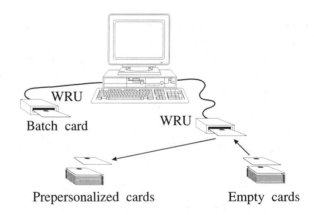

Figure 7.1 Prepersonalization process using batch cards.

---

[*] In Latin-derived languages, such as French or Spanish, objects usually have gender; the gender of the word *card* is feminine. In these languages, the term used above is the mother card; daughter cards coming from the same mother become sisters, and so on. These terms are widely used, since France has played a major role in the developing of smart cards.

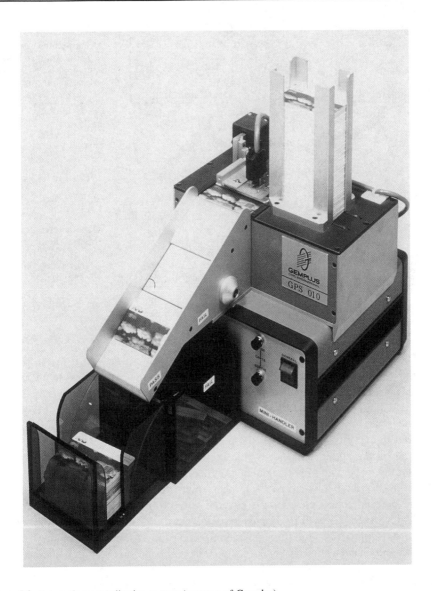

Figure 7.2 Automatic personalization system (courtesy of Gemplus).

7.1.2 Card Personalization

Consider the case of a company named GUTI, Inc., which specializes in services for customers of high standing. This time the company is preparing a new service consisting of a syndicated lottery combined with the state lottery. The customers invest a variable amount of money weekly and the collected sum is spent on lottery tickets. Winnings are proportionally redistributed. All the transactions are made electronically.

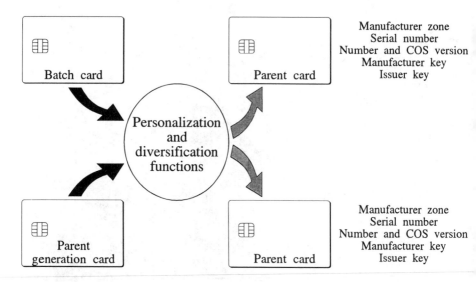

Figure 7.3 Preparation of different parent cards for the same batch card.

The capabilities of our smart card are similar to those described in the previous chapter. The card shall undergo double personalization: a general process to characterize the cards pertaining to the application, and a specific process to identify every customer. In a second step, the card file structure will be defined.

The issuer reserves the master key as the issuer key. The same master key is created and stored in every card. Whenever the master key is required for file handling, it will be entered by the application, not by the human manager. Therefore, only one attempt for master key presentation is permitted. (Actually, the control software package does not hold the master key; it is stored in another smart card whose access is restricted by signature. Special access protection is covered in the following chapters.)

As for the PIN, it will be employed as the main user identification. Alphanumeric keys are not appropriate for this application, since the terminals where the cards are introduced only have a numeric keyboard. On the other hand, an eight-digit number (smart card's secret codes are typically 8 bytes long) is too long to be remembered and keyed in each time the card is used. Therefore, PINs are made up with a small padding function that automatically adds four characters (e.g., GUTI) to a four-digit number. The number for each customer is selected at random. In this way, the users only have to enter four digits, as in PINs for banking and financial applications in magnetic stripe cards. Three consecutive wrong PIN attempts are permitted.

The personalization process continues with the allocation of three bytes for a general serial number; this number is given to all the cards issued by the company. The creation program automatically assigns the serial number using a counter. These bytes are write-protected and readable through the master key. The same protection is used for an application serial number of the same length.

7.1.3 File Structure

A file named 01, containing two 25-byte records, is created to store the first and last names of the customer (Figure 7.4). The file is write-protected by the master key, but reading is not restricted. Another file (02) containing a single 4-byte record will store the expiry date (month and year). (A de facto standard in smart cards indicates that all external card data, either embossed or stored in the magnetic stripe, should also be stored in the card memory. Although this rule is not stated in any official standard, everybody follows it.)

The main application requires a purse file (03) for the transactions. Debit operations become protected by the PIN while the crediting and the topping up of the card are controlled by the master key. In this way, bets are controlled by the users, while winnings and new funds are introduced under issuer control.

The customer's first quota is $1,000. This amount is stored in the purse file, after checking personal data and serial number(s) of the card in order to avoid mistakes. The card is ready for embossing and any other external ID.

The above described card personalization and file structuring can be easily performed with the card functions presented in the previous chapter and a few extra lines of code.

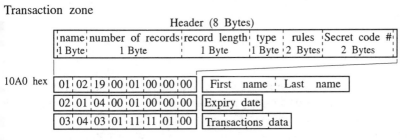

Figure 7.4 Contents of the secret and user/application areas in the example.

It is advisable to follow every write command with the corresponding read command to ensure that all data have been correctly stored and that the desired protections are active. A program derived from *kike.c* may be used for this checking.

7.2 CARD MANAGEMENT

Once the card is given to the customer, a new managing software package comes into operation. In this simple application, the tasks of such a program are limited to purse control and a few extra features such as PIN change. A third package within the application will take care of less common situations, such as card malfunctioning and blocking, service renewal, and so on.

7.2.1 Ordinary Managing

Transactions are carried out with standard WRUs used as peripherals for personal computers. The application is simple enough to allow WRUs to care for routine operations, printing receipts for the customers while keeping relevant data in their memory. However, we want to use the functions of the previous chapter, not an assembler WRU program. Moreover, data should be transmitted daily to a central computer; therefore, personal computers are advisable. Transmitted data are enciphered using the company's card-based standard procedure.

The customer identifies him/herself with the PIN. The number is directly keyed in using the WRU keyboard, out of sight of the company employee. The purse is automatically updated every time the card is used. Once properly identified, the customer may choose between several possibilities: to bet a fixed amount next week or every week until otherwise stated, collect his/her winnings if any, or refill the card with fresh money. A receipt summarizing the transaction and the relevant figures of the purse (balance, credit, and debit) is printed.

He/she may also modify the PIN as many times as desired. As an extra precaution, the old PIN is requested again for the PIN change, and the function is time-limited (we do not want anybody manipulating the card while the customer is tying his/her shoe laces). The new PIN is requested again to confirm (the number is not shown anywhere, so it is advisable to double check it).

7.2.2 Troubleshooting

Some less common situations have also been considered in designing the application. Lost, damaged, and expired cards are simply renewed using the data of the former card. The other exceptional situation, forgotten PIN, deserves a careful analysis.

Cards are usually designed to avoid cross-linking between secret codes. A master key may show some privileges that other secret codes lack: card reactivation or erasing, for example. However, reading, erasing, or modifying a secret code is not usually permitted for security reasons. This raises some problems when designing applications where the cards should not block irreversibly.

Our customer has forgotten his/her PIN. He/she had previously modified the original random number assigned by the personalization program. The card blocks after the third wrong attempt. The customer sends the card back to the issuer. A card reactivation function, like the one shown in the previous chapter, would be useless, since it simply allows some extra attempts (three in our case) to enter the correct PIN. What can we do to recover the data? In the above application, the answer is quite simple: since all the transactions are performed on line, all the relevant data are stored in the computer. Therefore, we can erase the whole card and restore the file structure. The updated information is written in the files and a new PIN is created.

Let us imagine now a similar application where off-line transactions are allowed. The user has changed the PIN and has blocked the card afterwards (the new PIN is not registered when the function is invoked). Now the problem is that PIN-protected files cannot be recovered; we are trying to avoid a loss of valuable data.

Technically, there are at least two ways of dealing with this situation, both requiring special personalization steps. If the card files have access-rules bytes with an OR bit (see previous chapter), the issuer may design an application where sensitive information is stored in files read-protected either by the PIN or by the master key. Should the PIN be forgotten by the user, the issuer may recover the information, erase the card, and restore the file structure and data back in the card again using only the master key.

The second procedure is rather involved. A master-key-protected pseudo-PIN file is created during the personalization process, and an initial PIN is written. An encrypted version of that PIN is allocated in the actual PIN memory area. The encryption procedure employs the standard card facilities. Every time the user is requested to enter the PIN, a PIN checking function encrypts the keyed number with the same procedure and the result is sent to the card in a PRESENT-PIN command. The remaining steps (such as PIN acceptance or rejection and increasing the wrong attempts counter) are automatically performed by the card as if it were working with a real PIN.

If the user wants to modify his/her PIN, a PIN generation function is called. This function performs the following tasks:

- Requests the former PIN;
- Requests the new PIN;
- Stores the new PIN in the pseudo-PIN file;
- Encrypts the new PIN;
- Invokes the CHANGE-PIN command, using the result of the encryption procedure as the new PIN.

Note that the PIN memory area must be used in order to take advantage of the usual card services. A pseudo-PIN file with no PIN counterpart would be more difficult to operate, and might ultimately jeopardize the security of the card. Speaking of security, the pseudo-

PIN file strategy depicted above need not be less secure than the regular PIN. All master key operations may be enciphered; even the pseudo-PIN file content may be an enciphered version of the user key.

A final point on this subject: although the above methods are technically feasible, they are not necessarily honest (or indeed legal), since both methods partially violate the privacy of users' data. Whether this violation matters or not depends on a number of factors, the kind and scope of the specific application probably being the most important. Besides legal questions, our opinion is that users of these applications should be informed in advance that their PIN (or their data) can be read by the issuer.

7.3 MULTIPURPOSE CARDS

In the good old days, when cards were designed for specific applications, things were much simpler, and both card issuer and card personalizer were the same person or the same organization. Nowadays, multipurpose smart cards are the name of the game; a single card may hold several applications with different scope, protection requirements, and complexity. One can easily realize that people dealing with software design in a health care environment, for example, would hardly ever coincide with developers of financial packages. A new concept, card personalizers, has been coined to describe indepen- dent developers that prepare applications for someone else's cards, much like people develop software for personal computers.

In this context, the issuers' job is getting closer to that of system managers of mainframe computers or networks: allocation of resources and overall system control. Card personalizers, on the other hand, develop single applications following the issuer's guidelines. (The issuer may also be, and usually is, one of the card personalizers, of course.) The final product is a smart card where all the applications are stacked together, sharing resources but keeping their privacy to some extent.

Suddenly, a new type of problem has arisen. Unless we issue as many cards as applications that our user requires (thus producing packs of cards like the current ones), we must agree with other personalizers on crucial details concerning data handling and storage. Even worse, the applications need not materialize at the same time or in the same place; in a multipurpose card, the eventual presence of unknown applications must be foreseen from the very first issue of the card containing perhaps just one application.

7.3.1 Issuers' Cards Versus Users' Cards

The underlying idea is much more involved than simply adding up unrelated applications. The whole world of card services has been customarily based on *issuers' cards*; in other words, current issuers are companies offering or selling services to customers via a convenient portable information medium: *their* cards. A typical user owns a credit card from X, another credit card from Y, a third card for gas stations, and a fourth card as a pass card for admittance in his/her favorite squash club. The multipurpose (also called *multifunction*) card would substitute for all the above with a single card. At first glance, it looks like a previous agreement between issuers would suffice to launch multipurpose cards.

However, this need not be the end of the story. The smart card concept is evolving toward users' cards provided by issuers who prepare cards to accept applications from different card personalizers. Again, our user owns a card holding two credit lines, gas, and squash services. It is not just another card, however, but *the user's* card. Next summer, our user spends a week in a new condo near a sunny beach. The first day, he/she gives this card to the receptionist, who stores a new time-limited application that permits our hero to access the condo and the parking lot. During that week, the user decides to spend some time (and some money) in a nice casino near the beach. The casino clerk stores an access pass and an electronic purse with the desired amount of money from one of the credit lines in the card. After a week, timeout expires the condo pass. Somewhere in the card memory, a flag is set to indicate that the application is no longer active, and so it can be overwritten. The casino pass is valid for one year; hence, that application is held.

The above situation is likely to be quite common soon. Smart cards would become as personal as current calling cards ("Here's my card"). Legal arguments and common sense suggest the existence of a prime issuer, who should be responsible for general maintenance, recovery, and renewal of cards, overall troubleshooting, and perhaps licensing of applications from card personalizers (e.g., modifying their code to permit card access for data storage from the applications). Anyway, the card layout would be ultimately decided by the user. The card would be linked to its owner as a driver's license is.

7.3.2 Technical Requirements

Besides legal matters, the advent of multipurpose customized cards raises several technical questions concerning both hardware and software. Eventually, smart cards should be more rugged to avoid failures from heavy use. Moreover, the number of reading/writing cycles of EEPROM will have to be improved (current typical values are about 10,000 cycles), and a larger user/application memory is desirable.

On the software side, the instruction sets or card operating systems must increase their flexibility. For example, the card described in the previous chapter could not be employed as it is, if only just because selective erasing requires entering the file protecting secret codes in advance. Commands to reorganize memory, crunching memory gaps from obsolete applications (more powerful than the crunching instruction of the previous chapter), must be included. Allocation and protection of memory would become a much more crucial issue; although files may be securely protected from the outside world, special care should be taken to avoid data scrambling from other applications sharing the same secret codes. Once the codes are entered, files would be vulnerable to the action of not-so-well-behaved applications, let alone viruses.

Strict access control mechanisms aside, the file hierarchical structure described in ISO 7816/4 is intended to solve most of the file managing pitfalls in multifunction cards (Figure 7.5). Each application can be logically placed in a different branch of the directory tree, owning a dedicated file that watches data flow to and from its branch. The master file at the root may look after general matters of the card, including data flow to and from the outside world.

7.3.3 Intersector Data Communications

Let us be now more positive in facing another problem derived from multifunction cards, namely, data sharing and communications between different applications. This obviously requires a new set of standards. In the world of standardization, this subject is called *intersector data communications*. The problem of having alien applications in the same card sharing common data may be overcome by solving a more general problem: providing standards for communications between smart cards and hosts. Any application accomplishing these standards could bring data from other standardized applications, perform the requested task, and take the relevant data back to the other applications (Figure 7.6). To achieve this, two conditions ought to be met in advance.

- The meaning of shared data has to be the same for all the applications in the pool (i.e., all the applications must ''speak'' the same language, even the same data format).
- Unique identifiers for all the companies involved in the transactions must be provided.

The main effort in inter-sector data communications is being carried out in Europe. The CEN is the European Community organization for standards. It is currently preparing a set of European norm (EN) inter-sector standards within its technical committee, CEN/TC 224 ''Machine readable cards, related device interfaces and operations.'' (This includes all kinds of information-holding cards, such as magnetic stripe cards.) These drafts, currently at the proposal stage, will eventually become parts of EN 726, the general European standard on this subject. Table 7.1 summarizes the parts and responsible groups of this standard.

Fortunately, most organizations involved in standardization, either national or international, have mutual agreements to adopt standards prepared by other organizations. ISO standards, for example, are usually accepted as EN standards and vice versa, though different numbering systems are employed.

As these lines are being written, several CEN/TC 224 working groups (WG) are preparing proposals for dealing with different aspects of card-host communications. Off- and on-line situations are being contemplated; payment messages and methods for prepayment and autobilling are being separately studied. As a rule, transactions involving payments are considered a predominant part of inter-sector interchange, albeit not the

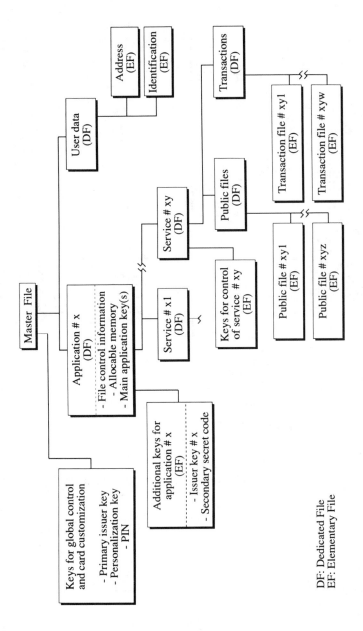

Figure 7.5 Allocation of applications in multifunction cards with hierarchical file structure.

DF: Dedicated File
EF: Elementary File

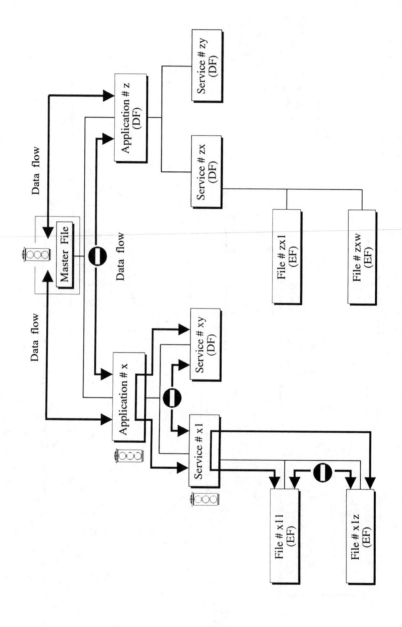

Figure 7.6 Data flow in multifunction cards is controlled by the master file and dedicated files.

only inter-sectorial messages for which standardization is required. Payment methods would become Part 5 of EN 726.

Table 7.1

Working Groups and Standards Related to Multifunction Smart Cards

Organization	Stage	Number	Year	Title/Content
ISO/IEC	IS	23166	1988	Codes for the representation of names of countries
CEN	prEN	3166	1992	
ISO/IEC	IS	639	1988	Codes for the representation of names of languages
ISO/IEC	IS	4217	1990	Codes for representation of currencies and funds
CEN	prEN	24217	1992	
ISO/IEC	IS	7812	1987	Identification cards; numbering system and registration
CEN	EN	27812	1989	procedure for issuers' identifiers
ISO/IEC	DIS	7812-1	1992	Identification cards; identification of issuers
				Part 1: Numbering system
ISO/IEC	IS	7813	1985	Identification cards, financial transaction cards; data processing,
	IS		1990	data storage devices, banking documents, financial
	DIS		1993	documents, identity cards, specifications, physical properties
CEN	EN	27813	1989	
ISO/IEC	CD	7816-5	1992	Identification cards; IC(s) cards with contact
				Part 5: Registration system for applications in ICC code
ISO/IEC	IS	8583	1987	Bank-card-originated messages; interchange message
	DIS		1992	specifications; content for financial transactions
CEN	EN	28583	1991	
ISO/IEC	IS	8825	1990	Information technology; open systems interconnection;
				specification of basic encoding rules for ASN.1
ISO/IEC	IS	8859-1	1987	Information processing—8-bit single-byte coded graphic
				character set
				Part 1: Latin alphabet N°. 1.
ISO/IEC				Banking: PIN management and security
	IS	9564-1	1991	Part 1: PIN protection principles & techniques
	IS	9564-2	1991	Part 2: Approved algorithm(s) for PIN encipherment
ISO				Financial transaction cards; messages between the integrated
				circuit card and the card-accepting device
	IS	9992-1	1990	Part 1: Concepts and structures
	DIS	9992-4	1993	Part 4: Common data for interchange
	CD	9992-5	1991	Part 5: Organization of data elements
CEN/TC 224/ WG9				Requirements for IC cards and terminals for telecommunication use
	prEN	726-1	1993	Part 1: System overview
	prEN	726-2	1993	Part 2: Security framework
	prEN	726-3	1993	Part 3: Application-independent card requirements
	prEN	726-4	1993	Part 4: Application-independent card-related terminal requirements

Table 7.1 (*cont.*)
Working Groups and Standards Related to Multifunction Smart Cards

Organization	Stage	Number	Year	Title/Content
	prEN	726-5	1993	Part 5: Payment methods
	prEN	726-6	1993	Part 6: Telecommunication features
CEN/TC 224/ WG7	WD	Work Item D.1.2.	1993	Rules for PIN handling in an intersector environment Part 1: PIN presentation
CEN/TC 224/ WG2	WD	Work Item D.1.3.	1993	Specifications (formats and codes) for identification and registration procedures
CEN/TC 224/ PT02	WD	N69	1993	Intersector data elements

Notes: ASN.1 = Abstract Syntax Notation One; CD = committee draft; CEN = *Comité Européen de Normalisation*; DIS = draft international standard; EN = European norm (standard); IC = integrated circuit; ICC = integrated circuit card; IEC = International Electrotechnical Commission; IS = international standard; ISO = International Organization for Standardization; PIN = personal identification number; prEN = project European norm; PT = project team; TC = technical committee; WD = working document or working draft; WG = working group.

WG4, for example, is preparing definitions for inter-sector data elements, such as the format and recommended access conditions for each smart card data element interchanged between sectors, the methods of enabling unique identification of data, and the authorities and procedures for the registration of eventual data elements. More than 40 data elements have been proposed to date, including IDs for chip manufacturer, card manufacturer, issuer, and personalizer; country code; language; card and application expiry date; verification methods and remaining verification attempts; and cryptographic algorithm identifier. Each of these items is described in terms of purpose, format, content, and access conditions. Some item definitions and scope are borrowed from ISO standards, especially ISO 7816/4 (almost the official standard by now) and the draft of 7816/5 (a new part of ISO 7816 concerning "Numbering system and registration procedures for application identifiers"). Whenever applicable, the data element tags (one or two bytes announcing the data element involved) are the same as the ASN.1 tags for Open System Interconnection (OSI), as described in ISO 8825.

WG5 is in charge of communications between device and host. Besides definitions of essential terms, the standard would include specifications on the structure and identification of messages, source and destination, routing, and updating. Other groups deal with the requirements of specific sectors; for example, WG6 is involved in the definition of standard man-machine interfaces, not only the ergonomic aspects, but also special features for handicapped people, such as ridges on the card surface allowing blind people to recognize and properly orient the card for insertion. WG8 studies new card types, like plug cards and minicards. WG11 is involved in terrestrial transportation (i.e., not airlines), while WG12 is devoted to health care cards.

The above paragraphs are intended to show that there is intense activity regarding the issue of card-host data communications standards and, indirectly, multipurpose smart card applications. The above mentioned drafts and working documents will presumably become actual standards throughout 1993 and 1994. The second half of this decade will probably be the starting point for general use of multipurpose cards.

7.4 CONCLUSIONS

In this chapter, the issuer and/or card personalizer role in smart card applications development has been reviewed. As cards become the preferred medium for performing routine transactions in more areas, the standard requirements would limit the number of issuers, at least in the early stages, simply because quite demanding conditions would have to be met in order to achieve the status of ''official'' issuer in multipurpose environments. Independent application developers will be restricted to indoor applications, such as access and presence control within a building or company premises (in other words, customized applications for a small number of users). Once the data structure and security conditions are firmly established, however, there will probably be a niche for independent developers in open applications, much like the shareware world in personal computers, though to a lesser scale.

Current smart cards feature powerful tools to avoid unauthorized handling of sensitive data. Time is needed, however, for the average user to trust in the privacy and security of data stored in cards. As customers' trust increases, more industrial and service sectors will begin to consider the implementation of smart cards to offer their products.

In the next chapter, examples of smart card applications in different sectors are given. This time, we will look for actual applications already implemented in one or several countries, ranging from the classic example of massive telephone services to specific solutions in quite distinct areas.

Chapter 8

Applications: The Present

In the last two chapters of the book, we will turn our attention to applications. This chapter will cover applications already implemented in various sectors. The next one will deal with recent advances in smart card use, and will include forecasts on future applications. Needless to say, it is not possible to include all the applications currently used worldwide. Instead, applications representative of the different areas (Figure 8.1) are presented, emphasizing how smart card facilities are used.

The worldwide sales of smart cards were about 12 million in 1991 and 20 million in 1992. The estimated figure for 1993 is about 35 million cards (i.e., 15% of the overall sales of chip cards). This percentage is constant, or increases slightly, throughout the years. Even so, estimations for 1995 are double the 1993 figure. Should a major credit card company or a national health service decide to implement a multimillion card application for their customers, these estimations would require major revision.

Smart card applications may be broadly divided into two groups, financial and nonfinancial applications. Magnetic stripe cards are mainly focused towards the first group; many millions of cards are used worldwide in banking and electronic sale transactions. Smart cards, however, are mainly used for nonfinancial applications of the second group. The success of financial magnetic stripe cards for on-line banking and electronic sale applications is certainly one of the main reasons for this uneven share of the market.

8.1 FINANCIAL APPLICATIONS

The historical relationship between smart cards and financial organizations resembles a frustrated love. Smart cards, being a perfect partner and well-designed to fulfill the requirements of the many services offered by banking corporations, have not yet found their privileged place in the financial world. Five years ago, a large increase in the use of smart cards for financial applications was predicted in the short term (i.e., now). These

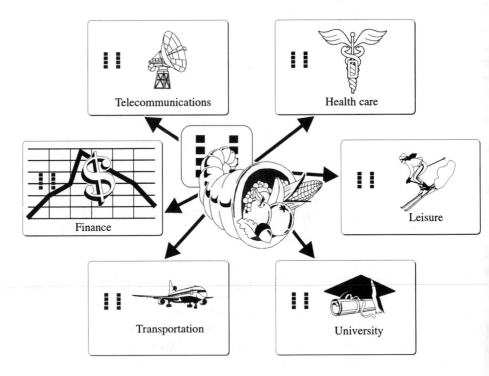

Figure 8.1 Main areas where smart cards are used.

forecasts have not been fulfilled; yet some people are currently predicting a similar card boom in the near future.

Several possible reasons may explain this apparent cul-de-sac. It is not just that magnetic stripe cards are successfully accomplishing the usual needs of financial organizations, but some other related issues are deterring, or at least constraining, the general use of smart cards in banking and finance.

- Surely one of the main reasons is price. Smart cards are six to ten times more expensive, on average, than magnetic stripe cards. This should not be a problem, since the price of the card is relatively small and might be charged directly or indirectly to the customer. The real problem is the updating of the ubiquitous writing/reading devices (ATMs, EPOSs) in many cities worldwide.
- Off-line transactions, being a clear advantage of smart cards, are somewhat in opposition to traditional banking modus operandi. Most financial organizations are based on centralized computer centers linked to their terminals by point-to-point lines or secure networks. On-line management of magnetic stripe cards is a natural extension of such networks. Off-line transactions rely on other security parameters, loosening the tight centralized control of bank mainframes. Moreover, off-line

transactions are not immediately known by the bank; the whole idea is disturbing for many financial managers.

• Like lasers in their early days, financial smart cards have been labeled "a solution looking for a problem." The underlying idea is that smart cards cannot do anything better than magnetic stripe cards with improved materials and devices. Highly sophisticated countermeasures may keep forgery, dud, and uncovered payments down to acceptable limits. Card malfunctioning or PIN failures are solved by rejecting the transaction or by swallowing the card and gently suggesting that the customer come back during office hours the next day. However, these arguments are based on current applications of magnetic stripe cards. Smart cards can facilitate new services not possible with magnetic card technology. These services have been resisted by financial institutions because they do not fit into current magnetic technology.

It might seem that the view of the future of financial smart cards is quite pessimistic. This is not the case. We think that smart cards are here to stay; they will eventually find their way to the core of financial systems; their unavoidable arrival, however, will probably be at a more even pace——and more peaceful——than predicted by many authors. Looking at the latest manufacturer and issuer trends in smart cards, it seems that financial smart cards, always associated with magnetic stripes, will be first offered to selected clients as an extra bonus, permitting some new services (Figure 8.2) not yet quite defined. There have already been some initiatives concerning the subject from the main credit card companies, albeit restricted to specific areas or countries. The following examples present some of the more interesting applications and experiences of smart card technology in finance.

8.1.1 Super Smart Cards

Super smart cards, also called very smart cards, go beyond the capabilities of regular smart cards. In 1988, the so-called SuperSmart Card, a joint development of Visa International, Inc., and Toshiba Corp. began field tests in Japan and the United States. The same size as a conventional credit card (just 0.76 mm thick), it featured a microprocessor and memory circuitry like other smart cards, a 16-alphanumeric-character liquid-crystal display, a 20-key keyboard, a 3V lithium battery, and a standard magnetic stripe (some models employ a magnetic-head transducer emulating the signals of regular magnetic stripes). The battery life for average use is estimated to be about three years. The card could also be used as a clock, calendar, calculator, and note pad.

The card was designed to be a completely independent payment system, either as standalone cash card or as point-of-sale terminal. For example, if the customer wanted to buy some goods from a shop, he/she switched on the card, which displayed the date and time, allowed the selection of an account, and required the holder to enter the PIN. Once the code was verified, the card became "open to buy" up to a previously established

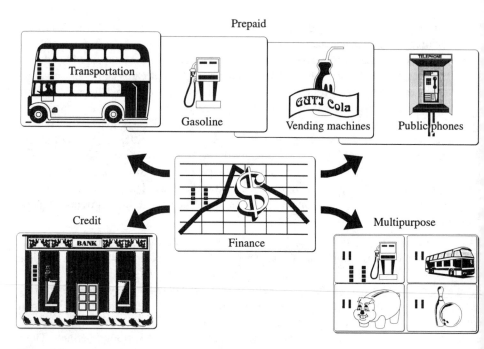

Figure 8.2 Prepaid, credit, and multipurpose cards used in finances.

limit. The customer could then check previous purchases and decide whether he/she wanted to charge the new purchase to that account. The amount (specifying currency if needed) was then entered via the keyboard and shown to the store clerk. Once the amount was agreed on, the transaction was confirmed by pushing a key ("YES"). The card then displayed an authorization code, which was copied by the clerk on to the receipt and to the store records.

Super smart cards have been selected as the first example to emphasize the opposing opinions derived from the subject of financial smart cards. For a security purist, this is the only smart card that guarantees the confidentiality of user data (as long as the user handles the card safely). Other smart cards require an external keyboard to enter sensitive data such as the PIN; therefore, a forged terminal might store this information without the user's consent, or even falsify the information stored in or retrieved from the card. However, there are some arguments against the card: it is the most expensive smart card technology and the least developed product; moreover, no standards have so far been proposed for such cards. Although some of these arguments may be overcome in the future, the question of user (and financial company) acceptance of this technology still remains. Some specialists have pointed out ergonomic problems with the keypad and the display in connection with the restricted size of the card. Anybody who has tried a credit-card sized solar calculator would probably agree that handling of these devices is quite clumsy.

At present, the authors are unaware of further development or exploitation of such super smart cards, albeit some interesting experiences based on these cards have been proposed e.g., a solution to avoid user traceability from electronic transactions. With this system, the user handles "electronic cash" previously stored in his/her card. The money cannot be spent by anybody else; still, the user's privacy is protected; that is, nobody involved in the transaction can find out who has performed it.

8.1.2 Prepaid Cards

Many current financial applications of smart cards are based on prepaid cards. The idea is quite simple: the card carries a certain amount of money that has been previously paid for by the cardholder. The main use of these cards is intended to be the substitution for cash in low-value transactions (e.g., $20 or less). A PIN might be required for high-value transactions, whereas the lowest ones would be automatically accepted; no authorization is required.

Prepaid cards take advantage of the off-line capabilities of smart cards; indeed, on-line transactions below a reasonable amount of money are not economically viable, if at all practical. In many cases (e.g., parking meters, food and drink dispensers, telephone calls), on-line operations are simply not feasible, while off-line ones are fast and inexpensive. Within this framework, smart cards would substitute for coins or bank notes just as magnetic stripe cards are substituting for checks. Although such payments are individually small, the potential of this market is amazing. For instance, it is estimated that 360 billion payment transactions are performed every year in the U.S. Of these, more than 270 billion are below $2, and 30 billion between $2 and $10. Presently, about 300 billion are cash transactions, while 60 billion are made using any bank-related facility.

In the U.S., CoreStates Financial Corp. has recently launched an electronic purse system based on their network of ATMs, Money Access Service (MAC). In the first months of 1993, the MAC network began the distribution of the first 5,000 cards of this new service; it is planned to reach 200,000 by the end of the year. MAC cards combine magnetic stripe and chip, allowing on-line and off-line transactions. Besides 13,000 ATMs, some 17,000 EPOSs participate in the application. The card may potentially be used with any equipment that accepts coins or notes, such as public telephones, photocopiers, laundry machines, and soft drink dispensers. Thus, MAC expects other participants to join, so that the card be usable in many other automated devices. There are many other examples of prepaid smart card applications. A major Danish initiative, Danmønt/Dancoin, is discussed in Section 8.1.4.

8.1.3 Banking Cards

Many banks worldwide have already adopted smart cards for business and financial applications. Examples of prepaid, credit, and debit smart cards can be found in several countries. Not surprisingly, many applications have evolved in small countries, or less developed ones, where there is no tradition of magnetic stripe banking cards, ATMs, or EPOSs. By the time the banks of these countries needed some kind of plastic money they found a quite mature smart card technology which compared favorably to magnetic stripe. Many of them decided to adopt the new technology, avoiding an eventual substitution of their cards in the future. Examples are found in Indonesia, with the prepaid debit card of EximBank; Guatemala, with the Elite bank card; and Malaysia, with the Smart Savings Passbook from the Bank of Islam.

France, the homeland of smart cards, finished in 1992 the distribution of its Smart Bank Cards based on Bull CP8 technology. This is certainly a major event in the world of financial smart cards; for example, currently, you can see the well-known golden shape of chip contacts on the top of French VISA cards (magnetic stripes are still on the back of course). France has at present the largest smart-card-based banking system in the world, with more than 21 million smart cards by the end of 1992.

Norway, a much less populated country, adopted financial smart cards to solve the problem of high communication costs of on-line transactions (because of the tough Norwegian orography and its low population density). The Norwegian banks managed to launch 1.2 million smart cards, a remarkable feat for a country of less than 4.5 million inhabitants. However, current economic difficulties have temporarily curtailed this application.

In February 1988, the Swiss PTT launched a pilot project with a view to replacing its magnetic stripe Postomat card with a new hybrid card, Postomat Plus, which also included a chip. The Postomat Plus (now called Postcard) smart card in Switzerland could be used for card withdrawals from ATMs belonging to the Swiss PTT, and also for paying for goods at checkout points of one big supermarket chain. The experience was quite successful, with more than 500,000 cards in circulation after two years. Other uses have been included in the card, such as remote payment, POS identification, prepayment, and retailers. The use of Postcard cards as subscriber identity modules for GSM (see Section 9.2.1) is under study.

8.1.4 Multifunction Financial Cards

Danmønt/Dancoin is a nationwide initiative in Denmark to provide prepaid cards on an open multipurpose basis. A joint venture of the Danish public telephone company and Danish Payment Systems, Danmønt (the Danish word for Danish coins, hence the English name Dancoin) intends to spread smart cards within this country of 5 million inhabitants. The trial period started in September 1992 and finished at the end of March 1993.

The main goal of Dancoin, as in other prepaid cards, is the replacement of small cash transactions with electronic off-line transactions. However, the importance of this experience comes from the high number of involved sectors: telephones, vending machines, banks, buses, trains, taxis, post offices, parking meters, and many others. After a period

/here there will be as many card issuers as providers of services, the application will volve into a single, fully multipurpose rechargeable card, which has been announced for 994. The complete system is expected to be fully implemented in 1995. By this date, ie impact on present customers' habits is predicted to result in a 1% annual decrease of ash transactions.

.2 HEALTH CARE CARDS

Iealth care is one of the major application areas of various types of cards. Intense activity n patient cards, either as a single subject or associated with computerization of health ecords, can be detected from statements made at several annual conferences, scientific ongresses, and symposia around the world. Browsing through the proceedings of these neetings, one can find contributions from many countries where implementations of card pplications for health services are suggested (Figure 8.3). Most applications are in the ilot project stage, and the national health services of many countries are using or testing ifferent cards for their patients. It is therefore reasonable to expect a rapid increase of ealth care card applications in the near future.

.2.1 Health Care Card Market

ard manufacturers are well aware of the huge number of cards involved in any nationwide ealth care application; hence, manufacturers are trying to demonstrate the advantages of

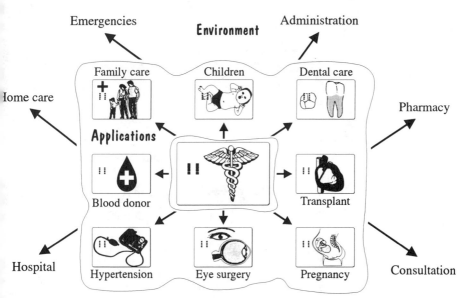

igure 8.3 Health-care areas where smart cards are used. Inset: examples of current applications.

using their particular cards (or technology) for such applications. For this reason, almo
every card technology (plastic, microfilm, bar code, magnetic stripe, optical, smart)
looking for a niche in the health care market.

When considering health care applications, it is important to realize that many ca
types may be used (Figure 8.4), depending on the kind and scope of the required inform
tion. For example, cards for administrative management (i.e., containing no clinical data
have requirements that are different from those of patient cards that store sensitive inform
tion. High-risk patients, or patients demanding special attention, may be provided wit
improved (and more expensive) cards, as compared to average users. Specific groups
the population (e.g., children) also require cards holding specific information (in this cas
growth and weight follow-up, vaccination calendar, allergies, etc.). Finally, handicappe
people and chronic patients such as diabetics should theoretically own specialized car
adapted to their diseases.

Health is a major concern to many people, and so data protection is an importal
issue when dealing with patient's health data. Unlike the case of financial cards, howeve

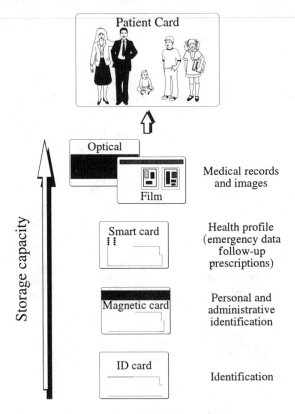

Figure 8.4 Cards of different technology may be used in health care environments.

he main argument is not protection against forgery, but privacy of data, somewhat protected by law in many countries. This privacy of data ought to be guaranteed, and its access be carefully restricted to appropriate professionals (such as physicians, nurses, pharmacists) within limited time spans.

3.2.2 Selecting a Technology for Health Care Cards

Although the ultimate solution in health care cards would probably have to be based on multipurpose or hybrid cards, several countries have adopted diverse solutions for solving, at least partially, the needs of their citizens. Simple magnetic stripe cards may be employed for identification purposes, perhaps including some critical health care data such as blood type, allergies, immunizations, and drug sensitivities. Smart cards may potentially offer a complete set of services, ranging from administration to prescriptions, emergencies, appointments, and so on. Moreover, smart cards are clearly advantageous from the security point of view. The use of smart cards in health care, however, is challenged by the manufacturers of optical cards, who argue that medical histories usually contain too much data, for which the limited storage capacity of smart cards is not appropriate (though internationally accepted coding schemes for diagnoses, procedures, and drugs are currently available, allowing considerable savings of storage space compared to natural language). Megabyte optical cards, as opposed to kilobyte smart cards, allow the storage of full medical records, along with digital images (e.g., radiographic) of the patients when needed.

Magnetic stripe cards aside, the question of choosing a card technology is ultimately related to several alien factors, namely, the mobility of the users and the level of information sharing between health centers. When the users look frequently for health care outside their assigned center, and networking for transferring health information is not fully implemented, the best solution is an optical card capable of holding as much relevant data as possible. Where a single health center is used, it would be advisable to keep the entire medical record at the assigned center, and to give the user a smart card containing just the most critical data for emergencies and standard coded versions of clinical and disease data (which can be translated to natural language by external software when reading the card). Additionally, extra services like automatic appointments, administration, and prescriptions might be included.

Japan is developing the most experience in optical cards, while European countries prefer smart cards, hybrids (chip and magnetic stripe in the same card), or various cards (magnetic stripe cards for the average population and smart cards for high-risk groups, children, elderly people, or chronically ill patients). The activity in the U.S. is still reduced, though the situation may change soon if President Bill Clinton's plans for health care are put in force: ''my plan will replace expensive billing, coding, and utilization-review functions with a simplified billing system. Everyone will carry 'smart cards' coded with his or her personal medical information.'' [1]

8.2.3 Data Management of Patient Cards

Regardless of the technology, the use of patient cards has intrinsic advantages for the user, providing that data privacy is guaranteed.

- Access to card data may be controlled by a PIN.
- Alternatively, access may be given by another card held by the health professional
- Health professional cards may in turn give privileges for accessing specific memory areas, depending on the kind of professional and the situation.
- The user may choose to leave the card safely at home or to carry it continuously. This should be taken as a user's right.
- More importantly, the user may even choose to give the card to any health professional, to be selective, or to refuse to give the card. Obviously, this applies to cards storing health data, not to cards for administration data.

Mobility is another area where patient cards are advantageous. The card gives every person the possibility of moving around the territory where his/her health insurance company is established, carrying a portable ID and/or a personal medical record, which may be used to request immediate health care anywhere. For instance, the French card DIALYBRE, for patients requiring dialysis, is being extended throughout the French territory, enabling those patients to move freely around the country. The European Community (EC) is studying the use of smart cards within its research program AIM (Advanced Informatics in Medicine). The final goal of these cards would be the definition of a European health care card, allowing EC citizens to obtain health care in any EC country "regardless of where they come from, regardless of where they are."

Let us summarize the ideas of Sections 8.2.1–8.2.3. A health care card may be used for the following functions.

- *Identification.* The patient identifies him/herself to the health service when requesting a service. The patient demonstrates that he/she is eligible for the service offered by this provider. This function is presently restricted to health insurance services.
- *Health Payments.* Health insurance companies are using cards to reimburse payments made in advance by the users, and to compensate for the services of the providers (i.e., health professionals).
- *Communications.* Cards may be used as portable information media between different health professionals. For example, a primary care physician may ask for a specific checkup from another health center storing information in the patient's card. The results are sent back using the same card. The physician then inserts a prescription, which is received by the pharmacist.
- *Health Records.* Cards may carry complete (or summarized) patient records, which are available to the users and health providers at any time.
- *Information.* External information may be printed on the card, including advertisements for the health care company, name and address of the assigned primary health care center, and telephone numbers for appointments and emergencies.

8.2.4 Canadian Health Care Projects

Several pilot projects involving cards in health care environments have been conducted in Canada in the past few years. Some pilots have just finished, while others are still continuing. The Encounter Card Pilot Project of Ontario finished its eight month field test in February 1993. The project involved 3,000 patients in northwestern Ontario. Six areas are presently being evaluated to determine the effectiveness of the system: interaction between patients and health professionals, information given to the users, individual health improvement, communications between health services, information accessibility in emergencies, and drug management. Special attention is also being paid to the acceptance of the system by health professionals and patients, as well as the security and confidentiality of sensitive data. For example, the Ontario Ministry of Health, sponsor of the project, received copies of all consultation records, where the patients' identity information was modified to protect their privacy. Patients' data in the support computers were protected as well. Should this pilot experience be successful, the use of smart cards for health care will be extended to the whole province.

Another major health care smart card project was launched in Quebec. The Quebec government decided to launch the project at the end of 1991, beginning an 18-month field test. The experience was sponsored by the Quebec Health Insurance Board and supported by a multidisciplinary research group at Laval University in Quebec. The field test was developed in the town of Rimouski (35,000 inhabitants). Up to 12,000 smart cards were used. Specific groups of the population were selected for the experience: elderly people (over 60 years), pregnant women, children up to 18 months of age, and the whole population of Saint Fabien de Rimouski. Card contents were divided into five areas: identification, vaccinations, prescriptions, medical history, and emergency.

The Quebec health care system is mostly financed by public funds, which refunds the physicians fees and the pharmaceutical services of retired and welfare people. Patients are free to choose their physicians and health centers, thus producing a spread of medical data. The Quebec Patient Smart Card was designed bearing in mind these principles (i.e., managing fragmented information while preserving freedom). As in the previous case, special efforts were made for patients to avoid what one of the designers called the *Big Brother Syndrome* (i.e., the feeling of being watched or scrutinized through the cards and support computer systems). During project development, for example, patients within the test areas were free to join the project or not. After joining, they were free to withdraw or simply not to use their cards at any time. Additionally, patients were told that, by presenting their cards, they were actually authorizing the health professional to read its contents; in an emergency situation, just holding the card authorizes the health professional to read it if the patient is unconscious. Anyway, patients could decide not to authorize the inclusion of specific medical information in their cards. These precautions eventually produced wider acceptance of the cards.

It is too early to ascertain whether these experiences will result in nationwide or provincewide applications of health care cards. Well-conducted projects like these, with clearly defined goals and ensuring data confidentiality, provide health authorities with the best examples of the advantages of employing smart cards in health care. Other Canadian health care projects using smart cards include:

- The Canadian Armed Forces card, allowing the Armed Forces physicians to store prescriptions in the cards;
- The Green Shield Smart Card project in Windsor, Ontario, involving 10,000 smart cards containing emergency medical and pharmaceutical information;
- The New Brunswick Health Card project, for drug therapy;
- The Health Information Register in Vancouver, for the follow-up of elderly and chronically ill patients.

8.2.5 French Health Care Projects

France is today the leading country in card applications concerning health care (and many other areas). The nationwide, magnetic-stripe-based, Santé-Pharma system is spread across the whole country, involving most of its pharmacies; estimations of the current number of issued cards are well above 1 million. A new payment procedure within the system is currently managing over 25,000 payments per month. As for smart cards, first experiences and field tests in France began as early as 1984, while the first health cards for public circulation were issued in 1985 at Blois (*Carte Santé* project).

The *Caisse Nationale d'Assurance Maladie* (CNAM, the French National Health Insurance Service) has participated in many card projects for several years. The French public Social Security is compulsory, covering practically 100% of the French population. It works on a pay-for-service/refund basis; that is, the patient pays for the service directly to the health professional and then asks for reimbursement. This generates a huge amount of administrative documents (there were 800 million reimbursement claims in 1992, each producing several documents). Moreover, the Social Security Department does not cover medical expenses in full, but only about 75% (in primary care). For this reason, many French people (over 80%) have complementary health insurance, either from private or from mutual (i.e., nonprofit) insurance companies. The complementary health insurance plans are often negotiated in bulk by employers for their employees. These companies cover the remaining 25% and/or offer additional services, increasing red tape.

There are more than 30 health-care-related card projects currently running in France, most of them based on smart cards. Some applications have been used for several years, while others, especially those from private companies or designed for special care, are just starting their implementation. Most projects also include cards for the health professionals. SESAM/VITALE, the most extensive of the projects, had distributed nearly 200,000 cards by the end of 1992; when fully implemented, the system will manage 27 to 30 million cards (one card per family) containing administrative data. SANTAL, one of the most important health care card projects, had issued 32,000 cards by that time. Some experiences, like HIPPOCARTE, are finishing their trial periods. Other applications, like DIALYBRE for dialysis patients or TRANSVIE for blood donors and transfusion procedures, are designed for specific health care requirements.

SESAM is a project developed by CNAM, whose main aim is to ease the administration of health services. It is based on Bull CP8 cards and takes advantage of the widely spread Minitel workstation terminals (Figure 8.5). National insurance cards are given to patients, while health professionals hold their own cards. Cards are periodically updated using Minitels. Card reading and writing is done by a portable input machine, MPS, which can be connected to telecommunication networks. The physician uses the MPS to store data regarding patient treatment and the pharmacist reads these data and records the medication codes according to the prescription. The information is collected every evening by the Social Security, and the refund process starts automatically.

The smart card employed by the SESAM system is called *VITALE*. The ultimate goal of the project is to provide a VITALE card to every person who is insured by CNAM; this amounts to about 30 million people (each card covers the insured person and his/her family). The coverage of the system will encompass the entire French population, more than 55 million people. VITALE cards are defined as ''portable family administrative files.''

Figure 8.5 Minitel-compatible terminal with slots for magnetic stripe and smart cards (courtesy of Telesincro).

The first SESAM trials began in 1985 in four test areas: Rennes, Blois, Lens, and Charleville-Mézières, involving 5,000 cards in each place. In 1990, the second phase started, distributing 100,000 cards in Boulogne-sur-Mer. The distribution of VITALE cards across the entire country began in 1992.

MUTUSANTE from the *Mutuelle Médicale et Chirugicale des Alpes* (Alpes Surgery and Medical Mutuality), is an example of an administrative application sponsored by a mutual company. It was launched in 1987 and includes, besides administrative data, the prepayment of health care services such as laboratory analysis and drug prescriptions. By 1990, the project had distributed over 60,000 cards free of charge to its members.

C3S from the *Fédération des Mutuelles de France* (France Mutuality Federation), is another administrative application, similar to MUTUSANTE. The C3S project began in 1990, issuing 25,000 cards in several places around the country: Sisteron, Digne, Nice, Toulon, Marseille, Menton, and Aulnoys. Besides financial data, the card contains some related to health: permanent data, such as emergency (the same data as defined in the European Health Emergency Card), blood group, missing organs; and temporary data, such as pregnancy or special treatments. There are also areas for specific health risks derived from the kind of work the user does, chronic diseases, and regular checkups. By 1991, 130,000 mutuality members had received their cards. The project was expected to be completed in 1993, amounting to more than 500,000 cards.

SESAM/VITALE, MUTUSANTE, and C3S are three examples of smart card applications issued by administrative health care organizations. Other experiences, controlled or issued by health institutions, are focused on health data. Within this group, SANTAL is the most important experience in health care cards in France.

The *SANTAL* project was first launched in the Saint-Nazaire region by an association of the same name involving eight hospitals, primary care physicians, laboratories, the Social Security, and mutual organizations. The project received unusually large financial support (8 million FF, about $1.5 million), with the target of providing CP8 smart cards free of charge to about 30,000 patients. The card contains some administrative data (patient identity and medical insurance) and a medical area, but not a true medical record, which includes essential information for emergencies, such as blood group, medical history, artificial limbs, previous hospitalization, dates of admission, current drug treatment, and allergies. SANTAL has 27,000 patients, hundreds of health professionals, four public hospitals, four private clinics, and eleven laboratories participating in the project.

DIALYBRE is a project sponsored by the *Fondation de l'Avenir* (Foundation for the Future), and was launched in 1988. The card, containing a small medical file, is given to all patients treated by haemodialysis as a result of renal failure. The pilot employed 500 smart cards. Once the project is completed, these patients will be able to travel throughout France, being attended to in any place through a national DIALYBRE network. Further plans will extend the system to other EC countries, thus increasing the mobility of these patients.

HIPPOCARTE is a project started in May 1990, which has developed a portable medical record in a smart card. It is a private initiative, the cards being offered to patients at 150 FF ($30). To involve health professionals, the card readers are given free for the first year. The application is based on Minitels and uses the same card readers as other applications. Several thousand HIPPOCARTE cards had been distributed in the Caen area by the end of 1991. (A similar experience called BIOCARTE was developed at Lille in 1986.) It was announced that SANTAL, DIALYBRE, and HIPPOCARTE readers would be unified by 1992.

TRANSVIE was originally designed as a smart card for blood donors in the Brest area. The field tests began in 1986 with some 5,000 cards and were carried out over three years. After this period, the card evolved towards multipurpose applications (within health care), extending its initial scope to the Greater Brest Area (200,000 inhabitants), and was intended to be a medical link between the patient and the health care system (i.e., a portable health file).

With so many health care card applications running at the same time, the *Carte du Professionnel de Santé* (*CPS*, Health Professional Card) has been a natural spin off. This card intends to make different systems compatible so that security and coherence in the communication of health data may be achieved. The CPS card provides nationwide identification of health professionals, and would be used as a single key for access to medical data in any system. Different access privileges are given, depending on the professional status and qualification within the system. The card would also be used as an electronic signature for the professional to add to or modify the data stored in the patient cards.

8.2.6 U.K. Health Care Projects

The Exeter Care Card is a remarkable health care card project, and has been running since 1989 in Exmouth (Devon), where the main concern is the handling of medical data, as opposed to administrative data (although these are also included). To save space in the 2K Bull CP8 smart card, a five-character alphanumeric hierarchical classification is used, which allows coding of pathologies according to international standards such as the International Classification of Diseases and many others. A data compression technique is also used.

The one-year trial period was carried out between 1989 and 1990, involving primary care physicians, dentists, pharmacists, two hospitals, and 8,500 smart cards. Cards were used for identification purposes, access to patient records, and drug prescriptions. Computers at different places were not linked up. Laptop computers for home visits were also used. Compatibility between external personal computers was granted to allow the use of the systems already installed.

After the trial period, an evaluation was carried out and presented to the health authorities to decide the future of the project. The experience has been considered very successful, since currently some 27,000 out of 34,000 inhabitants of Exmouth have a smart card, which is used at physicians' offices, pharmacies, and hospitals. The cards are being read by at least four computer systems.

Other, smaller projects involving health care cards have been conducted in Britain: Rhydyfelin-Pharmacy (Wales) issued 2,500 smart cards, mainly used as electronic prescription media, Southport experimented with a community nursing service based on SRAM memory cards, and the West London Hospital has been testing an optical memory card for its maternity service.

8.2.7 Italian Health Care Projects

Italy is conducting several health care card projects. Three of them, located at Lombardy, Sardinia, and Umbria, are supported by the Ministry of Health. Smart and optical cards are being used in these projects. The largest project is Salus, in Lombardy, with 60,000 Bull CP8 smart cards. It was launched in January 1989 for an 18-month trial period focused on hospital emergency services and physicians. The cards contain data on several at-risk pathologies (e.g., hypertension, allergies, cardiologic risks, high-risk pregnancy), as well as general health data (e.g., blood group, current drug prescriptions, hospitalizations). This project is quite similar to SANTAL in France. The Sardinia project was developed using 20,000 optical cards and is concerned with medical records, family and personal histories, clinical problems, and emergency data. The Umbria project is based on 44,000 CP8 smart cards. Its main areas are nephrology, cardiology, and hypertension. None of these or other (much smaller) projects have resulted in general use applications yet.

8.2.8 Health Care Cards in Other European Countries

The Spanish INSALUD, the National Health Care service, is distributing magnetic stripe cards for administrative and identification purposes. Several limited studies on patient smart cards have been carried out, but none has been accepted for general use yet. Some smart-card-based proposals for selected patient groups, such as children and high-risk and chronically-ill patients, are currently under study. Moreover, two small-scale pilot projects, blood-donor cards and blood pressure follow-up for hypertensive patients, are currently running.

Portugal studied the possibility of adopting a magnetic stripe card for general use, but finally a simple paper card was selected, while the eventual implementation of smart cards was analyzed. In the meantime, a geographically limited project for diabetic patients based on smart cards has been prepared.

Sweden has been using embossed health care cards for 25 years. In 1989 a pilot project on drug prescriptions based on smart cards was initiated in Tjörn, an island near Gothenburg. Several studies on specific health care areas, like ophthalmology, maternity, or administration, have been announced. There are also plans to introduce a health care professional card.

Germany began a pilot field test involving 2,200 physicians and dentists and 1.2 million patients, using magnetic stripe cards for identification purposes. The test should have been completed by 1992. Some legal difficulties have precluded the general use of smart cards for the moment. Limited smart card projects for vaccinations and diabetes are currently being carried out.

The Medical Technical Research Institute of Switzerland launched in 1989 a smart card project called SANACARD. The card contained administrative information and personal data like blood group, allergies, and vaccinations. Some 3,000 cards were distributed in Basel, Davos, and Lausanne.

The Netherlands has made a big effort in medical data transfer based on interactive videotext (EDIFACT). Nearly 40 projects have been developed in this field since 1983. The relative success of this system has somewhat delayed the implementation of health care cards. Nevertheless, it was announced in 1992 that the next generation of projects related to medical data exchange will use smart cards for communications. Quite recently, the Academic Hospital of Maastricht has begun using smart cards.

8.3 UNIVERSITY CARDS

University research groups have been traditionally involved in smart card applications. It is not surprising, therefore, that smart card applications for university services are quite common (Figure 8.6). It is not surprising either that university-related applications were initiated in the early days of smart cards.

8.3.1 French Universities

The first appearance of a university record card took place in 1983 at the University of Paris VII. The card (CP8) stored the student's academic information, recording his/her progress, yearly course selection, and qualifications. In other words, the card stored the academic curriculum of the holder, while offering a number of extra functions related to services within the campus facilities.

A major project was started in 1985 at the University of Science and Technology of Lille. The card follows the guidelines of the Paris University card, but several new features have been included. By 1989, the trial period had finished, and more than 5,000 students had their own smart card. The card includes administrative data and academic information as above; moreover, it is used for identification purposes and access to the university library, dramatically improving the handling of scientific books and journals. The card may also be used for obtaining health care, since a health care insurance company, SMENO (a mutual company based in Lille), accepts the student card as a membership card.

The original smart card at Lille was Bull CP8. Currently, cards from Sligos, developed in conjunction with TRT-Philips, are being used (*Carte SUP*). This project is currently

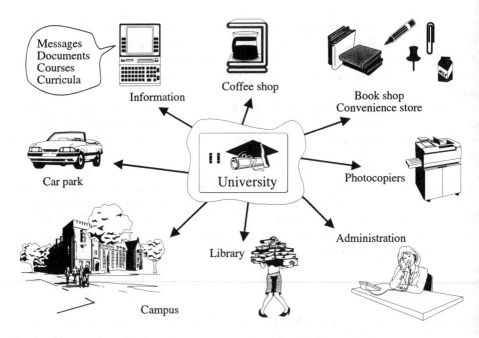

Figure 8.6 Current applications of smart cards in universities and colleges.

supported by the French Education Ministry, which aims to extend the experience to all French universities. The final product will be a multipurpose card with three kinds of applications: data files, access control, and electronic purse. Data include academic records, course registrations, and medical data. Access to individual rooms, libraries, laboratories, and leisure areas is controlled with the card. Other French universities like Campania, Toulouse, and Bordeaux were scheduled to join the project in 1992. Over 23,000 cards are currently in use; three times as many are expected to be used in the second phase of the project.

8.3.2 Italian Universities

The largest smart card application for universities is currently located at the University of Rome, La Sapienza. This was approved in 1987, starting with 5,000 smart cards delivered to students of the Faculty of Economics. The so-called *libretto elettronico* (electronic record) was intended to solve administrative and management problems for both students and staff. La Sapienza is one of the largest universities in Europe (and in the world), with some 180,000 students, more than 40 curricula, 7,000 members of academic staff, and 6,000 members of administrative staff. On average, every student generates 30 paper records per year (i.e., more than 5 million documents).

The student card works on 50 self-service terminals spread around the campus, allowing the students to consult their curricula, ask for documents, or obtain information from their faculty or the whole university. The terminals are interactive, so that the student may request changes in the courses, if applicable, or documents. If the documents do not need to be certified, they are obtained on line by the terminal's built-in printer. Certificate requests are transmitted to a networked computer which generates the document automatically, so that the student may eventually collect it from the faculty's office.

The members of academic staff are provided with a different smart card version that can be used, upon PIN identification, for recording the students' examination results (in the university's database and in the students' cards), as well as for requesting any kind of academic information. More than 1,000 terminals are available for this application. Examiners may also identify the students by means of their cards, thus ascertaining that the students are correctly registered and entitled to take the examination. The members of administrative staff have another smart card version, which is used for updating the database information and to issue new cards for fresh students, and backups for lost and damaged cards.

More than 250,000 cards are currently in circulation. New features are planned for implementation in the cards, including privileged access to restricted areas or electronic purse functions. Quite recently, the 900-year-old University of Bologna also adopted smart cards, their scope being quite similar to that of the La Sapienza cards.

8.3.3 U.S. and Canadian Universities

There has been some activity in the U.S. concerning smart cards. Between 1989 and 1990, over 10 universities and colleges tested different uses for smart cards, especially for access control to dormitories and dining halls, soft drink vending machines, and photocopying. At Queens College (Charlotte, North Carolina) and Trinity College (Burlington, Vermont), the projects were discontinued, largely because of high cost.

Loyola College (Baltimore, Maryland) began a multipurpose smart card project in 1990. Cards are used for transactions in the book and convenience stores, soft drink vending machines, and post office. There is also a plan to use the card for access control to car parks, buildings and rooms, book lending, academic and medical records, and photocopies. Another multipurpose application is running at Duke University (the first higher education center in the U.S. that employed cards). The project began in 1985 with magnetic stripe cards.

The University of Georgia employs hybrid magnetic stripe/smart cards. There was an initial application for access control to buildings (dormitories) which was designed on magnetic stripe cards. The project was extended for controlling access to individual rooms. The hybrid card uses the magnetic stripe with the already installed hardware for accessing the buildings, and the chip for room access. The Southern College of Technology (Atlanta, Georgia) has a similar application based on smart cards.

Florida State University has combined two applications in the same card. Besides access control, the card can be used for financial transactions using ATMs of Florida banks.

At Calgary University (Canada), smart cards have been used to solve a fraud problem in public photocopying. New digital audio tape techniques, now widely available, are a real challenge for magnetic stripe cards. In Calgary, the students managed to copy the stripes of unused photocopy cards onto pieces of audio tape. Forged cards were prepared by simply fixing the tape on a card-sized piece of plastic, making a card virtually identical to the original one. The fraud has been drastically cut by replacing the magnetic stripe system with a smart-card-based system.

8.3.4 Other Universities

Similar applications are being installed in several universities around the world. Most of them are focused on administration. For instance, different pilot projects have been developed at the universities of the Balearic Islands (Spain), Oslo (Norway), Melbourne (Australia), Tilburg (Netherlands), Vienna (Austria), and Singapore. The scope is similar to that of the above described applications. For example, Oslo has an initial access control application which will eventually extend to telephone services. Tilburg is using the cards for book rental and lending at the university library.

8.4 TELECOMMUNICATION AND COMPUTER CARDS

Public telephone applications are by far the largest users of chip cards. Over 200 million telephone chip cards will be used this year throughout the world. This figure has been achieved mostly in Europe (more than 80 million in France), since several major countries have selected other solutions. For instance, this year Japan will use over 400 million magnetic cards for public telephones. (Incidentally, Japan's NTT is presently considering the possibility of using smart cards for "semipublic" telephones in restaurants, hotels, parlors, etc. These phones cannot be operated with magnetic telephone cards.)

Telephone chip cards cannot be strictly considered smart cards, since they lack microprocessors. Yet there is some "intelligence" in the cards, since they are able to perform a simple program prepared during card manufacturing. The program is normally linked to the chip by hardware (wired logic). A small amount of memory (usually less than 100 bytes) is included in the chip.

These tiny siblings of smart cards are remarkably reliable and cost-effective. From 1985 to 1992, the manufacturing failure rate decreased from 14,000 to 400 cards per million. Another 400 cards per million fail during the life cycle (i.e., when customers are using them). Therefore, the overall failure rate is less than one card in every thousand. On the other hand, overhead costs for using chip cards are negligible relative to the final card price and are largely made up for by reductions in vandalism and thefts in public telephones.

Actual smart cards are also employed in telecommunications, computers, and consumer electronics (Figure 8.7), as shown in the following sections. Some phone services use smart cards. Besides GSM communications, which are reviewed in the next chapter, integrated services including phones and smart cards have recently been commercialized. Cards can protect data communications and storage in mainframes and personal computers. Smart cards are also used in other telecommunication services, with the well-known example of pay TV being the most important.

8.4.1 Follow-Me Phones

Siemens (Germany) offers a phone exchange where the extensions are not associated with physical phones, but with smart cards. With this system, the phones of a company may be personalized. Every person entitled to use the service has a smart card, which contains the extension number assigned to him/her. The number belongs to the user, meaning that it can be given to other people or printed on his/her calling cards. However, the number is not linked to any specific phone in the system. When the user arrives at his/her office, he/she inserts the smart card in a slot of the phone and enters his/her PIN. The phone

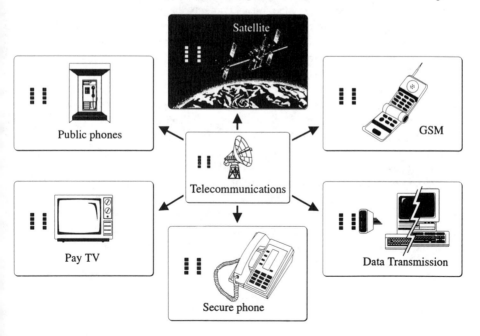

Figure 8.7 Smart cards in communications and consumer electronics.

then becomes the recipient of the calls for the number stored in the card. If the user has to go to or work temporarily in another office or in a meeting, he/she simply takes the card and inserts it in the nearest phone, and the calls are automatically transferred to the new location. If a card is not inserted in any phone, its calls are transferred to a central exchange. As extra protection, there is a time interval between calls, after which the card requests the user to re-enter the PIN. This time is predefined by the user. This avoids improper use of the phone if the user forgets to remove the card when leaving the office.

The card may have another function: voice encryption/decryption. The voice is distorted when sent through the line and is recovered at the other end. To use this feature, both telephones must belong to the same system. Data may also be sent using the same line. It is even possible to switch between voice and data in the same connection.

For outgoing calls, the card may contain instructions restricting time and/or distance of the calls the user is allowed. Moreover, phone charges may be individually distributed, since they are registered in every card. Since the application is independent of physical phones, the user is charged for his/her calls regardless the phone he/she is employing.

8.4.2 Data Security in Computers

Smart cards may be used as security locks for computers. The absence of the card or the failure to present the correct PIN may lock the keyboard or the system. Disks may also be protected by cards, either enciphering its contents using the card facilities, or storing in the card some crucial information on the data structure. In either case, unauthorized attempts to read the disk files only produces meaningless garbage.

Smart cards have been traditionally associated with security issues; most major card companies (e.g., Bull, Philips, and Gemplus) have developed applications where cards are associated with computer units, terminals, and peripherals. In personal computers, the card WRU is externally connected to the computer; internal units that fit into 3.5-in drive bays are also available. Communications between different computers may be protected, too. Before being sent through the network (or by modem), data are encrypted by the smart card. Another card at the other end decrypts the message.

Smart cards may also be used in networked shared mainframes. For instance, the headquarters of a Swiss bank corporation has installed a smart-card-based access system covering its 1,500 personal computer terminals, servers, and mainframes. Each authorized user has a smart card where his/her access privileges are specified. Every card holds a user PIN, as well as passwords for accessing different levels of servers or mainframes within the system. Additional security features such as timeout when the terminal is unattended and card expiring dates are also included.

Other sophisticated proposals for data security are discussed in the next chapter.

8.4.3 Pay TV

Pay TV channels are found in atmospherically transmitted, satellite, and cable TV. Channel Plus (Channel +) in several European countries is an example of the first kind, while some channels of ASTRA satellites are examples of the second. Image and sound information of pay TVs is codified in such a way that TV monitors of nonusers display scrambled images when tuning into one of these channels.

Pay TV companies must deal with two issues. First, the service should be only available to their customers; this is achieved with the scrambling procedure. The customers are provided with a descrambling device that is connected between the antenna (or the cable) and the TV monitor to decode the signal. Second, since these services are usually rented, the issuer must ensure that the service is disconnected from those customers who have delayed their payments. This feature should be teleoperated for obvious reasons.

Channel +, for example, delivers a two-component system. The first component is a *black box*, which performs the connections to the antenna and TV monitor, and the electronic unscrambling. The device is lent to the customers at the beginning of the contract, for which a deposit is required. The second component is a smart card. Actually, its shape is not that of a card, but rather a plastic key. It has the usual golden contacts, indicating that a chip is embedded in the key. For the system to work, the smart key has to be inserted into the box. The key contents may vary from one system to another, but the scope is the same. The key holds some essential information that is required by the electronics for unscrambling the TV signal. The descrambling sequence is changed every few seconds, thus largely squeezing out piracy. Once the rental period has expired, the scrambling rules are changed, and the key does not work. Upon renewal of the service, the key is given the new scrambling algorithms for the next period. This can be simply done by giving the user a new key. The Channel+ system, more conveniently, reprograms the old key at the customer's home, sending the required instructions in the teletext area of the TV signal. Alternatively, an order for the key to block can be sent using the same medium. The system is also employed for sending personalized messages to the customers (e.g., for birthdays) or to remind them that the rental payment has not been received.

8.5 MISCELLANEOUS

Smart cards have found a place in many other activities. Card applications can be spotted worldwide in amazingly variable areas. Prepaid cards are used for public transport in trams, buses, trains, and subways. There are sport cards for practicing golf, ski, or squash. Cards are being employed by hotels, gas stations, trade centers, cinemas, and theaters. Cards are carried in cars for highway tolls, in ships, and in oil-drilling platforms. Apple-shaped cards are the only dress for clients of several nudist beaches, where the cards have demonstrated their reliability in a hostile environment like sea water. The examples given below spotlight a few of the less common uses of smart cards.

8.5.1 Certification of Coins

Smart cards are being used to protect gold coins against forgery. The possession of an original gold coin makes it relatively easy to make copies using less expensive metals or alloys with the same density. The forged coins are covered with pure gold afterwards. Chemical analysis may discover the fraud, but the coin is irreversibly damaged.

Smart Cards USA has proposed a new system. Every coin is associated with a smart card. A unique electronic signature of the coin, based on measurements of conductivity and absorption of several radio-frequencies (using a radiotransmitter specifically designed for this application), is obtained for every coin and stored in its card. Data are protected by the card's standard security tools. The card is used in every further sale of the coin. The system is currently used by international coin dealers at the Universal Coin Corporation.

8.5.2 Electronic Benefits Transfer

U.S. social services are investigating the use of smart cards for replacing traditional food stamps and checks. The applications are called *electronic benefit transfer* (EBT). The Department of the Treasury has initiated an EBT project, and another six are being carried out by state governments. EBT is an ideal framework for off-line transactions in different environments, the selection of smart cards for these applications being a natural one. There are EBT applications based on magnetic stripe and the combination of the stripe with a chip card. The use of cards will reduce costs for both the official agencies and the recipient (e.g., charges for check cashing).

Applications in this area are not technically appealing. However, their implementation requires the use of multiple EPOSs for reaching the areas where the EBT is applied, including rural sites. In statewide applications, EPOSs should be extended to stores in other states located near the state borders. The same problem arises in electronic check cashing in ATMs. Many benefits could be delivered with the same EBT card (e.g., food stamps, Social Security annuity, veterans programs, Families With Dependent Children, Medicare, Medicaid), thus producing further cost savings. However, cooperation between all involved administrations would be necessary.

8.5.3 Peanut Card

The U.S. Department of Agriculture (USDA) has for several years been running an application for distribution of peanut quotas between producers. Peanut production involves some 70,000 farmers spread over 20 states. These farmers deliver their crops to 500 buying sites administered from 400 offices. Each farmer is reimbursed at "full quota rate" for his/her quota share; excess production is labeled "export only," its rate being much lower (less than 50%) than the quota rate.

A national quota is decided each year; the quota is proportionately assigned to states, which in turn divide their quotas by counties and individual producers. Under the old system, production records generated more than a million pieces of paper, and marketing errors were quite common. Once the smart card system was implemented, each producer received a smart card containing some identification and administrative fixed data, an electronic purselike record of deliveries storing the updated quota balance, and a balance of payments owed to the producer. At the buying site, operators carrying secure ID smart cards validate every transaction. Transfer of these transactions to the central computers of the official agencies results in reimbursements to the farmers using the corresponding rate. The application was designed and delivered by Micro Card Technologies, Inc., in collaboration with IBM, which supplied the terminals and the software. By 1990, more than 100,000 cards and 1,000 terminals were in service. Plans to extend the concept to a similar quota system for tobacco producers were announced by the USDA.

8.5.4 British Gas Card

In the United Kingdom, several services such as gas and electricity have been customarily offered under a prepayment basis. Under the old system, the client had to insert coins in the corresponding meter to obtain the service. The coins were periodically collected by the company's personnel. Besides the need to have coins at any time, the system was quite inconvenient because it stimulated thefts. Even worse, the burglars used to take the entire meter, since that was easier than extracting the coins (and the customer had to buy a new one).

These systems have been replaced by a new, cashless, prepaid strategy. Electricity is currently being obtained through an electronic key, while British Gas has adopted a smart card solution called *Quantum*. The Quantum meter system consists of a gas meter controlled by a smart card. The card is recharged in nearby ATMs or gas offices. Once the bought credit is stored in the card, this is inserted in the gas meter, which automatically takes the credit and puts it into the meter. Emergency credit is provided when the money runs out. The amount due for the borrowed gas is eventually subtracted when the recharged card is inserted again in the meter. Other features of the system include partial payments for unpaid bills and emergency credit, as well as a "budget" feature that lets the user choose how much credit he/she wants to use during a particular period of time (this is useful for short-term renting).

Cards are personalized by the meter itself. Cards cannot be used in a different meter; therefore, lost and stolen cards are useless. When a customer loses the card, a replacement card is provided. The new card must be inserted in the meter for personalization, and then it can be charged as usual.

8.6 CONCLUSIONS

This chapter, though extensive, has merely scratched the outer surface of current smart card applications. Smart cards are becoming the natural choice for many applications besides the classical financial cards. These applications are perhaps less noticeable, as their range seldom extends above 1 million cards. Still, chances are growing for everyday people in many countries to hold a smart card in their wallets. Smart cards are currently common in France and, to a lesser extent, in other European countries. The "critical mass" of smart card applications is being reached in many places, while the lack of infrastructure and expertise as barriers for smart card implementation is being overcome. The continuous spawning of smart card applications, or perhaps a few nationwide applications, will produce a snowball effect sooner or later. Smart cards are here to stay, and their impact on the everyday habits of the population is steadily increasing. The next chapter considers advanced card technologies for current applications and some anticipated trends.

REFERENCES

[1] "The Clinton Health Care Plan," *The New England Journal of Medicine*, Vol. 327, No. 11, p. 804, 1992.

Chapter 9
Applications: New Trends

Can the future of smart cards be extrapolated from present achievements or will it be decided by unforeseen findings and applications? Smart card evolution in the last few years and state-of-the-art applications allow us to deduce the characteristics and market trends of smart cards in the near future (e.g., three years). However, as mentioned in the previous chapter, market trends derived from current applications may be dwarfed by the sudden decision of any government or financial company concerning the use of smart cards in any nationwide or worldwide application. This would be a quantum leap in smart card forecasts; more than ever, there are clear signs in several countries that this event is about to happen.

In this last chapter, several areas where there is a high level of activity which is not fully translated to smart card implementations will be reviewed. Again, the list is not exhaustive. Biometric tests, covered in the first section, shall be taken as the most important issue in this context. The development of reliable, inexpensive biometric tests for user ID would open many new areas to smart card applications and would confirm their superiority in many others, notably finance-related applications. The second section focuses on the use of smart cards in the GSM. Besides its intrinsic importance, it is an example of service personalization, pointing to multifunction personal cards. The third section reviews new trends in Europe from the point of view of cross-border applications. The EC research and development (R&D) programs are paying attention to smart cards in quite distinct areas, which may be taken as the paradigm of new European trends. Finally, in the last section we will show our (perhaps not impartial) view on the future of smart cards, including some long-term forecasts.

9.1 BIOMETRICS

Unique ID of human beings and animals may be achieved by measuring any permanent biological attribute whose variability compares to or exceeds the applicable population.

Fingerprints are the most typical example in humans; many other features have been analyzed and proposed for ID purposes. Smart cards for ID and access control may include biometric data. These data are stored in the card and compared to real-time measurements obtained by an external device on the person whose identity is being checked. If both sets of data match within predefined tolerances, the ID is positive. The thresholds established for these tolerances ultimately determine the level of security. In other words, since no test is completely irrefutable, tolerances must be adjusted according to the application.

Automated ID from biometric data may be required in quite different environments. Biometric parameters employed for remote ID in telephone calls requesting access to services, for example, are more restricted than EPOS recognition for credit or access of authorized visitors to restricted areas. On the other hand, social acceptance of several biometric techniques (e.g., retinal patterns, fingerprints, or dental records) may advise the selection of less intrusive techniques, unless security is of paramount importance for the application. DNA sampling is an extreme example of an intrusive technique.

9.1.1 Adjusting Discrimination Levels

Let us assume that the parameters obtained from the biometric measurements have been joined in a single variable whose discrimination power is being analyzed. Repeated readings on the persons being identified give values for this variable that are plotted in Figure 9.1(a). The graph is a classical Gaussian curve derived from the frequency histogram. For any given person and variable, the width of the Gaussian curve should ideally be zero; that is, all the measurements should give the same value. In practice, however, there is always some deviation, hence a finite Gaussian width.

In the same figure, the values of the same variable for other people are presented as a second Gaussian curve. (This need not be the case, since it depends on the algorithm chosen for the computation. The actual shape of the second curve does not affect the reasoning below.) As can be seen in the figure, some overlap between the curves is produced. The overlapping area limits the discrimination of the test. The curves are not to scale; overlapping of real biometric tests is usually below 1%.

The dotted line (discrimination level) between the curves divides the figure into four areas: true acceptance (TA), false acceptance (FA), true rejection (TR), and false rejection (FR). TA and TR areas completely cover their Gaussian curves, except the small portions located on the other side of the discrimination level (i.e., FR and FA). Should the line be placed as in Figure 9.1(a), the real card owners would be correctly identified most of the time (TA area) and rejected on a few occasions (FR area). On the other hand, some other people would be incorrectly identified as card owners (FA area).

The location of the discrimination level should be adjusted depending on security requirements. Figure 9.1(b) shows a discrimination level for which the acceptance of false owners is virtually impossible (FA area is nearly zero), thus improving the system security. The penalty is that real owners will have a higher rejection rate (FR area is increased).

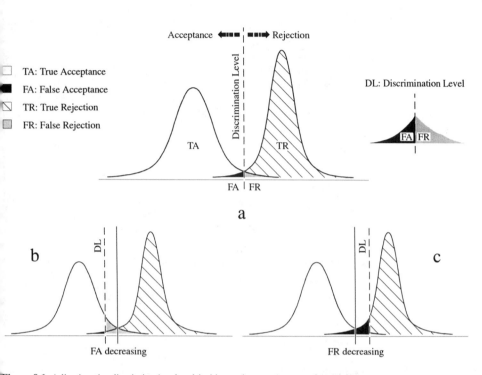

Figure 9.1 Adjusting the discrimination level in biometric tests (see text for details).

This is the strategy that must be applied to sensitive restricted areas or services (e.g., in financial or military applications).

Figure 9.1(c) shows the opposite situation, where the discrimination level has been moved to prepare a "permissive" system. Card owners are now correctly identified almost every time (FR area is reduced), but an increased number of noneligible people (FA area) are also accepted. At first glance, it seems that this situation should not be tolerated in actual applications. This is not the case, as shown in one of the examples given below.

9.1.2 Biometric Techniques

Automated recognition and human recognition work on different assumptions. The human brain is a massively interconnected system, which is unbeatable in pattern recognition. Humans recognize easily the face and voice of people they know. They are not so good, however, in distinguishing other features such as hand geometry or vein patterns. After all, many hands have similar shapes, requiring precise quantitative measurements for identifying every person. These measurements may be easily obtained with a relatively simple device.

There is no perfect biometric system for all the applications. Rather, some biometric techniques (Figure 9.2) may be more suitable for certain environments, depending on,

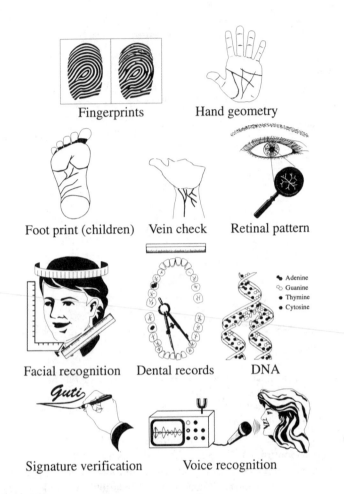

Fingerprints   Hand geometry

Foot print (children)   Vein check   Retinal pattern

Facial recognition   Dental records   DNA

Signature verification   Voice recognition

Figure 9.2 Biometric tests.

among other factors, the desired security level and the number of users. For instance, unattended recognition has different requirements than attended; outdoor applications reduce the number of practical biometric devices, and demonstration of claimed identity needs specific tests as compared to eligibility for access regardless of ID. Finally, the required amount of memory needed to store the biometric data (even applying data compression) may become a relevant factor in some applications.

Fingerprints have traditionally been employed as an ID tool in law enforcement. Present systems take advantage of decades of experience in extracting ID features from prints. Optical and ultrasonic devices have been proposed for fingerprint detection (Figure 9.3), since they currently have low FR and very low FA. Some problems arise, however, in its implementation in consumer applications, the social acceptance not being the least

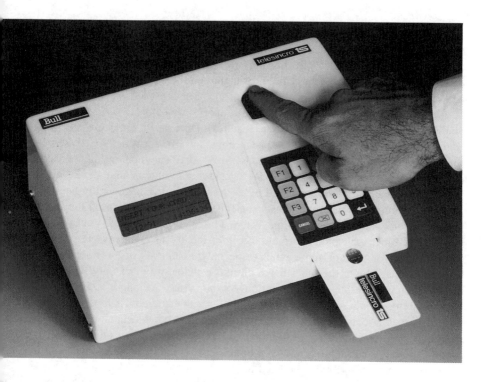

Figure 9.3 Fingerprint recognition system associated to smart cards (courtesy of Telesincro).

important. Dirty surfaces may impair the performance of the system, especially in optical devices. Ever more stringent hygiene demands must be borne in mind. For these reasons, the system may be inappropriate for unattended and/or outdoor applications. In some countries where fingerprints have been traditionally used in ID cards for citizens (i.e., not only for arrested suspects), social rejection is greatly reduced, allowing very large ID applications such as EXPO'92 in Spain (see section 9.1.3 below). In the U.S., the Los Angeles Department of Public Social Services is using a fingerprint-based ID system called *Automated Fingerprint Image Reporting and Match* (AFIRM) to identify eligible members within its relief benefit programs. The U.S. Immigration and Naturalization Service is also using fingerprints, among other biometric techniques, for several alien ID applications.

Hand geometry has features similar to fingerprints, though perhaps its social acceptance is higher. Similar devices are used in both cases; in fact, combined measurements may be simultaneously obtained, at least theoretically, using the same device. Hand geometry should in principle be less accurate than fingerprints, because it has a lower number of parameters and less variability. However, the technology is much more recent, and thorough comparisons are needed. In the meantime, manufacturers have managed to offer reliable products, as demonstrated by their use in applications with strict security requirements, such as the U.S. Department of Energy, Hanford Site, where nuclear and chemical waste are disposed of. The Hanford Site is implementing a personal ID system based on smart card badges carrying information on the cardholder's hand geometry for access control.

Signature verification is a typical example of so-called *behavioral* features (i.e. biometric data not based on anatomical features). Devices for signature recording range from bar code scanners to digitizing pads. Signatures are not usually analyzed as prints since the size, height, width, and orientation may vary. The input systems instead detect motion, relative trajectories, speed, and/or acceleration of the penlike device given to the user. The precise algorithm employed by each manufacturer is generally kept secret.

Recognition by signature takes some time for the user to sign on the input board. This is a disadvantage for applications where a large number of people must be identified in a limited time; for example, admittance to a factory or company premises. It is not suitable either for outdoor applications (especially unattended ones), since hardware can be easily damaged. On the other hand, current technology offers very low FR and FA. In these circumstances, the best applications for this system are indoor accesses to restricted areas or services, where only a few persons (tens or hundreds at most) are allowed to enter. One subtle detail of signature verification (and other behavioral tests) is that it requires a positive action from the individual being identified: in other words, the user is not identified if he/she does not want to be. This should be taken into account in some applications; for instance, those related to immigration or social benefits.

Retinal pattern recognition devices have been offered as commercial products for several years. Early models faced social rejection, not only for privacy considerations but for an extended misleading belief concerning eye injury by continuous use of these devices. Extensive tests on the new models have proved the reliability of the system. Moreover, retinal scans have low memory requirements, very low FR and negligible FA, making this technique quite useful in high security environments, even in outdoor applications. Sandia National Laboratories are testing retinal scanners to improve their security specifications. Although less developed, similar arguments may be applied to *vein patterns* measured in the hands or wrists of the persons being identified.

Voice recognition is probably the biometric system that attracts the most R&D from private organizations, universities, and administrations. Systems range from those requiring the pronunciation of a fixed sentence to recognizers of random sentences, either selected by the machine or by the user. The main pitfall of this technique, relatively high FR, has been steadily reduced as the technology improves. However, sophisticated voice reproduction by digital techniques may impair the reliability of these systems, especially in unattended sites, unless countermeasures are adopted. On the positive side, voice recognition has the highest social acceptance and is suitable for outdoor applications.

Facial recognition is an attempt to make computers mimic human capabilities. Special computation techniques like neural networks are being investigated for this purpose; current results, however, are far from those of the human brain, since the systems usually lack tolerances on position, lighting, and orientation of the face. Nevertheless, they have proved useful in helping human operators find out the identity of people by reducing the number of possible identities within the population database. Gemplus employs a different approach for facial recognition (Figure 9.4). Its off-line system consists of a smart card containing a compressed file with a digitized picture of the cardholder. The card is read by a portable terminal which shows the picture and ID data in a miniature color display. The ID is then performed by a human operator. McCorquodale has developed a similar system.

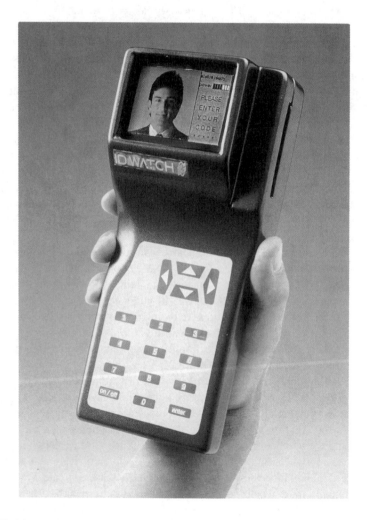

Figure 9.4 Facial recognition by human operators based on data stored in a smart card (courtesy of Gemplus).

9.1.3 Some Biometric Experiences

Smart cards containing biometric data have been used for ID purposes, access control and related applications in many countries and environments. Some consumer market applications for immigration, social benefits, and military purposes are being implemented or designed. Several examples have been shown in the above section. We will now describe two rather different experiences implemented in Spain in 1992 when it celebrated in 1992 two major international events: the Universal Exposition EXPO'92 in Seville and the 1992 Olympic Games in Barcelona. At least two biometrics-related smart card applications were prepared for these events. EXPO'92 was an exhibition of the history, culture, and latest technological achievements of most countries of the world; each country prepared its own pavilion. There were several other pavilions focusing on specific topics such as nature, discoveries, space, and navigation. Hundreds of cultural events took place as well. During the six months of the exhibition, it received 48 million people, averaging 250,000 visitors per day, increasing up to more than 400,000 visitors on peak days.

Magnetic stripe tickets for one day or three days could be obtained at any time, their price being about $40 and $100, respectively. Prior to the exhibition opening, moreover, personalized season passes were sold. The price of these passes was $300 each. Clearly, the idea was to stimulate people to visit the exhibition, since the season pass price for six months was quite low compared to daily tickets. The initiative was so successful that the selling of personal season passes had to be discontinued after more than 180,000 were sold; otherwise the exhibition would have collapsed under a flood of season cardholders.

The application for EXPO'92 season passes was developed on smart cards prepared by the *Fábrica Nacional de Moneda y Timbre* (FNMT, Spanish National Factory of Coins and Stamps, which also manufactures Spanish telephone chip cards) under Bull license. The main concern of FNMT developers was to guarantee that the cardholders did not lend (or rent) their cards to other visitors. A biometric system based on fingerprints was adopted. As mentioned in the previous section, fingerprints are routinely used in Spanish ID documents; therefore, no social rejection of this system was experienced. The same system and card was used for the 30,000 EXPO'92 workers.

Season cardholders were instructed to use specific admittance gates, where fingerprint readers were placed. No special security requirements were needed for this application, but speed was essential to avoid severe bottlenecks at the admittance gates. In these circumstances, the solution was to loosen the parameter ranges for positive matching, thus minimizing the number of false rejections. An FA increase was obviously produced, but it was not important in this case. For example, if the cards were able to reject 9 out of 10 false cardholders (a modest result for a biometric test), this rate would have been enough to dissuade most would-be trespassers. The system manufacturers reckoned an average time for recognition of about 8 sec; actually, tests took about 30 sec in the first weeks, the time being reduced to 15 sec after two months.

The opposite case (i.e., high security level, low number of users) was faced by the developers of the application for ID and access to the air traffic control tower of Barcelona airport, which was rebuilt for the 1992 Olympic Games. Fewer than 200 persons are allowed to enter the tower, but security is obviously a major concern in this environment. The application was developed by 2IS on McCorquodale cards. Signature recognition was selected. The parameters of three signature samples of permitted users were stored in their smart cards. A limited number of attempts was given to the users, the signatures being compared to the average of the three signatures stored in the card. If a successful match was achieved, the parameters of this signature were stored in the card, substituting for the oldest data. Therefore, the signature samples are continuously updated, the three most recent ones being stored in the card. This avoids signature time-drift problems shown by many users.

9.2 GLOBAL SYSTEM FOR MOBILE COMMUNICATIONS

Mobile phones have become popular in the last few years. A cellular system of repeaters and links manages to keep track of the users' physical location, transferring their calls to the phones, regardless of where they are within the coverage area of the system. As the area and the number of users grow, the problem of locating every user increases.

Nationwide coverage has been achieved in several countries. However, this is not enough in many small or medium-size countries, especially in Europe. Indeed, many users are frequent travellers that often cross their country borders. A new transnational system, based on smart cards, has been launched in Europe to satisfy this demand. Among other companies, Gemplus is particularly active in this area.

GSM is an international mobile phone system based on digital transmission and cellular infrastructure. First agreements for defining such a system were signed by 17 European countries in 1987. The specification was finished in 1990. The first commercial launch took place in 1992. At the time of writing, the second phase of the project is about to end; 30 countries have joined the project in the meantime. Besides the original European members, countries from Eastern Europe, Africa, and Asia and also Australia and New Zealand are currently implementing GSM. At present, over 1 million GSM subscribers are registered. This figure is dwarfed when compared to the nearly 7 million regular mobile phones in Europe. Forecasts, however, are quite favorable for the GSM system: it is expected that GSM users will reach this number by the end of the decade.

9.2.1 System Design

GSM takes advantage of both digital transmission and smart card features to achieve a powerful tandem. Digital signals on a 900-MHz carrier allow high-quality voice transmission, data transmission, fax and message services, encryption/decryption of messages, and extra services. The smart card is primarily used for user authentication. Within GSM, the users' cards become their Subscriber Identity Modules (SIM). When a card is inserted into a mobile phone, the system uses the card data and PIN checking to generate an international management subscriber identity (IMSI). This ID allows the service provider to bill the calls to the corresponding national operator. It is important to realize that the subscriber is identified through the card; therefore, the card may be removed from the user's mobile phone and inserted into another phone of the same system. In this way GSM services can be obtained in taxis, airplanes, boats, rental cars, or any public telephone (see below). Moreover, mobile equipment may be rented and used by any subscriber again being billed in his/her country of origin through IMSI.

9.2.2 GSM Equipment and Services

Three kinds of mobile equipment are used in GSM (Figure 9.5). The highest power is provided by units permanently attached to a vehicle. Medium-power portable units are carried in a suitcase, while low-power pocket-sized units (handsets) can be carried in the belt or in a handbag. The first two types employ regular ISO 7816 smart cards. Handsets are too small for these cards to fit in; therefore, 25 × 15-mm rectangular plug-in cards are used. It should be noted that the size of these cards has not been standardized (a first

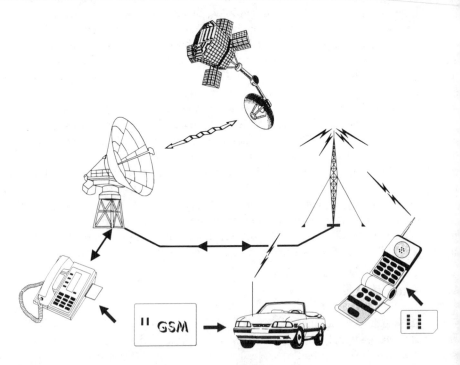

Figure 9.5 Regular and plug-in smart cards employed in the GSM system.

European draft from CEN/TC 224 has recently been submitted to the CEN members). The functional behavior of the contacts is quite similar to regular smart cards, except that programming voltage is not supplied. (This is not a crucial issue; most regular cards do not currently require programming voltage.) The remaining electrical signals follow ISO 7816/3; the transmission protocol is T = 0. EEPROM memory sizes range from 2K to 8K. No magnetic stripe and no embossing are permitted.

The subscription identity is kept in the smart card. To avoid conflicts between subscribers owning credit-card- and plug-in-sized smart cards, the former can also be inserted into handsets. The plug-in card may remain inside, the SIM of the credit-card-sized card overriding the plug-in card's SIM as long as it is inserted. In this way, the handset owner may lend his/her equipment to any other GSM subscriber.

Phase I of GSM offers several supplementary services such as messages, PIN disabling, and reduced key-in for frequently used numbers. Phase II includes charge calculations and supplementary services. Since the user identity is guaranteed through a card, it is possible to adapt the cards for working in public pay phones; moreover, different GSM service providers may issue personalized cards. New features are planned eventually to be included, such as emergency health care records and electronic purse.

9.3 NEW TRENDS IN EUROPE

Europe is still the main producer and consumer of smart card applications. International projects are supported by several organizations, the EC R&D programs being the most representative. In this section, two particularly active areas are used as examples of present EC-supported European activities in smart cards. It goes without saying that many other national and international applications are currently being designed or tested in Europe. The importance of EC programs, however, is enhanced by the impact and scope of the funded applications; indeed, partners from at least two (and usually three or more) EC countries are required for the commission to support any project. This feature gives international character to any application derived from these projects; their results, more-over, are often adopted as EC directives for further development. In our opinion, the existence of numerous smart-card-related EC R&D projects leads to two conclusions: on the one hand, there exists a strong interest in supporting a largely European technology; on the other hand, a sharp increase of transnational smart card applications should be expected in the next few years.

9.3.1 Smart Cards in Transportation

DRIVE is an EC R&D program devoted to improving road transport through new systems and technologies. As in other EC programs, partners from several EC countries join in research consortia. Several approved initiatives involve smart cards. DRIVE I was launched in January 1989 and lasted three years. In January 1992, DRIVE II started and included other smart card projects, as well as extensions of the most promising DRIVE I projects. (A similar program, called *Intelligent Vehicle Highway Systems* (IVHS), has recently been launched in the U.S.)

The PAMELA project was funded by DRIVE I to develop a two-way communication system between moving vehicles and fixed roadside beacons. Such a system may be used to have beacons deliver traffic information (i.e., emergency situations, and weather-related traffic difficulties) to drivers. The vehicles may in turn warn of their presence to traffic control. A smart card was included in the system as a tool for nonstop toll payments. Microwave transponders developed in this project have demonstrated their reliability even in multilane, high-speed (100 mi/h) tests. The application has been extended in DRIVE II to other uses, such as car parking and road pricing. The new project, ADEPT, has included some non-EC European partners, such as Norway and Sweden.

Another DRIVE I project, SMART, performed a detailed study on potential smart card applications in transport. The main conclusions of this study were twofold.

- The lack of coordination was limiting the market penetration of smart cards.
- Current cards were not yet fully prepared for multipurpose environments.

These conclusions eventually led to an increased European effort in standardization and technology of smart cards.

BARTOC studied the application of smart cards as a payment system for public transport. Since smart cards are too expensive for single fares, their use as season tickets was proposed. These cards may eventually become City Cards, usable for payment of different urban services such as libraries, swimming pools, car parks, and public transport.

Besides ADEPT, DRIVE II has also funded several projects related to smart cards. CASH intends to produce a common functional specification for automatic debiting in Europe. GAUDI involves five European cities (Trondheim, Marseille, Dublin, Bologna, and Barcelona) in a project on urban debiting by smart cards. The Dublin work package includes a multifunction smart card for payment of buses, subways, parking fees, and highway tolls, as well as telephone calls. The bus company intends to implement the system in the full fleet, issuing about 100,000 IC cards. Marseille is investigating the use of contactless cards for hands-off ticketing. Most of these DRIVE II projects are still active, their term being up in 1994.

To complete this section on European transport, the largest current application of contactless cards should be mentioned. It is not an international project, but entirely British. The Greater Manchester Passenger Transport Executive ordered 500,000 contactless cards from GEC Card Technology (U.K.). One million cards will be used when the application is fully implemented. The cards will be used in Greater Manchester's 2,700 buses, trams, and rail stations.

9.3.2 CAFE Project

The ESPRIT EC program supports R&D activities in information technologies. Several card-related projects have been supported by this framework. CRYPTOCARD intends to develop a microprocessor associated to a standard crypto-coprocessor for high-security smart cards. MORECO and MORESYS are involved in multifunction smart cards for electronic badges allowing hands-off access through infrared bidirectional transmission.

CAFE (Conditional Access For Europe) is a 3-year ESPRIT project aiming at the definition and demonstration of high-security techniques for international payments, communication, and personal information using an "electronic wallet." The definition phase intends to establish the requirements of financial companies and retailers for cashless payments. The building of prototypes and tests are foreseen in the second phase. The project also involves security experts, social researchers, semiconductor manufacturers, and electronic designers.

Thirteen partners from six EC countries (Germany, Denmark, France, Netherlands, U.K., and Belgium) and one non-EC country (Norway) have joined the CAFE project. From contacts with a large number of service providers, a comprehensive list of objectives has been prepared. These include open payment and data, commercial and legislation issues, a simple (yet highly reliable) security kernel, facilities for service providers to install their applications while keeping their privacy, and standardization through CEN and ISO.

The CAFE scope is more ambitious than financial applications. CAFE devices should ultimately replace the entire content of our wallets or purses (i.e., credit cards, transport tickets, ID documents, driver's license, passport, health care data, and, of course, cash). This raises a huge number of technical, commercial, and legal problems. Although it is technically feasible to mimic all the above items by electronic means, these electronic replicas ought to be commercially and legally acceptable. Perhaps legal acceptance of official documents in electronic format will be the hardest issue in the short term.

In this context, the American Bar Association has recently adopted a resolution encouraging the "development of legal standards . . . for information in electronic form" and "the use of . . . security techniques to assure the authenticity of information in electronic form." Moreover, the ABA supports action by federal and state governments to "recognize that information in electronic form . . . may be considered to satisfy legal requirements regarding a writing or signature to the same extent as information on paper or in other conventional forms." [1]

It should be noted that no mention of smart cards is made in the CAFE project. In fact, one of the issues under consideration is the physical shape, size, and capabilities of the electronic wallets defined in the project (provided a single model is adopted; CAFE may be even defined ultimately as a software concept to be implemented in different platforms). However, regardless of the external appearance of the final device, the smart card philosophy will be behind the scenes.

9.4 CONCLUSIONS: THE FUTURE

Smart cards have currently found niches in many areas, especially in nonfinancial applications. At present, however, smart cards have become popular in only a few countries;

little activity is found in some of the greatest economic powers, like the U.S. and Japan. Some events should come about allowing smart cards to mature as the best alternative to dozens of objects routinely carried by many people: coins, bank notes, checks, ID documents, access passes, transport tickets, medical prescriptions, credit cards, health records, keys, phone tokens, and so forth.

- The financial world should involve smart cards in services for regular clients (not only VIPs), as in France.
- The unit card price should drop to a fraction of the current price in order to reach multimillion consumer applications.
- At the same time, technology improvements must contribute to this decrease by improving card performance; multipurpose cards compete favorably with lower priced products because of their functionality.
- A socially acceptable, legally recognized, fast, versatile, and inexpensive biometric test for ID should be developed; this might be achieved by improving and/or combining some of the existing tests or by finding an entirely new one.

The financial world may move towards smart cards through hybrid cards featuring magnetic stripe and chip, as in the MAC network in the U.S. This would allow the use of current ATMs and EPOSs, while the chip would complement these devices by offering extra services or by authenticating off-line users through secure PINs or biometric tests.

The increasing fraud in financial magnetic stripe cards would indeed contribute to this decision. After the implementation of financial smart cards, France reported a 5% decrease in card fraud for the first time in 1991 (even though the number of transactions increased by 15%). In the same year, card fraud in the U.K. (magnetic stripe) increased by about 25%. Should these trends continue, the dropping of smart card prices would eventually lead to massive replacements of magnetic stripe cards by smart cards. Less developed countries, with no magnetic stripe tradition, are already leap-frogging directly to the new technology. Some developed European countries have also adopted financial smart cards. It does not seem too optimistic to predict the generalization of financial smart cards (with some remarkable exceptions) by the end of the century. Quite probably, there will be no sudden replacement of magnetic stripe cards, but rather a step-by-step adaptation of financial services to these media.

In the long term, the smart card market should evolve to multifunctionality. People would realize that the number of cards in their wallets or purses is steadily declining, as is the need to carry coins or bank notes. The acceptance of this should not be a problem, unless users consider the cards an intrusion of their privacy. For example, several financial applications may be merged into the same card, together with prepaid services (phone, transport). Sharing on the same card health data or personal documents, however, would hardly be acceptable. To implement such a personal card, a change in smart card image must be achieved. As mentioned previously, this change, in our opinion, would ultimately lead to the concept of a user's card, as opposed to an issuer's card. Issuers would become service providers, their influence on the card contents being restricted to specific areas dictated by the users.

The underlying idea is personal, not personalized, cards. One or several biometric tests (signature and any other nonbehavioral test) will reciprocally link the card and its owner. Service providers will offer personalized applications to be implemented in the user's personal card, at the user's will. Card issuers will take care of general management, replacement, and renewal of the user's personal cards.

What will be the final format of personal cards? At this time, not even the physical shape of the devices is definite yet. Let us assume a credit-card-sized system (Figure 9.6), bearing in mind that physical shape is not really relevant. To maintain compatibility with current systems, it should have a magnetic stripe for many years. It must feature an intelligent system controlling incoming and outgoing data and authenticating the card users and the external devices. If memory-consuming applications are desired, the storage capacity of current smart cards should be substantially increased. Alternatively, extra memory might be added as WORM optical memory, as in current optical cards, or as new erasable media such as magneto-optical materials. In either case, the stored information could be controlled by the microprocessor (e.g., through data encryption). Other features, like bar codes and pictures, may also be included.

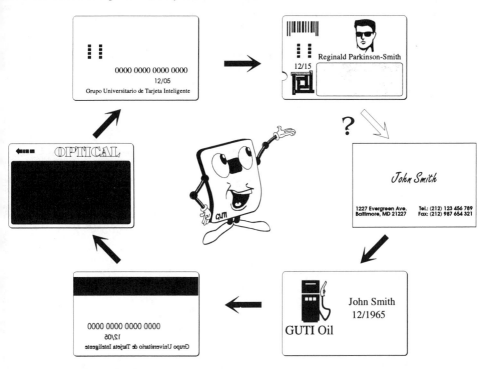

Figure 9.6 Peering into the future: from calling cards to personal smart cards.

New calling cards are coming. At the end of the book, we have come full circle, returning to the beginning. Dream or nightmare, the implementation of single personal smart cards is technologically feasible now, and should be economically attractive in a few years. On one not so distant day, somebody will arrive at someone else's office and, after shaking hands, he/she will show a plastic rectangle to the other person while saying "Here's my card." That day, smart cards will have found a permanent place in our society.

REFERENCES

[1] Baum, Michael S. "Trust . . . The Missing Piece of the Puzzle," *Proceedings of Cardtech/Securtech*, Arlington, VA, pp. 423–426, April 1993.

Appendix A
Title

A.1 ISO 7816/2 AND 7816/3

A.1.1 Smart Card Contacts

Table A.1 shows the position of the *centers* of smart card contacts as measured from the upper and left card edges. The minimum size of each contact is 2.0×1.7 mm. These values are derived from the ISO 7816/3 standard. C4 and C8 are RFU. Some smart card models from a number of manufacturers (e.g., Gemplus and McCorquodale) have only six contacts, since C4 and C8 are not installed. Nevertheless, these cards meet ISO standards.

Table A.1
Position of Chip Contact Centers (mm)

Contact	French Standard		ISO Standard	
	Left Edge	Upper Edge	Left Edge	Upper Edge
C1	11.25	17.54	11.25	20.08
C2	11.25	15.00	11.25	22.62
C3	11.25	12.46	11.25	25.16
C4	11.25	9.92	11.25	27.70
C5	18.87	17.54	18.87	20.08
C6	18.87	15.00	18.87	22.62
C7	18.87	12.46	18.87	25.16
C8	18.87	9.92	18.87	27.70

A.1.2 ATR Parameters

The cards' working parameters are encoded in their ATR bytes. ISO usually associate ATR bytes, nibbles, or bits with actual parameters through tables. However, parameter can also be obtained from ATR bytes through simple formulas. Names and uses of AT bytes are explained in Chapter 5.

Elementary Time Unit

etu is defined as the time elapsed for the transmission of one bit. Initial etu is used initiate communications. A different etu (work etu) may be solicited by the card or agree on (negotiated) between the card and the WRU by means of a PTS procedure.

- Cards with internal clock: initial etu = 1/9600 sec; work etu = $(1/D) \times (1/9,60C$ sec.
- Cards without internal clock: initial etu = $372/f$ sec; work etu = $(1/D) \times (F/f)$ se

where D is the bit rate adjustment factor (derived from TA_1 LSN); F is the clock ra conversion factor (derived from TA_1 MSN); and f is the clock frequency in hertz; th minimum f is always 1 MHz; the maximum frequency is also derived from TA_1 MSN.

Calculation of Parameters D, F, f, N, I, and P

For D *factor*, let y be the decimal value of TA_1 LSN. Then $y = 0, 6, 7, 8$ are RFU; D $2^{(y-1)}$ for $0 < y < 6$; and $D = 2^{-(y-1)}$ for $8 < y < 16$.

For F *factor*, let z be the decimal value of TA_1 MSN, and b_4, b_3, b_2, and b_1 th nibble bits. Then $z = 0$ means internal clock; $z = 7, 8, 14, 15$ are RFU; $F = 186(1 + z$ $b_3z - 3b_3)$ for $0 < z < 7$; and $F = 256(1 + z + b_3z - 3b_3)$ for $8 < z < 14$.

For f *frequency (maximum frequency)*, let z be the decimal value of TA_1 MSN, an b_4, b_3, b_2, and b_1 the nibble's bits. Then f is undefined for $z = 0, 7, 8, 14, 15$; $f = 5$ MH for $z = 1$; $f = 2(1 + z + b_3z - 3b_3)$ MHz for $1 < z < 7$; and $f = 2.5(1 + z + b_3z - 3b_3)$ MH for $8 < z < 14$.

N *(extra guard time)* is directly coded in byte TC_1, from 0 to 254 etu. If $N = 255$ then the extra guard time is −1. Guard time is always $12 + N$.

I *(maximum programming current)* is coded in bits b_7 and b_6 of TB_1. Values 0C 01, and 10 correspond to 25, 50, and 100 mA, respectively. Value 11 is RFU.

P *factor (programming voltage)*, N is coded in bits b_5 through b_1 of TB_1. The decim value of these bits, from 5 to 25, is the voltage in volts. $P = 0$ means that VPP shoul not be connected. If TB_2 is sent, then TB_1 voltage must be disregarded. TB_2 encodes th programming voltage, using the entire byte, in tenths of volts (5.0V to 25.0V).

.1.3 Protocol Type T = 1

Most current cards employ the $T = 0$ protocol, described in Chapter 5. $T = 1$, an asynchronous half-duplex block transmission protocol, will surely be the second fully standardized protocol for smart card communications. The eventual standard (an amendment of ISO 816/3, at present in draft form) may differ from the data and comments below. Some T 1 concepts are discussed below.

- A block is defined as the smallest data unit for communications between WRUs and smart cards using this protocol. Blocks are made of three (sometimes two) fields: prologue, information, and epilogue.
- Fields in turn are made of subfields. The prologue field contains three 1-byte subfields for node address, protocol control, and length. The information field may contain from 0 to 254 bytes. The epilogue field holds the error detection code (1 or 2 bytes).
- Blocks may carry either application information or control data. These include handling of transmission errors.
- Block integrity must be checked upon reception before processing its information.
- Block starts and block ends should be separately detected.
- The protocol may be initiated by ATR or PTS. The first block is always sent by the WRU. Once the protocol is started, the sender and receiver roles are alternated.
- As a consequence, if either the WRU or the card want to send more than 254 data bytes, a chaining procedure must be used. The information is divided into blocks, which are sent separately. After receiving each block, the receiver switches to sender, sends a ''receive-ready'' block (see below), and becomes a receiver again.

Block elements include prologue, information, and epilogue fields, which are discussed below.

- For the *prologue field*, the node address byte is split into nibbles. The MSN identifies the block destination and the LSN identifies the source. Both destination and source are encoded using the three LSBs of their nibbles. The MSB of each nibble is used for VPP control. The protocol control byte is used to define block types. There are information blocks for carrying information, supervisory blocks for data control, and receive-ready blocks for acknowledgment. Supervisory blocks may contain an information field. Receive-ready blocks do not. The length byte encodes the size of the information field (00 to FE hex). FF hex is RFU.
- The *information field* is optional, since it depends on the block type. When present, its contents also depend on the block type: information blocks carry application data, whereas supervisory blocks carry control data.
- The *epilogue field* is one or two bytes long and is used for error detection. One-byte epilogues hold an XOR of all the preceding block bytes (i.e., a check sum). Two-byte epilogues contain the block cyclic redundancy check (CRC, as defined

in ISO 3309). The use of check sums or CRCs is announced by the card using an ATR TC byte other than TC_1.

A.2 ISO 7816/4 AND RELATED EN STANDARDS

By the time of writing (September 1993), ISO 7816/4 had not been approved. The last vote for the draft to become a draft international standard (DIS), a previous step to becoming an official standard, was taken in May 1993. The DIS status was then rejected partially because of some inconsistencies in the document, which are mentioned below.

A.2.1 Status Bytes

Status bytes SW1 and SW2 are used in ISO 7816/3 to denote the processing state in the card. ISO 7816/4 suggests more standardized values, other than 90 00 hex, for obtaining information about the card status. All SW values below are given in hexadecimal format. As a rule, SW1 describes the issue, while SW2 gives more specific details. SW2 = 00 always means that no extra information can be given. SW1 = 90, 61, 62, or 63 are used for advising that the card process is completed. SW1 = 64 to 6F (except 66, which is RFU) indicate that the process has been aborted. In the first case, the process may have had normal termination (SW1 = 90 or 61), or a problem may have been found (SW1 = 62 or 63).

- SW1 = 90: The process is correctly completed.
- SW1 = 61: This byte is reserved for block transmission. The card is indicating that more data bytes are to be sent. The number of remaining bytes is then coded in SW2. The WRU must issue the corresponding command to get these bytes.
- SW1 = 62: Warning. Some problem has arisen. The state of nonvolatile memory is unchanged. Further information is included in SW2. SW2 = 00, 81 to 85. For instance, SW2 = 81 indicates that returned data may be corrupted.
- SW1 = 63: Warning. Some problem has arisen. The state of nonvolatile memory is changed. Further information is included in SW2. SW2 = 00, 01, 80 to 8F. For instance, SW2 = 01 indicates that the last write has filled up the file.

Current drafts of European standards include more suggestions for SW2 values. For example, when SW1 = 62, SW2 = C0 means that the selected file is irreversibly blocked. Other Cx values are for denoting "on-line transaction required," "too many off-line transactions," and "unsuccessful password" card blocking. Remaining password verifications are encoded in an SW2 nibble. Dx values are similarly used for external authentications.

The process is usually aborted (SW1 = 64 to 6F except 66) for two reasons: execution errors (64 and 65) and checking errors (67 to 6F). Execution errors are again separated, depending on whether the nonvolatile memory has been changed (SW1 = 65) or not (SW1

= 64). Very few SW2 values are suggested for execution errors. Moreover, only SW2 = ¶0 is indicated for several checking errors, such as 67 (incorrect command length), 6B (incorrect command parameters), 6D (wrong instruction code), 6E (instruction class not supported), and 6F (no precise diagnosis). The remaining checking errors employ several SW2 values. The same SW2 value may have different meanings, depending on SW1. For instance, SW2 = 81 may be interpreted as "logical channel not supported" (SW1 = 68, CLA not supported), "command incompatible with file organization" (SW1 = 69, command not allowed), or "function not supported" (SW1 = 6A, wrong P1/P2 parameters). The case SW1 = 6C (incorrect data length) is unique. In this error, SW2 is used for specifying the correct data length.

A.2.2 Historical Bytes and Data Elements

As in the previous case, historical bytes were used before ISO 7816/4 started, though they were restricted to supplementary ATR information, which was used ad libitum by the manufacturers. At present, 7816/4, 7816/5, and European norms related to inter-sector data elements (CEN TC224/PT02/N277) have suggested some structure of these bytes, thus allowing different cards to share the same application (or different applications to share the same card). This structure is given by using the historical bytes as data elements. Data elements are defined as information items for which a name, a description, and a format have been specified. They have a TLV format: a unique, file-independent, identification tag (ISO 8825), followed by the data element length and value. The notation is derived from ASN.1 objects of OSI. Encoding of these elements is described in ISO 8859/. Data elements are located by default in the historical bytes and/or the ATR file described within the ISO 7816/4 hierarchical file structure. Alternatively, the ATR file may contain the path of the elementary file where the data elements can be found.

Data Elements in Historical Bytes

When data elements are contained in the historical bytes, they are made up of three fields:

- *Category indicator* (1 byte, mandatory). When 00, three other bytes are included: card life status (CLS), SW1, and SW2. When 80, the status is given in a TLV object, whose tag is 8.
- *TLV objects* (optional) following ASN.1 encoding rules, with tag = 4X and length = 0Y. This is replaced by XY, the object being completed with Y data bytes. Several TLV groups are declared, such as country/isser indicator, selection data, card issuer data, preissuing data, and card capabilities.
  - *Country indicators* (XY = 1Y) are coded with three digits following ISO 3166. *Issuer indicators* may announce the issuer ID number as defined in ISO 7812 (then XY = 2Y).

- *Selection data* (XY = 31) contain information concerning the existence of an ATR file (default file ID 2F 00) and/or a DIR file (default file ID 2F 01).
- *Card issuer data* (tag = 5X) are not described in ISO, but in ENs. The tag size is either 1 byte (50 - 5E) or 2 bytes (5F xx). Some data are declared as mandatory and some others as optional. For instance, the IC serial number (TLV = 56 04 xx yy zz ww) is declared mandatory and read-only. Another important object is the expiry date (TLV = 5F 21 04 xx yy zz ww), in which the date is expressed as YY MM. When the card has no expiry date, the four data bytes are set to 00. (Note: apparently, the tags of this and the remaining optional TLV objects below do not follow the XY rule described above. This issue is not explained in the current ISO draft.)
- *Preissuing data* (tag = 6X) are used for indicating card and IC manufacturers, IC type, mask version, and so on. Some elements overlap the previous 5X objects. For example, the IC manufacturer is also identified by tag 54.
- *Card capabilities* (tag = 71, 72 or 73) include information on file handling, such as DF selection method (name, file identifier, path, etc.), and EF handling (relative addressing, record ID, record number).
- *Status information.* As mentioned above, if the category indicator is 00, 3 bytes are included: CLS, SW1, and SW2. CLS = 00 indicates that no CLS is provided. SW1, SW2 = 00 00 is used when no status is indicated. SW1, SW2 = 90 00 indicates an error-free normal status.

ATR File Data Elements

The card may include an ATR file (default ID 2F 01). The structure and contents of this file are the same as the historical ATR bytes. Data elements are combined with tags and lengths making ASN.1 objects. Table A.2 shows optional TLV examples of data elements.

Table A.2
Examples of Data Elements in ATR Files

Bytes	Length (Bytes)	Description
1	1	Tag = 59 for IC card identification number
2	1	L = XX = N, length of IC card identification number
3 to $N + 2$	N	V = IC card identification number
$N + 3$	1	Tag = 56 for IC serial number
$N + 4$	1	L = 04 = 4 bytes for card numbering
$N + 5$ to $N + 8$	4	V = XX XX XX XX, card number
$N + 9$ to $N + 10$	2	Tag = 5F 21, application expiry date
$N + 11$	1	L = 04 = length of application expiry date
$N + 12$ to $N + 15$	4	V = XX XX XX XX 4 digits in the format YY MM

Non-ATR File Data Elements

Data elements may also be found in an EF other than the ATR file. In this case, the ATR file must contain an ASN.1 object where the coding and location of that EF is included i.e., the object format is tag + coding indicator + path). EF-contained data elements may or may not be coded as ASN.1 objects.

The use of ASN.1 objects outside the ATR file must be denoted in the data element location indicator described above. Table A.3 shows an example of the ATR file contents where the presence of an EF containing data elements is indicated. The contents of this EF would be the same as shown in Table A.2.

If data elements are not coded as ASN.1 objects, the order of data elements within the EF is announced in the ATR file location indicator. Variable-length data elements in the EF are preceded by a single byte denoting their length, while fixed-length data elements are not. For instance, the contents of the ATR file could be as shown in Table A.3 (except the coding indicator, which is 01 in this case). The EF contents are shown in Table A.4. Note that the contents are the same as in the previous cases, except that tags and lengths are not used. The IC card identification number does include its length, since it is variable.

A.2.3 Basic Interindustry Commands

As was seen in Chapters 5 and 6, card commands are made of several encoded elements e.g., CLA, INS, P1, P2). ISO 7816/4 enhances the use of these elements, especially CLA,

Table A.3
Contents of an ATR File Denoting an EF With ASN.1 Objects

Bytes	Length (Bytes)	Description
1, 2	2	Tag = 5F 2E for data element location indicator
3	1	L = 07 = N, length of data element location indicator
4 to 10	7	V = 59 tag for IC card identification number
		56 tag for IC serial number
		5F 21 tag for application expiry date
		00 coding indicator (ASN.1)
		XY ZW path from MF (file identifier)

Table A.4
Data Elements in a non-ASN.1 Elementary File

Bytes	Length (Bytes)	Description
1	1	L = XX = N, length of IC card identification number
2 to N + 1	N	V = IC card identification number
N + 2 to N + 5	4	V = XX XX XX XX, card serial number
N + 6 to N + 9	4	V = XX XX XX XX, application expiry date (YY MM)

Table A.5
INS Codes Defined in ISO 7816/4

Name	INS	P1-P2	LCf	Data Field	LEf	Response (Data Field (Status Not Shown))
		Command				
Read binary	B0	Offset of the first byte to read in data units from the beginning of the file	Empty	Empty	Number of bytes to read	Data read (LEf bytes)
Write binary	D0	Offset of the first byte to write in data units from the beginning of the file	Number of bytes to be written	String of bytes to be written	Empty	Empty
Erase binary	0E	Offset of the first byte to erase; 00 00 indicates the beginning of the file	Empty or 02	Empty, erase up to the end of the file; present (>P1-P2) offset of first byte not to erase	Empty	Empty*
Read record	B2	Record identifier or number of the first record to read 00 means current record	Empty	Empty	Number of bytes to read	Partial read of one record or record sequence; complete read of one record; read of multiple records up to the file end
Write record	D2	Indicating either append to or update the record (records are TLV objects in the data field of the message)	Length of the subsequent data field	Parameters and data to be written (tag, record identifier, length, whole data bytes of the record)	Empty	Empty
Select file	A4	P1: selection control (file identifier, file name, path) P2: selection options (file control information format, first or only occurrence)	Empty or length of data field	If present according to P1-P2: file identifier, path from MF, from current DF, file name	Maximum length of data expected in response	Information according to P2 (at most LEf bytes)

Table A.5 (*cont.*)
INS Codes Defined in ISO 7816/4

Name	INS	Command				Response (Data Field (Status Not Shown))
		P1-P2	LCf	Data Field	LEf	
Verify	20	P1 = 00 P2 file selection mode (implicit selection, current file, parent file, master file)	Number of bytes of the verification data	Verification data	Empty	Empty[†]
Internal authenticate	88	P1: reference of the algorithm in the card P2: reference of the secret key as seen from the current file (MF or DF)	Number of bytes of the data field	Authentication-related data (e.g., challenge)	Maximum number of bytes expected in response	Authentication-related data (e.g., response to the challenge)
External authenticate	82	P1: reference of the algorithm in the card P2: reference of the secret key as seen from the current file (MF or DF)	Number of bytes of the data field	Authentication-related data (e.g., response to the challenge)	Empty	Empty[†]
Get response	C0	P1: sequence number P2 = 00	Empty	Empty	Maximum length of data expected in response	Information according to LEf[‡]
Envelope	C2	P1: sequence number, last Envelope command, more Envelope to follow	Number of data bytes	Data sent to the card	Empty	Empty

[*]When SW1 = 63, the erase is successful, but after using an internal retry ₃outine.
[†]SW1= 63: verification is unsuccessful. SW2 may indicate the number of retries.
[‡]SW1 = 61: more data bytes are available; the number of bytes is coded in SW2. A new Get Response command using SW2 information must be issued.

which is not usually used by current 7816/3 cards. Moreover, standardization of INS values performing specific tasks is initiated. CLA contains information in both nibbles. The MSN of the CLA byte indicates whether the command follows the structure and coding specified in this part of the 7816 standard; the LSN role, moreover, is conditioned by the MSN value. CLA = 8X, 9X are used by cards whose instruction sets are defined by the manufacturer, whereas CLA = AX to EX are reserved for cards whose instruction sets follow 7816/4. When CLA = AX, the LSN contains information concerning secure messaging. b_4 and b_3 denote the secure messaging format (e.g., included in a TLV object). b_2 and b_1 are used for indicating logical channel numbers. (A logical channel is a logical link between the interface device and a file, either MF, DF, or EF.) Eleven INS codes are defined (6X and 9X codes are not used for historical reasons). The codes are shown in Table A.5. As can be seen in the Table, the basic card functions have been declared. The possibility of sending more than 256 bytes using the T = 0 protocol is also given.

Appendix B

Listings of Software Modules Shown in Chapter 6

Listing 6.1
ser_port.h, Header File of Serial Port Communication Functions

```
/*-------------------------------------------------------------------------*
 *   File:          ser_port.h                                             *
 *   Description:   constant and function declarations for managing serial ports of PC *
 *                  compatible computers.                                  *
 *-------------------------------------------------------------------------*/

#ifndef SER_PORT
#define SER_PORT

/* Port numbers */
#define COM1            0
#define COM2            1

/* Hex values of format data parameters */
#define DATA_BITS_5     0x00
#define DATA_BITS_6     0x01
#define DATA_BITS_7     0x02
#define DATA_BITS_8     0x03
#define STOP_BITS_1     0x00
#define STOP_BITS_2     0x04
#define NO_PARITY       0x00
#define ODD_PARITY      0x08
#define EVEN_PARITY     0x18
#define NO_INTERRUP     0x00

/* USART registers offset */
#define RX_REG          0               /* Reception register */
#define TX_REG          0               /* Transmission buffer register */
#define DIV_LSBY        0               /* Least Significant Byte of the divisor latch */
#define DIV_MSBY        1               /* Most Significant Byte of the divisor latch */
#define INT_MASK        1               /* Interruption mask */
#define INT_PEND        2               /* Interruptions pending */
#define DAT_FORM        3               /* Data format */
#define MOD_CTRL        4               /* Modem control */
#define ERR_STAT        5               /* Errors/status */
#define MOD_STAT        6               /* Modem status */

/* Masks for UART 8250 registers */
#define READYTRX        0x20            /* UART 8250 ready to transmit */
#define ERR_MASK        0x1E            /* Generic error in UART 8250 */
#define DATA_READY      0x01            /* Data ready for reading */

/* Masks for line control register of the serial port */
#define DATA_BITS_MASK  0x03
#define STOP_BITS_MASK  0x04
#define PARITY_MASK     0x18
```

```
/* Maximum baud rate employed by the 8250 */
#define MAX_BAUD        115200L                              /* = clock frecuency/16 */

/* Masks for status interpretation */
#define TIME_OUT        0x80
#define DATA_READY      0x01

/* Maximum waiting time for a character (secs.) */
#define MAX_TIME        10

/* Base direction of serial ports */
#define COM1_BASE       0x3F8
#define COM2_BASE       0x2F8

/* Macro to compute base direction of port "port_no" */
#define base_dir(port_no)    (port_no==COM1?COM1_BASE:COM2_BASE)

/* Type definition */
typedef enum {ERROR_TX, OK_TX} t_err_tx;

/* Function prototypes */
t_err_tx SetSerPort (                                        /* Sets port parameters */
                    unsigned port_no,                        /* port number */
                    unsigned char data_bits,
                    unsigned char stop_bits,
                    unsigned char parity,
                    unsigned baud_no,                        /* baud rate */
                    unsigned char interrupt_mask);

unsigned char ReadStatus (int port_no);                      /* Reads port status */

t_err_tx SendByte (unsigned port_no, char c);        /* Sends byte "c" through port "port_no" */

t_err_tx ReceiveByte (int port_no, char *c);        /* Receives byte "c" through port "port_no" */

t_err_tx SendString (int port_no, char *s, int no_bytes);/* Sends string "s" through port "port_no" */

#endif
```

Listing 6.2
wru_guti.h, Header File of Managing Functions for the WRU

```
/*----------------------------------------------------------------------------------------*
 * File:          wru_guti.h                                                               *
 * Description:   routines for building WRU messages.                                      *
 *----------------------------------------------------------------------------------------*/

#ifndef WRU
#define WRU

#include "ser_port.h"

/* Constant definitions */
#define MAX_BUFFER          600                          /* Maximum number of bytes */
#define STX                 '\2'                          /* Start of text character */
#define ETX                 '\3'                            /* End of text character */
#define MAX_LOOPS           50              /* Max # of chars before starting message */
#define WRU_ANS_LEN         1                              /* Length of wru answer */
#define PON_HEAD            "ON"                           /* "Power on card" header */
#define POFF_HEAD           "OF"                          /* "Power off card" header */
#define IN_HEAD             "IN"                        /* "Input instruction" header */
#define OUT_HEAD            "OU"                       /* "Output instruction" header */

#define MENS_HEADTAIL_LEN   4                 /* Header and trailer lengths of any message */
#define WRU_MENS_LEN        2          /* Header and trailer lengths of messages to wru */
#define SC_HEAD_LEN         2                         /* Header of messages to sc */
#define NO_CARD_BYTE        '0'                     /* WRU byte meaning "no card inserted" */
#define UN_CARD_BYTE        '1'                /* WRU byte meaning "unknown card inserted" */
#define AS_CARD_BYTE        '2'      /* WRU byte meaning "unknown asynchronous card inserted" */
#define SY_CARD_BYTE        '3'          /* WRU byte meaning "synchronous card inserted" */
#define GC1_CARD_BYTE       '4'     /* WRU byte meaning "asynchronous GC1 card inserted" */
#define GC2_CARD_BYTE       '5'     /* WRU byte meaning "asynchronous GC2 card inserted" */
```

```
define GCJ_CARD_BYTE        '6'                /* WRU byte meaning "asynchronous GC Jet card inserted" */
define GC_ERROR_BYTE        'A'                    /* WRU byte meaning "something is wrong" */

* Type definitions */
ypedef enum {                                                      /* Instruction type */
                INPUT,                                           /* Sending data to card */
                OUTPUT                                     /* Receiving data from the card */
                } t_instr;

ypedef enum {                                              /* Card types recognized by WRU */
                NO_CARD,                                         /* No sc inserted */
                SY_CARD,                                         /* Synchronous sc */
                UNKN_CARD,                                          /* Unknown sc */
                ASY_CARD,                                    /* Asynchronous sc */
                GC1_CARD,                                              /* GC1 sc */
                GC2_CARD,                                              /* GC2 sc */
                GCJ_CARD                                               /* GCJ sc */
                } t_sc;

* Function prototypes */
_err_tx MesToWru ( char *message,                                  /* Message to send */
                unsigned char no_bytes);                     /* Number of bytes to send */

_err_tx MesToSc ( unsigned char no_bytes,                    /* Number of bytes to send */
                t_instr instruction,          /* Type of instruction: incoming or outgoing */
                char *message);                                    /* Message to send */

_err_tx MesFromWru (char *message,                                 /* Message received */
                unsigned char *bytes_no);

_err_tx MesFromSc ( char *wru_st,                                   /* Reader Status */
                char *card_ans);                                    /* Card Answer */

_err_tx CardType ( char *wru_answer,                              /* String to analyze */
                t_sc *sc);                                      /* Pointer to result */

_err_tx WruType ( char *wru_answer,                              /* String to analyze */
                t_sc *sc);                                      /* Pointer to result */

_err_tx WruAnswer ( char *wru_answer,                            /* String to analyze */
                t_sc *sc);                                      /* Pointer to result */

_err_tx TxRxMessage (int no_bytes,                      /* Number of bytes to transmit */
                t_instr instruction,                            /* Instruction type */
                char *message,                                    /* Message to send */
                t_sc *sc,                                              /* Sc type */
                char *card_ans);                                    /* Card answer */

_err_tx PowerOnCard (t_sc *sc,                                         /* Sc type */
                char *ans_to_reset);                       /* Card answer to reset */

_err_tx PowerOffCard (t_sc *sc);                                       /* Sc type */

#endif
```

Listing 6.3
wru_guti.c, Functions for Managing the WRU

```
/*------------------------------------------------------------------------------*
 * File:        wru_guti.c (Writing/Reading Unit)                               *
 * Description: Routines for building WRU messages.                             *
 *              These functions are wru-dependent, call to level 0 communication routines, *
 *              and are called for PC/WRU communications and PC/SC communications through WRU. *
 *------------------------------------------------------------------------------*/

#include    <string.h>
#include    <stdio.h>

#include    "wru_guti.h"

int port =  COM1;                                     /* Global variable: Active port number */

/*------------------------------------------------------------------------*
 * TRANSMISSION FUNCTIONS:                                                 *
 * MesToWru: Function for sending messages from PC to WRU.                 *
```

```
*       This function prepares message's header and trailer, computes      *
*       message checksum and calls to ser_port SendString.                 *
*       This function is also called by next function.                     *
*  MesToSc: Function for sending messages to the smart card.               *
*       This function prepares a message header depending on the instruction *
*------------------------------------------------------------------------*/
t_err_tx MesToWru (char *message, unsigned char no_bytes)
{
char buffer[MAX_BUFFER];                                    /* String sent to the reader */
char *string = buffer;                                      /* Pointer to buffer */
unsigned char chk = 0x00;                    /* Exclusive OR on all characters of the message body */

*string++ = STX;                                                    /* Message header */
*string++ = no_bytes;

while (no_bytes--) {          /* Computing the checksum and preparing the message at the same time */
    *string++ = *message;
    chk ^= *message++;}
*string++ = ETX;                                            /* Message trailer */
*string = chk;                                              /* Message checksum */
return (SendString (port, buffer, no_bytes+MENS_HEADTAIL_LEN));   /* Sending message */
}


t_err_tx MesToSc (unsigned char no_bytes, t_instr instruction, char *message)
{
char buffer[MAX_BUFFER];

if (instruction == INPUT) strcpy (buffer, IN_HEAD);   /* Message header depends on instruction case */
else strcpy (buffer, OUT_HEAD);

strncat (buffer, message, no_bytes);
return (MesToWru(buffer, no_bytes+SC_HEAD_LEN));                    /* Sending message */
}

/*------------------------------------------------------------------------*
 * RECEPTION FUNCTIONS:                                                    *
 *  MesFromWru: receives a string from WRU.                                *
 *      This function waits for STX character detection and keeps          *
 *      receiving characters until ETX is received.                        *
 *  MesFromSc: receives a string from sc.                                  *
 *      This function calls to MesFromWru and divides the message into two *
 *      parts: WRU answer and card answer. The function uses "AsciiToHex"  *
 *      to transform the card answer into hexadecimal. "AsciiToHex" uses   *
 *      "HexVal", an internal function.                                    *
 *------------------------------------------------------------------------*/

t_err_tx MesFromWru (char *message, unsigned char *bytes_no)
{
int i = 0;
char c;
t_err_tx status;
unsigned char chk = 0x00;                                   /* Message checksum */

while ((status = ReceiveByte (port, &c)) && c != STX && i++ < MAX_LOOPS);
if (i >= MAX_LOOPS || !status)                              /* Waiting for STX character */
    return ERROR_TX;
if (!ReceiveByte (port, bytes_no))                          /* Receiving number of characters */
    return ERROR_TX;
i = 0;
do {                           /* Receiving characters and computing checksum until ETX is found */
    status = ReceiveByte (port, message);
    if (*message != ETX) chk ^= *message;}
while (status && *message++ != ETX && i++ <= *bytes_no);
if (!status || i != *bytes_no + 1) return ERROR_TX;
if (ReceiveByte (port, message) != OK_TX)                   /* Receiving checksum */
    return ERROR_TX;
if (*message != chk)                                        /* Checking checksum */
    return ERROR_TX;
return OK_TX;
}

t_err_tx MesFromSc (char *wru_st, char *card_ans)
{
char buffer[MAX_BUFFER];
unsigned char bytes_no;

if (!MesFromWru (buffer, &bytes_no)) return ERROR_TX;       /* Receiving message */
strncpy (wru_st, buffer, WRU_ANS_LEN);                      /* Getting wru status */
```

```
trncpy (card_ans, buffer+WRU_ANS_LEN, bytes_no);              /* Getting sc answer */
eturn OK_TX;


/*-----------------------------------------------------------------*
 * READER ANSWER ANALYSIS FUNCTION:                                *
 *     CardType: identifies type of card from WRU answers.         *
 *               WRUs, besides card answers if any, return strings in which *
 *               card type is coded.                               *
 *-----------------------------------------------------------------*/

t_err_tx CardType (char *wru_answer, t_sc *sc)

switch (wru_answer[0])
    {
    case NO_CARD_BYTE: *sc = NO_CARD; break;                       /* No sc inserted */
    case AS_CARD_BYTE: *sc = ASY_CARD; break;        /* Asynchronous sc but unknown model */
    case UN_CARD_BYTE: *sc = UNKN_CARD; break;                /* Unknown sc inserted */
    case GC1_CARD_BYTE: *sc = GC1_CARD; break;                   /* GC1 sc inserted */
    case GC2_CARD_BYTE: *sc = GC2_CARD; break;                   /* GC2 sc inserted */
    case GCJ_CARD_BYTE: *sc = GCJ_CARD; break;                   /* GCJ sc inserted */
    case SY_CARD_BYTE: *sc = SY_CARD; break;           /* Synchronous sc inserted */
    default : return ERROR_TX;
    }
return OK_TX;
}

/*-----------------------------------------------------------------*
 * TRANSMISSION AND RECEPTION FUNCTION:                            *
 * TxRxMessage: sends a message to a card and gets its reponse through WRU  *
 *-----------------------------------------------------------------*/

t_err_tx TxRxMessage (int no_bytes, t_instr instruction, char *message,
                      t_sc *sc, char *card_ans)

char read_st[MAX_BUFFER];                                    /* Internal variable */

if (!MesToSc (no_bytes, instruction, message))                /* Sending message */
    return ERROR_TX;
if (!MesFromSc (read_st, card_ans))                          /* Receiving answer */
    return ERROR_TX;
return (CardType (read_st, sc));                   /* Analysis of the device answer */
}

/*-----------------------------------------------------------------*
 * FUNCTIONS FOR WRU CONTROL                                       *
 *    PowerOnCard: WRU waits for a card to be inserted, powers up, and *
 *         resets the card. The card answers using its ATR (Answer To Reset). *
 *    PowerOffCard: WRU waits for card removal. After card removal, WRU sends *
 *         its general status to computer.                         *
 *-----------------------------------------------------------------*/

t_err_tx PowerOnCard (t_sc *sc, char *ans_to_reset)

char read_st[MAX_BUFFER];                                    /* Internal variable */

if (!MesToWru(PON_HEAD, WRU_MENS_LEN))                         /* Sending message */
    return ERROR_TX;
if (!MesFromSc (read_st, ans_to_reset))                      /* Receiving answer */
    return ERROR_TX;
return (CardType (read_st, sc));                   /* Analysis of the device answer */
}

t_err_tx PowerOffCard (t_sc *sc)

char read_st[MAX_BUFFER];
unsigned char aux;

if (!MesToWru(POFF_HEAD, WRU_MENS_LEN))                        /* Sending message */
    return ERROR_TX;
if (!MesFromWru (read_st, &aux))                             /* Receiving answer */
    return ERROR_TX;
return (CardType (read_st, sc));                      /* Analysis of WRU answer */
}
```

Listing 6.4

sc_tools.h, Header File Containing Card Constants and Function Prototypes of Auxiliary Functions

```
/*------------------------------------------------------------------------*
 * File:        sc_tools.h                                                 *
 * Description: Card tools definitions.                                    *
 *------------------------------------------------------------------------*/

#ifndef SC_TOOLS
#define SC_TOOLS

#include "wru_guti.h"

/* Message format */
#define CLA        0                            /* Instruction class */
#define INS        1                            /* Instruction code */
#define P1         2                        /* Instruction parameter 1 */
#define P2         3                        /* Instruction parameter 2 */
#define P3         4                           /* Length of data field */
#define DATA       5                /* String of data bytes sent in command */

/* Constants */
#define NULL_BYTE   0

/* Error constants */
#define OK_CONSTANT      '\x90'                /* SW1 value for correct command */
#define ERROR_CONSTANT   '\x62'     /* SW1 start value for codification of many errors */
#define ERROR_OFFSET     '\x80'     /* SW2 start value for codification of many errors */

/* t_error_card type definition */
typedef enum {  OK_CARD,                            /* Message transmission was ok */
                E_TX_RX_CARD,                            /* Transmission error */
                E_NO_CARD,                          /* No card inserted in reader */
                E_UNKN_CARD,                           /* Unknown card inserted */
                E_DATA_CORRUPTED_CARD,            /* Returned data may be corrupted */
                E_END_OF_FILE_CARD,        /* End of file reached before end of reading */
                E_FILE_INVALIDATED_CARD,            /* Selected file is not valid */
                E_MEMORY_FAILURE_CARD,                      /* Memory failure */
                E_WRONG_LENGTH_CARD,                   /* Command length error */
                E_FUNCTION_NOT_SUPPORTED_CARD,          /* Function not supported */
                E_COMMAND_NOT_ALLOWED_CARD,           /* Command not recognized */
                E_WRONG_P1_P2_CARD,                      /* P1 and/or P2 wrong */
                E_INCORRECT_PARAMETERS_CARD,   /* Incorrect parameters in the data field */
                E_FILE_NOT_FOUND_CARD,                     /* File not found */
                E_RECORD_NOT_FOUND_CARD,                 /* Record not found */
                E_FILE_FULL_CARD,          /* Not enough memory space in record or file */
                E_P3_INCONSISTENT_CARD,        /* P3 is inconsistent with P1-P2 values */
                E_DATA_NOT_FOUND_CARD,                /* Referenced data not found */
                E_WRONG_P3_CARD,                         /* Wrong length P3 */
                E_WRONG_INS_CARD,                            /* Wrong INS */
                E_CLASS_NOT_SUPPORTED_CARD,           /* Class is not supported */
                E_NO_DIAGNOSIS_CARD              /* No precise diagnosis is given */
             } t_error_card;

/* Function prototypes */
void FillMessage (   char *message,                    /* Pointer to message array */
                     char data_CLA,                  /* Instruction class data */
                     char data_INS,                   /* Instruction code data */
                     char data_P1,                              /* P1 data */
                     char data_P2,                              /* P2 data */
                     char data_P3);                             /* P3 data */

t_error_card CardErrorAnalysis ( t_err_tx error,            /* ERROR_TX/OK_TX */
                                 t_sc sc,                    /* WRU status */
                                 char *card_ans);            /* Card answer */

#endif
```

Listing 6.5

sc_tools.c, Auxiliary Functions for Card Management

```c
/*----------------------------------------------------------------------------*
 * File:          sctools.c                                                   *
 * Description:   High level routines for internal use                        *
 *----------------------------------------------------------------------------*/

#include <stdio.h>

#include "sc_tools.h"

/*--------------------------------------------------------------------*
 * FillMessage: fills in the message fields CLA, INS, P1, P2, and P3. *
 * CardErrorAnalysis: analyzes the error given by the reader and returns *
 *                    the corresponding card error.                   *
 *--------------------------------------------------------------------*/
void FillMessage (    char *message, char data_CLA, char data_INS, char data_P1,
                      char data_P2, char data_P3)
{
message[CLA] = data_CLA;
message[INS] = data_INS;
message[P1]  = data_P1;
message[P2]  = data_P2;
message[P3]  = data_P3;
}


t_error_card CardErrorAnalysis (t_err_tx error, t_sc sc, char *card_ans)
{
if (error == OK_TX){
     if (sc == GC2_CARD){
          if ((*card_ans == OK_CONSTANT) && (*(card_ans+1) == NULL_BYTE))
                 return OK_CARD;
          else if (*card_ans == ERROR_CONSTANT){
               switch (*(card_ans+1)){
                    case ERROR_OFFSET+1: return E_DATA_CORRUPTED_CARD;
                    case ERROR_OFFSET+2: return E_END_OF_FILE_CARD;
                    case ERROR_OFFSET+4: return E_FILE_INVALIDATED_CARD;
                    default: return E_TX_RX_CARD;
                    }
               }
          else if ((*card_ans == ERROR_CONSTANT+3) && (*(card_ans+1) == NULL_BYTE+1))
                 return E_MEMORY_FAILURE_CARD;
          else if ((*card_ans == ERROR_CONSTANT+5) && (*(card_ans+1) == NULL_BYTE))
                 return E_WRONG_LENGTH_CARD;
          else if ((*card_ans == ERROR_CONSTANT+6) && (*(card_ans+1) == NULL_BYTE))
                 return E_FUNCTION_NOT_SUPPORTED_CARD;
          else if ((*card_ans == ERROR_CONSTANT+7) && (*(card_ans+1) == NULL_BYTE))
                 return E_COMMAND_NOT_ALLOWED_CARD;
          else if (*card_ans == ERROR_CONSTANT+8){
               switch (*(card_ans+1)){
                    case NULL_BYTE:      return E_WRONG_P1_P2_CARD;
                    case ERROR_OFFSET:   return E_INCORRECT_PARAMETERS_CARD;
                    case ERROR_OFFSET+2: return E_FILE_NOT_FOUND_CARD;
                    case ERROR_OFFSET+3: return E_RECORD_NOT_FOUND_CARD;
                    case ERROR_OFFSET+4: return E_FILE_FULL_CARD;
                    case ERROR_OFFSET+7: return E_P3_INCONSISTENT_CARD;
                    case ERROR_OFFSET+8: return E_DATA_NOT_FOUND_CARD;
                    default: return E_TX_RX_CARD;
                    }
               }
          else if (*card_ans == ERROR_CONSTANT+10) return E_WRONG_P3_CARD;
          else if (*card_ans == ERROR_CONSTANT+11) return E_WRONG_INS_CARD;
          else if (*card_ans == ERROR_CONSTANT+12) return E_CLASS_NOT_SUPPORTED_CARD;
          else if (*card_ans == ERROR_CONSTANT+13) return E_NO_DIAGNOSIS_CARD;
          else return E_TX_RX_CARD;
          }
     else return E_UNKN_CARD;
     }
else return E_TX_RX_CARD;
}
```

Listing 6.6

card_cmd.h, Header File of Card Functions

```
/*----------------------------------------------------------------------------*
 * File:           card_cmd.h                                                  *
 * Description:    Low level routines for GUTI cards                           *
 *----------------------------------------------------------------------------*/

#ifndef CARD_CMD
#define CARD_CMD

#include "sc_tools.h"

#define GUTI_CLA              0x0A                      /* CLA for the GUTI card */

#define MAX_REC_SIZE          500                        /* Maximum buffer size */
#define SW1                   1                         /* 1 byte reserved for SW1 */
#define SW2                   1                         /* 1 byte reserved for SW2 */

                                                    /* Electronic purse constants */
#define DATA_LEN              3                /* 3 bytes for transaction amount */
#define DATE_LEN              3                  /* 3 bytes for transaction date */
#define NUMBER_LEN            2                /* 2 bytes for transaction number */

#define MASTER_KEY_NO         0                          /* Secret Key constants */
#define PIN_NO                1

#define SK_LEN                8                           /* Secret Key length */

#define ENCRYPT_DATA_LEN      8                         /* Enciphering constants */

#define SERIAL_NO_LEN         8                  /* Special functions' constants */
#define REPORT_DATA_LEN       2

#define MAKE_FILE_LEN         10                    /* Maximum message lengths */
#define SELECT_FILE_LEN       5                             /* File commands */
#define WRITE_RECORD_LEN      245                             /* 240 + L */
#define READ_RECORD_LEN       5
#define MAKE_PURSE_LEN        15                   /* Electronic purse commands */
#define PURSE_COMM_LEN        8
#define PURSE_INFO_LEN        5
#define SK_COMM_LEN           13                        /* Keys / PIN commands */
#define REACT_KEYS_LEN        5
#define ENCRYPT_LEN           5                        /* Enciphering commands */
#define CHALLENGE_ANS_LEN     13
#define SPECIAL_LEN           5                         /* Special functions */

/*----------------------------------------------------------------------*
 * Function prototypes: FILE AND RECORD COMMANDS                         *
 *----------------------------------------------------------------------*/
t_error_card MakeFile ( char file_name,              /* Name of file to create */
                        char no_records,         /* Number of records in file */
                        char no_bytes,         /* Number of bytes in each record */
                        char access_rules_AB,    /* File Read/Write access rules */
                        char access_rules_CD,    /* File Read/Write access rules */
                        char codes_AB,            /* First pair of secret keys */
                        char codes_CD);          /* Second pair of secret keys */

t_error_card MakeWORM ( char file_name,              /* Name of file to create */
                        char no_records,         /* Number of records in file */
                        char no_bytes,         /* Number of bytes in each record */
                        char access_rules_AB,    /* File Read/Write access rules */
                        char access_rules_CD,    /* File Read/Write access rules */
                        char codes_AB,            /* First pair of secret keys */
                        char codes_CD);          /* Second pair of secret keys */

t_error_card SelectFile (char file_name);            /* Name of file to select */

t_error_card WriteRecord (char no_record,             /* Record number in file */
                          char no_bytes,            /* Number of bytes to write */
                          char *data);                        /* Data to write */

t_error_card WriteWORM ( char no_record,              /* Record number in file */
                         char no_bytes,             /* Number of bytes to write */
                         char *data);                         /* Data to write */

t_error_card ReadRecord (char no_record,             /* Number of record in file */
```

```
                    char no_bytes,                          /* Number of bytes in record */
                    char *data_read);                       /* Data read from file */

*-------------------------------------------------------------------*
* Function prototypes: ELECTRONIC PURSE COMMANDS                    *
*------------------------------------------------------------------*/
_error_card MakePurse ( char file_name,                     /* Name of file to create */
                    char *transaction_date,                 /* Transaction date */
                    char *credit_limit,                     /* Credit limit */
                    char access_rules_AB,          /* File Read/Write access rules */
                    char access_rules_CD,          /* File Read/Write access rules */
                    char codes_AB,                     /* First pair of secret keys */
                    char codes_CD);                    /* Second pair of secret keys */

_error_card Loan      ( char *amount_loaned);               /* Credited amount */

_error_card Payment   ( char *amount_paid);                 /* Debited amount */

_error_card PurseInfo ( char *remaining_balance,            /* Remaining balance */
                    char *transaction_number,               /* Transaction number */
                    char *transaction_date);                /* Transaction date */

*-------------------------------------------------------------------*
* Function prototypes: KEYS / PIN MANAGEMENT COMMANDS               *
*------------------------------------------------------------------*/
_error_card SetMasterKey (char max_no_present,    /* Maximum number of incorrect presentations */
                    char *MK);                              /* Master Key */

_error_card VerifyMasterKey (char *MK);                     /* Master Key */

_error_card ModifyMasterKey (char *MK);                     /* Master Key */

_error_card SetPIN    ( char max_no_present,      /* Maximum number of incorrect presentations */
                    char *PIN);                             /* PIN */

_error_card VerifyPIN ( char *PIN);                         /* PIN */

_error_card ModifyPIN ( char *PIN);                         /* PIN */

_error_card SetSK     ( char max_no_present,      /* Maximum number of incorrect presentations */
                    char no_SK,                             /* Secret key number */
                    char *SK);                              /* Secret key */

_error_card VerifySK  ( char no_SK,                         /* Secret key number */
                    char *SK);                              /* Secret key */

_error_card ModifySK  ( char no_SK,                         /* Secret key number */
                    char *SK);                              /* Secret key */

_error_card ReactKeys ( void);                    /* Reactivates SKs. MK required */

/*-------------------------------------------------------------------*
* Function prototypes: ENCIPHERING FUNCTIONS                        *
*------------------------------------------------------------------*/
_error_card Encrypt   ( char destination,         /* Data stored in RAM (0) or in EEPROM (!=0) */
                    char source);                 /* Data read from RAM (0) or from EEPROM (!=0) */

_error_card Decrypt   ( char destination,         /* Data stored in RAM (0) or in EEPROM (!=0) */
                    char source);                 /* Data read from RAM (0) or from EEPROM (!=0) */

_error_card Random    ( void);                              /* Generates a random number */

_error_card Challenge ( void);                    /* Used for authentication of the external system */

_error_card ChallengeAns (char *data);            /* Authentication data sent back from the wru */

/*-------------------------------------------------------------------*
* Function prototypes: SPECIAL FUNCTIONS                            *
*------------------------------------------------------------------*/
_error_card ReadSerialNo (char *data);                      /* Serial number */

_error_card WipeOutCard (void);                   /* Erase the whole card structure */

_error_card EraseFile (char no_records,           /* Number of records in file */
                    char no_bytes);               /* Number of bytes in each record */

_error_card CrunchCard (void);                    /* Crunches card data area */
```

```
t_error_card ReportSK  ( char no_SK,                                      /* Secret key number */
                         char *SK_encrypted,                                  /* SK encrypted */
                         char *SK_active,                                       /* SK active */
                         char *max_attempt,                           /* Maximum number of attempts */
#endif                   char *remain_attempt);                     /* Remaining number of attempts */
```

Listing 6.7
card_cmd.c, Functions for File Management

```
/*---------------------------------------------------------------------------*
 * FILE AND RECORD COMMANDS                                                   *
 * MakeFile: creates regular files.                                           *
 * MakeWORM: creates WORM (write once read many) files.                       *
 * SelectFile: selects a file.                                                *
 * WriteRecord: writes data into a record of the selected file.               *
 * WriteWORM: writes data into a record of the selected WORM file.            *
 * ReadRecord: reads data from a given record of the selected file.           *
 *---------------------------------------------------------------------------*/
t_error_card MakeFile ( char file_name, char no_records, char no_bytes, char access_rules_AB,
                        char access_rules_CD, char codes_AB, char codes_CD)
{
char message[MAKE_FILE_LEN];                                      /* Message sent to card */
t_sc sc;                                                                 /* Card type */
char card_ans[SW1+SW2];                                                /* Card answer */
t_err_tx error;                                                        /* ERROR/OK_TX */

memset (card_ans, NULL_BYTE, SW1+SW2);                               /* Clears the buffer */

FillMessage(message, GUTI_CLA, 0xA0, file_name, no_records, 0x05);  /* Message for creating file */
message[DATA]    = no_bytes;
message[DATA+1] = access_rules_AB;
message[DATA+2] = access_rules_CD;
message[DATA+3] = codes_AB;
message[DATA+4] = codes_CD;

error = TxRxMessage (MAKE_FILE_LEN, INPUT, message, &sc, card_ans);  /* Transmitting the message */
return (CardErrorAnalysis (error, sc, card_ans));                       /* Returning error */
}

/*-------------------MakeWORM----------------------------*/
t_error_card MakeWORM ( char file_name, char no_records, char no_bytes, char access_rules_AB,
                        char access_rules_CD, char codes_AB, char codes_CD)
{
char message[MAKE_FILE_LEN];
t_sc sc;
char card_ans[SW1+SW2];
t_err_tx error;

memset (card_ans, NULL_BYTE, SW1+SW2);

FillMessage(message, GUTI_CLA, 0xA6, file_name, no_records, 0x05);
message[DATA]    = no_bytes;
message[DATA+1] = access_rules_AB;
message[DATA+2] = access_rules_CD;
message[DATA+3] = codes_AB;
message[DATA+4] = codes_CD;

error = TxRxMessage (MAKE_FILE_LEN, INPUT, message, &sc, card_ans);
return (CardErrorAnalysis (error, sc, card_ans));
}

/*-------------------SelectFile----------------------------*/
t_error_card SelectFile (char file_name)
{
char message[SELECT_FILE_LEN];
t_sc sc;
char card_ans[SW1+SW2];
t_err_tx error;

memset (card_ans, NULL_BYTE, SW1+SW2);

FillMessage(message, GUTI_CLA, 0xA4, file_name, NULL_BYTE, NULL_BYTE);
```

```
error = TxRxMessage (SELECT_FILE_LEN, INPUT, message, &sc, card_ans);
return (CardErrorAnalysis (error, sc, card_ans));
}

/*--------------------WriteRecord--------------------------*/
t_error_card WriteRecord (char no_record, char no_bytes, char *data)
{
int i;
char message[WRITE_RECORD_LEN];
t_sc sc;
char card_ans[SW1+SW2];
t_err_tx error;

memset (card_ans, NULL_BYTE, SW1+SW2);

FillMessage(message, GUTI_CLA, 0xD2, NULL_BYTE, no_record, no_bytes);
for (i = 0; i < no_bytes; i++) message[DATA+i] = *(data+i);

error = TxRxMessage (DATA+no_bytes, INPUT, message, &sc, card_ans);
return (CardErrorAnalysis (error, sc, card_ans));
}

/*--------------------WriteWORM--------------------------*/
t_error_card WriteWORM (char no_record, char no_bytes, char *data)
{
int i;
char message[WRITE_RECORD_LEN];
t_sc sc;
char card_ans[SW1+SW2];
t_err_tx error;

memset (card_ans, NULL_BYTE, SW1+SW2);

FillMessage(message, GUTI_CLA, 0xD6, NULL_BYTE, no_record, no_bytes);
for (i = 0; i < no_bytes; i++) message[DATA+i] = *(data+i);

error = TxRxMessage (DATA+no_bytes, INPUT, message, &sc, card_ans);
return (CardErrorAnalysis (error, sc, card_ans));
}

/*--------------------ReadRecord--------------------------*/
t_error_card ReadRecord (char no_record, char no_bytes, char *data)
{
int i;
char message[READ_RECORD_LEN];
t_sc sc;
char card_ans[MAX_REC_SIZE+SW1+SW2];
t_err_tx error;

memset (card_ans, NULL_BYTE, MAX_REC_SIZE+SW1+SW2);

FillMessage(message, GUTI_CLA, 0xB2, NULL_BYTE, no_record, no_bytes);
error = TxRxMessage (READ_RECORD_LEN, OUTPUT, message, &sc, card_ans);

if (card_ans[no_bytes] == OK_CONSTANT && card_ans[no_bytes+1] == NULL_BYTE){     /* Data retrieve */
    for (i=0; i<no_bytes; i++) *(data+i) = card_ans[i];
    card_ans[0] = card_ans[no_bytes];
    card_ans[1] = card_ans[no_bytes+1];
    }

return (CardErrorAnalysis (error, sc, card_ans));
}
```

Listing 6.8

card_cmd.c (cont.): Purse File Management

```
/*----------------------------------------------------------------------*
 * ELECTRONIC PURSE COMMANDS                                            *
 * MakePurse: creates a purse file.                                     *
 * Loan: Updates purse credit.                                          *
 * Payment: Substract an amount from card credit.                       *
 * PurseInfo: returns information from a purse file: balance,           *
 *            last transaction number, and transaction date.            *
 *----------------------------------------------------------------------*/
```

```
t_error_card MakePurse ( char file_name, char *transaction_date, char *credit_limit,
                         char access_rules_AB, char access_rules_CD, char codes_AB, char codes_CD)
{
char message[MAKE_PURSE_LEN];                                          /* Message sent to card */
t_sc sc;                                                                     /* Card type */
char card_ans[SW1+SW2];                                                    /* Card answer */
t_err_tx error;                                                            /* ERROR/OK_TX */

memset (card_ans, NULL_BYTE, SW1+SW2);                                  /* Clears the buffer */

FillMessage(message, GUTI_CLA, 0xA2, file_name, NULL_BYTE, 0x0A);/* Message for creating purse file */
message[DATA]   = *transaction_date;
message[DATA+1] = *(transaction_date+1);
message[DATA+2] = *(transaction_date+2);
message[DATA+3] = *credit_limit;
message[DATA+4] = *(credit_limit+1);
message[DATA+5] = *(credit_limit+2);
message[DATA+6] = access_rules_AB;
message[DATA+7] = access_rules_CD;
message[DATA+8] = codes_AB;
message[DATA+9] = codes_CD;

error = TxRxMessage (MAKE_PURSE_LEN, INPUT, message, &sc, card_ans);    /* Transmitting the message */
return (CardErrorAnalysis (error, sc, card_ans));                        /* Returning error */
}

/*--------------------Loan--------------------------------*/
t_error_card Loan (char *amount_loaned)
{
int i;
char message[PURSE_COMM_LEN];
t_sc sc;
char card_ans[SW1+SW2];
t_err_tx error;

memset (card_ans, NULL_BYTE, SW1+SW2);

FillMessage(message, GUTI_CLA, 0x50, NULL_BYTE, NULL_BYTE, DATA_LEN);
for (i=0; i<DATA_LEN; i++) message[DATA+i] = *(amount_loaned+i);

error = TxRxMessage (PURSE_COMM_LEN, INPUT, message, &sc, card_ans);
return (CardErrorAnalysis (error, sc, card_ans));
}

/*--------------------Payment----------------------------*/
t_error_card Payment (char *amount_paid)
{
int i;
char message[PURSE_COMM_LEN];
t_sc sc;
char card_ans[SW1+SW2];
t_err_tx error;

memset (card_ans, NULL_BYTE, SW1+SW2);

FillMessage(message, GUTI_CLA, 0x52, NULL_BYTE, NULL_BYTE, DATA_LEN);
for (i=0; i<DATA_LEN; i++) message[DATA+i] = *(amount_paid+i);

error = TxRxMessage (PURSE_COMM_LEN, INPUT, message, &sc, card_ans);
return (CardErrorAnalysis (error, sc, card_ans));
}

/*--------------------PurseInfo----------------------------*/
t_error_card PurseInfo (char *remaining_balance, char *transaction_number, char *transaction_date)
{
int i;
char message[PURSE_INFO_LEN];
t_sc sc;
char card_ans[MAX_REC_SIZE+SW1+SW2];
t_err_tx error;

memset (card_ans, NULL_BYTE, MAX_REC_SIZE+SW1+SW2);

FillMessage(message, GUTI_CLA, 0x54, NULL_BYTE, NULL_BYTE, DATA_LEN+NUMBER_LEN+DATE_LEN);
error = TxRxMessage (PURSE_INFO_LEN, OUTPUT, message, &sc, card_ans);

if (card_ans[DATA_LEN+NUMBER_LEN+DATE_LEN] == OK_CONSTANT                   /* Data retrieve */
 && card_ans[DATA_LEN+NUMBER_LEN+DATE_LEN+1] == NULL_BYTE){
```

```
    for (i=0; i<DATA_LEN; i++) *(remaining_balance+i) = card_ans[i];
    for (i=0; i<NUMBER_LEN; i++) *(transaction_number+i) = card_ans[i+DATA_LEN];
    for (i=0; i<DATE_LEN; i++) *(transaction_date+i) = card_ans[i+NUMBER_LEN+DATA_LEN];
    card_ans[0] = card_ans[DATA_LEN+NUMBER_LEN+DATE_LEN];
    card_ans[1] = card_ans[DATA_LEN+NUMBER_LEN+DATE_LEN+1];
    }

return (CardErrorAnalysis (error, sc, card_ans));
}
```

Listing 6.9
card_cmd.c (cont.): Secret Code Management

```
/*---------------------------------------------------------------------------*
 * KEYS / PIN MANAGEMENT COMMANDS                                            *
 * SetMasterKey: writes Master Key. This function can be invoked only once.  *
 * VerifyMasterKey: enters Master Key. Unlock MK-protected features.         *
 * ModifyMasterKey: modifies the current Master Key. Old MK required.        *
 * SetPin: writes PIN. This function can be invoked only once.               *
 * VerifyPin: enters PIN.                                                    *
 * ModifyPin: modifies current PIN. Old PIN required.                        *
 * SetSK: writes a Secret Key.                                               *
 * VerifySK: enters a Secret Key.                                            *
 * ModifySK: modifies a Secret Key. Old Secret Key required.                 *
 * ReactKeys: reactivates the card if disabled. MK required.                 *
 *   MK and PIN-related functions have no special instructions in this card. *
 *   The same general instructions for SKs are therefore used.               *
 *---------------------------------------------------------------------------*/
t_error_card SetMasterKey (char max_no_present, char *MK)
{
int i;
char message[SK_COMM_LEN];
t_sc sc;
char card_ans[SW1+SW2];
t_err_tx error;

memset (card_ans, NULL_BYTE, SW1+SW2);

FillMessage(message, GUTI_CLA, 0x22, max_no_present, MASTER_KEY_NO, SK_LEN);
for (i=0; i<SK_LEN; i++) message[DATA+i] = *(MK+i);

error = TxRxMessage (SK_COMM_LEN, INPUT, message, &sc, card_ans);
return (CardErrorAnalysis (error, sc, card_ans));
}

/*--------------------VerifyMasterKey---------------------*/
t_error_card VerifyMasterKey (char *MK)
{
int i;
char message[SK_COMM_LEN];
t_sc sc;
char card_ans[SW1+SW2];
t_err_tx error;

memset (card_ans, NULL_BYTE, SW1+SW2);

FillMessage(message, GUTI_CLA, 0x20, NULL_BYTE, MASTER_KEY_NO, SK_LEN);
for (i=0; i<SK_LEN; i++) message[DATA+i] = *(MK+i);

error = TxRxMessage (SK_COMM_LEN, INPUT, message, &sc, card_ans);
return (CardErrorAnalysis (error, sc, card_ans));
}

/*--------------------ModifyMasterKey---------------------*/
t_error_card ModifyMasterKey (char *MK)
{
int i;
char message[SK_COMM_LEN];
t_sc sc;
char card_ans[SW1+SW2];
t_err_tx error;

memset (card_ans, NULL_BYTE, SW1+SW2);
```

```
FillMessage(message, GUTI_CLA, 0x24, NULL_BYTE, MASTER_KEY_NO, SK_LEN);
for (i=0; i<SK_LEN; i++) message[DATA+i] = *(MK+i);

error = TxRxMessage (SK_COMM_LEN, INPUT, message, &sc, card_ans);
return (CardErrorAnalysis (error, sc, card_ans));
}

/*--------------------SetPIN--------------------------------*/
t_error_card SetPIN (char max_no_present, char *PIN)
{
int i;
char message[SK_COMM_LEN];
t_sc sc;
char card_ans[SW1+SW2];
t_err_tx error;

memset (card_ans, NULL_BYTE, SW1+SW2);

FillMessage(message, GUTI_CLA, 0x22, max_no_present, PIN_NO, SK_LEN);
for (i=0; i<SK_LEN; i++) message[DATA+i] = *(PIN+i);

error = TxRxMessage (SK_COMM_LEN, INPUT, message, &sc, card_ans);
return (CardErrorAnalysis (error, sc, card_ans));
}

/*--------------------VerifyPIN----------------------------*/
t_error_card VerifyPIN (char *PIN)
{
int i;
char message[SK_COMM_LEN];
t_sc sc;
char card_ans[SW1+SW2];
t_err_tx error;

memset (card_ans, NULL_BYTE, SW1+SW2);

FillMessage(message, GUTI_CLA, 0x20, NULL_BYTE, PIN_NO, SK_LEN);
for (i=0; i<SK_LEN; i++) message[DATA+i] = *(PIN+i);

error = TxRxMessage (SK_COMM_LEN, INPUT, message, &sc, card_ans);
return (CardErrorAnalysis (error, sc, card_ans));
}

/*--------------------ModifyPIN----------------------------*/
t_error_card ModifyPIN (char *PIN)
{
int i;
char message[SK_COMM_LEN];
t_sc sc;
char card_ans[SW1+SW2];
t_err_tx error;

memset (card_ans, NULL_BYTE, SW1+SW2);

FillMessage(message, GUTI_CLA, 0x24, NULL_BYTE, PIN_NO, SK_LEN);
for (i=0; i<SK_LEN; i++) message[DATA+i] = *(PIN+i);

error = TxRxMessage (SK_COMM_LEN, INPUT, message, &sc, card_ans);
return (CardErrorAnalysis (error, sc, card_ans));
}

/*--------------------SetSK--------------------------------*/
t_error_card SetSK (char max_no_present, char no_SK, char *SK)
{
int i;
char message[SK_COMM_LEN];
t_sc sc;
char card_ans[SW1+SW2];
t_err_tx error;

memset (card_ans, NULL_BYTE, SW1+SW2);

FillMessage(message, GUTI_CLA, 0x22, max_no_present, no_SK, SK_LEN);
for (i=0; i<SK_LEN; i++) message[DATA+i] = *(SK+i);

error = TxRxMessage (SK_COMM_LEN, INPUT, message, &sc, card_ans);
return (CardErrorAnalysis (error, sc, card_ans));
}
```

```
/*---------------------VerifySK-----------------------*/
t_error_card VerifySK (char no_SK, char *SK)
{
int i;
char message[SK_COMM_LEN];
t_sc sc;
char card_ans[SW1+SW2];
t_err_tx error;

memset (card_ans, NULL_BYTE, SW1+SW2);
FillMessage(message, GUTI_CLA, 0x20, NULL_BYTE, no_SK, SK_LEN);
for (i=0; i<SK_LEN; i++) message[DATA+i] = *(SK+i);

error = TxRxMessage (SK_COMM_LEN, INPUT, message, &sc, card_ans);
return (CardErrorAnalysis (error, sc, card_ans));
}
/*---------------------ModifySK-----------------------*/
t_error_card ModifySK (char no_SK, char *SK)
{
int i;
char message[SK_COMM_LEN];
t_sc sc;
char card_ans[SW1+SW2];
t_err_tx error;

memset (card_ans, NULL_BYTE, SW1+SW2);

FillMessage(message, GUTI_CLA, 0x24, NULL_BYTE, no_SK, SK_LEN);
for (i=0; i<SK_LEN; i++) message[DATA+i] = *(SK+i);

error = TxRxMessage (SK_COMM_LEN, INPUT, message, &sc, card_ans);
return (CardErrorAnalysis (error, sc, card_ans));
}
/*---------------------ReactKeys----------------------*/
t_error_card ReactKeys (void)
{
char message[REACT_KEYS_LEN];
t_sc sc;
char card_ans[SW1+SW2];
t_err_tx error;

memset (card_ans, NULL_BYTE, SW1+SW2);

FillMessage(message, GUTI_CLA, 0x26, NULL_BYTE, NULL_BYTE, NULL_BYTE);

error = TxRxMessage (REACT_KEYS_LEN, INPUT, message, &sc, card_ans);
return (CardErrorAnalysis (error, sc, card_ans));
}
```

Listing 6.10
card_cmd.c (cont.): Enciphering Functions

```
/*----------------------------------------------------------------*
 * ENCIPHERING FUNCTIONS                                          *
 *  Encrypt: performs DES enciphering.                            *
 *  Decrypt: performs a data DES deciphering.                     *
 *  Random: generates an eight-byte random number.               *
 *  Challenge: Challenges the external system for authentication. *
 *  ChallengeAns: wru answer to a previous card challenge.       *
 *----------------------------------------------------------------*/
t_error_card Encrypt (char destination, char source)
{
char message[ENCRYPT_LEN];
t_sc sc;
char card_ans[SW1+SW2];
t_err_tx error;

memset (card_ans, NULL_BYTE, SW1+SW2);
```

```
FillMessage(message, GUTI_CLA, 0xE0, destination, source, NULL_BYTE);
error = TxRxMessage (ENCRYPT_LEN, INPUT, message, &sc, card_ans);
return (CardErrorAnalysis (error, sc, card_ans));
}

/*-------------------Decrypt----------------------------*/
t_error_card Decrypt (char destination, char source)
{
char message[ENCRYPT_LEN];
t_sc sc;
char card_ans[SW1+SW2];
t_err_tx error;

memset (card_ans, NULL_BYTE, SW1+SW2);

FillMessage(message, GUTI_CLA, 0xE2, destination, source, NULL_BYTE);
error = TxRxMessage (ENCRYPT_LEN, INPUT, message, &sc, card_ans);
return (CardErrorAnalysis (error, sc, card_ans));
}

/*-------------------Random----------------------------*/
t_error_card Random ()
{
char message[ENCRYPT_LEN];
t_sc sc;
char card_ans[SW1+SW2];
t_err_tx error;

memset (card_ans, NULL_BYTE, SW1+SW2);

FillMessage(message, GUTI_CLA, 0xE4, NULL_BYTE, NULL_BYTE, NULL_BYTE);
error = TxRxMessage (ENCRYPT_LEN, INPUT, message, &sc, card_ans);
return (CardErrorAnalysis (error, sc, card_ans));
}

/*-------------------Challenge----------------------------*/
t_error_card Challenge ()
{
char message[ENCRYPT_LEN];
t_sc sc;
char card_ans[SW1+SW2];
t_err_tx error;

memset (card_ans, NULL_BYTE, SW1+SW2);

FillMessage(message, GUTI_CLA, 0xE6, NULL_BYTE, NULL_BYTE, NULL_BYTE);
error = TxRxMessage (ENCRYPT_LEN, INPUT, message, &sc, card_ans);
return (CardErrorAnalysis (error, sc, card_ans));
}

/*-------------------ChallengeAns----------------------------*/
t_error_card ChallengeAns (char *data)
{
int i;
char message[CHALLENGE_ANS_LEN];
t_sc sc;
char card_ans[SW1+SW2];
t_err_tx error;

memset (card_ans, NULL_BYTE, SW1+SW2);

FillMessage(message, GUTI_CLA, 0xE8, NULL_BYTE, NULL_BYTE, ENCRYPT_DATA_LEN);
for (i=0; i<ENCRYPT_DATA_LEN;i++) message[DATA+i] = *(data+i);

error = TxRxMessage (CHALLENGE_ANS_LEN, INPUT, message, &sc, card_ans);
return (CardErrorAnalysis (error, sc, card_ans));
}
```

Listing 6.11

card_cmd.c (cont.): Special Functions

```
/*------------------------------------------------------------------------*
 * SPECIAL FUNCTIONS -- All these functions require MK.                    *
 *   ReadSerialNo: reads the card serial number.                          *
 *   WipeOutCard: erases entire card memory.                              *
 *   EraseFile: erases a file. MK and SKs protecting file writing required.*
 *              File must be selected.                                    *
 *   CrunchCard: allocates files in the lowest free memory addresses.     *
 *   ReportSK: returns SK presence and encryption, as well as remaining and*
 *             maximum number of incorrect entry attempts. Uses nibbles.  *
 *------------------------------------------------------------------------*/
t_error_card ReadSerialNo(char *data)
{
int i;
char message[SPECIAL_LEN];
t_sc sc;
char card_ans[MAX_REC_SIZE+SW1+SW2];
t_error_card error;

memset (card_ans, NULL_BYTE, MAX_REC_SIZE+SW1+SW2);

FillMessage(message, GUTI_CLA, 0xBA, NULL_BYTE, NULL_BYTE, SERIAL_NO_LEN);
error = TxRxMessage (SPECIAL_LEN, OUTPUT, message, &sc, card_ans);

if (card_ans[SERIAL_NO_LEN] == OK_CONSTANT && card_ans[SERIAL_NO_LEN+1] == NULL_BYTE){
    for (i=0; i<SERIAL_NO_LEN; i++) *(data+i) = card_ans[i];            /* Data retrieve */
    card_ans[0] = card_ans[SERIAL_NO_LEN];
    card_ans[1] = card_ans[SERIAL_NO_LEN+1];
    }

return (CardErrorAnalysis (error, sc, card_ans));
}

/*-------------------WipeOutCard-------------------------*/
t_error_card  WipeOutCard()
{
char message[SPECIAL_LEN];
t_sc sc;
char card_ans[SW1+SW2];
t_err_tx error;

memset (card_ans, NULL_BYTE, SW1+SW2);

FillMessage(message, GUTI_CLA, 0x02, NULL_BYTE, NULL_BYTE, NULL_BYTE);
error = TxRxMessage (SPECIAL_LEN, INPUT, message, &sc, card_ans);
return (CardErrorAnalysis (error, sc, card_ans));
}

/*-------------------EraseFile--------------------------*/
t_error_card  EraseFile(char no_records, char no_bytes)
{
char message[SPECIAL_LEN];
t_sc sc;
char card_ans[SW1+SW2];
t_err_tx error;

memset (card_ans, NULL_BYTE, SW1+SW2);

FillMessage(message, GUTI_CLA, 0x04, no_records, no_bytes, NULL_BYTE);
error = TxRxMessage (SPECIAL_LEN, INPUT, message, &sc, card_ans);
return (CardErrorAnalysis (error, sc, card_ans));
}

/*-----------------CrunchCard--------------------------*/
t_error_card  CrunchCard()
{
char message[SPECIAL_LEN];
t_sc sc;
char card_ans[SW1+SW2];
t_err_tx error;

memset (card_ans, NULL_BYTE, SW1+SW2);

FillMessage(message, GUTI_CLA, 0x06, NULL_BYTE, NULL_BYTE, NULL_BYTE);
error = TxRxMessage (SPECIAL_LEN, INPUT, message, &sc, card_ans);
```

```
return (CardErrorAnalysis (error, sc, card_ans));
}

/*--------------------ReportSK-----------------------------*/
t_error_card  ReportSK ( char no_SK, char *SK_encrypted, char *SK_active,
                         char *max_attempt, char *remain_attempt)
{
char message[SPECIAL_LEN];
t_sc sc;
char card_ans[MAX_REC_SIZE+SW1+SW2];
t_err_tx error;

memset (card_ans, NULL_BYTE, MAX_REC_SIZE+SW1+SW2);

FillMessage(message, GUTI_CLA, 0x28, no_SK, NULL_BYTE, REPORT_DATA_LEN);
error = TxRxMessage (SPECIAL_LEN, OUTPUT, message, &sc, card_ans);

if (card_ans[REPORT_DATA_LEN] == OK_CONSTANT && card_ans[REPORT_DATA_LEN+1] == NULL_BYTE){
    *SK_encrypted = ((card_ans[0] >> 4) & '\x01');
    *SK_active = (card_ans[0] & '\x01');
    *max_attempt = (card_ans[1] >> 4);
    *remain_attempt = (card_ans[1] & '\x0F');
    card_ans[0] = card_ans[REPORT_DATA_LEN];
    card_ans[1] = card_ans[REPORT_DATA_LEN+1];
    }

return (CardErrorAnalysis (error, sc, card_ans));
}
```

Listing 6.12
kike.c, A Test Program for Smart Cards

```
/*------------------------------------------------------------------------*
 * File:          kike.c                                                   *
 * Description:   Test program for card instructions.                      *
 *                Must be recompiled if changing SK protections or filenames. *
 *                A number of instructions has not been included. They may be added as new *
 *                cases in the switch instruction of main().               *
 *------------------------------------------------------------------------*/
#include <stdio.h>
#include <conio.h>
#include <string.h>

#include "wru_guti.h"
#include "card_cmd.h"

#define File_Name         0x27                                /* From 0x00 to 0xFE */
#define Access_Rules_AB   0x23    /* Read protection by code B; write protection by code A and B */
#define Access_Rules_CD   0x43        /* Read protection by code C or D; write protection by both */
#define Number_Records    1
#define Number_Bytes      10
#define DAT               "HI IM KIKE"

#define SK_0              "MASTERME"
#define SK_1              "PINPOINT"
#define SK_2              "IAMRIGHT"
#define SK_3              "IAMOKTOO"
#define SK_NEW            "WHATEVER"
#define SK_WRONG          "IAMWRONG"
#define MAX_NO_FAILS      3
#define CODES_AB          0x10                              /* Protected by Master Key and PIN */
#define CODES_CD          0x32              /* Protected by Secret Key 2 and Secret Key 3 */
#define NO_SK_2           0x02
#define NO_SK_3           0x03
#define NO_SK_NEW         0x0F


/*------------------------------------------------------------------------*
 * DisplayCardError: displays a short error message                        *
 *------------------------------------------------------------------------*/
void DisplayCardError (t_error_card card_error)
{
switch (card_error){
```

```
        case OK_CARD:
                        printf ("OK\n"); break;
        case E_TX_RX_CARD:
                        printf ("Transmission error\n"); break;
        case E_NO_CARD:
                        printf ("No card inserted\n"); break;
        case E_UNKN_CARD:
                        printf ("Not asynchronous card inserted\n"); break;
        case E_DATA_CORRUPTED_CARD:
                        printf ("Returned data may be corrupted\n"); break;
        case E_END_OF_FILE_CARD:
                        printf ("End of file reached before end of reading\n"); break;
        case E_FILE_INVALIDATED_CARD:
                        printf ("Selected file is not valid\n"); break;
        case E_MEMORY_FAILURE_CARD:
                        printf ("Memory failure\n"); break;
        case E_WRONG_LENGTH_CARD:
                        printf ("Command length error\n"); break;
        case E_FUNCTION_NOT_SUPPORTED_CARD:
                        printf ("Function not supported\n"); break;
        case E_COMMAND_NOT_ALLOWED_CARD:
                        printf ("Command not recognized\n"); break;
        case E_WRONG_P1_P2_CARD:
                        printf ("P1 and/or P2 are wrong\n"); break;
        case E_INCORRECT_PARAMETERS_CARD:
                        printf ("Incorrect parameters in the data field\n"); break;
        case E_FILE_NOT_FOUND_CARD:
                        printf ("File not found\n"); break;
        case E_RECORD_NOT_FOUND_CARD:
                        printf ("Record not found\n"); break;
        case E_FILE_FULL_CARD:
                        printf ("Not enough memory space in record or file\n"); break;
        case E_P3_INCONSISTENT_CARD:
                        printf ("P3 is inconsistent with P1-P2 values\n"); break;
        case E_DATA_NOT_FOUND_CARD:
                        printf ("Referenced data not found\n"); break;
        case E_WRONG_P3_CARD:
                        printf ("Wrong length P3\n"); break;
        case E_WRONG_INS_CARD:
                        printf ("Wrong INS\n"); break;
        case E_CLASS_NOT_SUPPORTED_CARD:
                        printf ("Class not supported\n"); break;
        case E_NO_DIAGNOSIS_CARD:
                        printf ("No precise diagnosis is given\n"); break;
        default:
                        printf ("I shouldn't be here. Something's going wrong");
        }
}

int main ()
{
t_sc sc;                                                         /* Smart card */
t_error_card card_error;
char card_ans[MAX_REC_SIZE+SW1+SW2];
char data_read[MAX_REC_SIZE];
char SK_encrypted;
char SK_active;
char no_attempt;
char no_remain;
char keyed_line[MAX_REC_SIZE];
int i = 0;
int len;

clrscr();
printf ("Hi, I'm Kike\n");
printf ("the brand new test program for smart cards\n");

if (!SetSerPort (COM1, DATA_BITS_8, STOP_BITS_1, NO_PARITY, 19200, NO_INTERRUP)){
    printf ("Bad port\n");                                       /* Setting serial port */
    return 0;
    }

printf ("Please, insert your card. I'm waiting...\n");           /* Inserting the card */
if (PowerOnCard (&sc, card_ans)){
    if (sc ==  NO_CARD){
        printf ("No card inserted\n");
        return 0;
        }
```

```
          else if (sc != GC2_CARD){                                      /* Unknown card */
              printf ("Unknown card. Please remove the card\n");
              PowerOffCard (&sc);
              return 0;
              }
     else{
          printf ("Transmission error\n");
          return 0;
          }

     do{
          clrscr();
          printf ("Choose the letters to make up the test sequence:\n");
          printf ("O - Power on, insert the card\n");
          printf ("F - Power off, remove the card\n");
          printf ("C - Creates a file\n");
          printf ("S - Selects a file\n");
          printf ("W - Writes record\n");
          printf ("R - Reads record\n");
          printf ("T - Sets a secret key\n");
          printf ("Y - Modifies a secret key\n");
          printf ("0 - Enters the MK\n");
          printf ("1 - Enters the PIN\n");
          printf ("2 - Enters the SK 2\n");
          printf ("3 - Enters the SK 3\n");
          printf ("G - Issues a wrong secret key in\n");
          printf ("P - Report of secret key\n");
          printf ("M - Generates a random number\n");
          printf ("E - Erases a file\n");
          printf ("K - Crunches the card\n");
          printf ("V - Reativates the keys\n");
          printf ("D - Erases the card\n");                   /* remaining instructions should be included here... */
          gets (keyed_line);
          len = strlen (keyed_line);
          for (i=0; i<len; i++){
               switch(keyed_line[i]){                                 /* ... and here as new switch cases */
                    case 'C':                                                /* Creating file */
                         printf ("Make a file\n");
                         DisplayCardError (MakeFile (File_Name, Number_Records, Number_Bytes,
                              Access_Rules_AB, Access_Rules_CD, CODES_AB, CODES_CD)); break;
                    case 'S':                                                /* Selecting file */
                         printf ("Select a file\n");
                         DisplayCardError (SelectFile (File_Name));break;
                    case 'W':                                                /* Writing record */
                         printf ("Write record\n");
                         DisplayCardError (WriteRecord (Number_Records, Number_Bytes, DAT));break;
                    case 'R':                                                /* Reading record */
                         printf ("Read record\n");
                         card_error = ReadRecord (Number_Records, Number_Bytes, data_read);
                         DisplayCardError (card_error);
                         if (card_error == OK_CARD){     /* Displaying the message received from record */
                              data_read[Number_Bytes] = '\0';
                              printf ("In the card is written: %s\n", data_read);
                              }break;
                    case 'T':                                                /* Setting a secret key */
                         printf ("Set a secret key\n");
                         DisplayCardError (SetSK (MAX_NO_FAILS, NO_SK_NEW, SK_1));break;
                    case 'Y':                                                /* Modifying a secret key */
                         printf ("Modify a secret key\n");
                         DisplayCardError (ModifySK (NO_SK_NEW, SK_NEW));break;
                    case '0':                                                /* Entering the Master Key */
                         printf ("Verify the Master Key\n");
                         DisplayCardError (VerifyMasterKey (SK_0));break;
                    case '1':                                                /* Entering the PIN */
                         printf ("Verify the PIN\n");
                         DisplayCardError (VerifyPIN (SK_1));break;
                    case '2':                                                /* Entering a secret key */
                         printf ("Verify secret key #2\n");
                         DisplayCardError (VerifySK (NO_SK_2, SK_2));break;
                    case '3':                                                /* Entering a secret key */
                         printf ("Verify secret key #3\n");
                         DisplayCardError (VerifySK (NO_SK_3, SK_3));break;
                    case 'G':                                                /* Entering a wrong secret key */
                         printf ("Issue Wrong Secret Key in\n");
                         DisplayCardError (VerifySK (NO_SK_NEW, SK_WRONG));break;
                    case 'P':                                                /* Showing secret key report */
                         printf ("Secret Key Report\n");
```

```
                    DisplayCardError (ReportSK (PIN_NO, &SK_encrypted, &SK_active, &no_attempt,
                    &no_remain));
                    printf ("SK presence indicator:%u\n", SK_active);
                    printf ("SK encryption indicator:%u\n", SK_encrypted);
                    printf ("Maximum fails:%u\n", no_attempt);
                    printf ("Remaining fails:%u\n", no_remain);break;
          case 'M':                                         /* Generating a random number */
                    printf ("Random number\n");
                    DisplayCardError (Random ());break;
          case 'E':                                         /* Erasing a file */
                    printf ("Erase a file\n");
                    DisplayCardError (EraseFile (Number_Records, Number_Bytes));break;
          case 'K':                                         /* Crunching the card */
                    printf ("Crunch the card\n");
                    DisplayCardError (CrunchCard ());break;
          case 'V':                                         /* Reactivating the keys */
                    printf ("Reactivate the keys\n");
                    DisplayCardError (ReactKeys ());break;
          case 'D':            /* Erasing the card. All the information and file structure is lost */
                    printf ("Erasing card\n");
                    DisplayCardError (WipeOutCard());break;
          default:
                    printf ("I don't understand the character %c. Try again\n", keyed_line[i]);
          }
       }
   printf ("Press Carriage Return to write next test sequence\n");
   printf ("Press Ctrl + Z to quit\n");
   } while (getchar () != EOF);

printf ("Please, remove your card\n");                                  /* Removing the card */
PowerOffCard (&sc);
return 1;
}
```

Listing 6.13
atr_iso.h Contains the Masks to Find the Historical Bytes Included in the ATR

```
/*---------------------------------------------------------------------------*
 * File:          atr_iso.h                                                  *
 * Description:   Header file of atr_iso.c, a program for interpreting smart card ATRs   *
 *---------------------------------------------------------------------------*/

#ifndef ATR_ISO
#define ATR_ISO

/* Constant definitions */
#define MAX_ATR         33                      /* Maximum number of ATR characters */
#define MAX_BYTES       31                      /* MAX_ATR - TS - TO */
#define RFU             -1                      /* Reserved for Future Use */
#define INT_CLOCK       -2                      /* Internal clock */
#define NO_VPP          0                       /* Vpp not connected */
#define DEF_FACTORF     372                     /* Default F factor */
#define DEF_MAXFREQ     5                       /* Default maximum frequency */
#define DEF_FACTORD     1                       /* Default D factor */
#define DEF_MAXPROGI    50                      /* Default maximum programming current */
#define DEF_MAXPROGV    5                       /* Default maximum programming voltage */
#define DEF_MINDELAY    12                      /* Default minimum delay */
#define DEF_PROTTYPE    0                       /* Default protocol type */
#define OFF_TS          0                       /* Offset of TS character */
#define OFF_TO          1                       /* Offset of TO character */

#define DIR_CONV        '\x3B'                   /* Direct transmission convention */
#define INV_CONV        '\x3F'                   /* Inverse transmission convention */
#define MASK_HIST       '\x0F'          /* Mask to find out the number of historical bytes */
#define MASK_TAi        '\x10'                   /* Mask for TAi detection */
#define MASK_TBi        '\x20'                   /* Mask for TBi detection */
#define MASK_TCi        '\x40'                   /* Mask for TCi detection */
#define MASK_TDi        '\x80'                   /* Mask for TDi detection */
#define MASK_FI         '\xF0'          /* Mask for maximum frequency and F factor */
#define MASK_DI         '\x0F'                   /* Mask for D factor */
#define MASK_II         '\x60'                   /* Mask for II parameter */
#define MASK_PI1        '\x1F'                   /* Mask for PI1 parameter */
#define MASK_T          '\x0F'                   /* Mask for protocol type */

/* Type definitions */
typedef enum { ERROR_ATR, OK_ATR } t_err_atr;
```

```
typedef enum {                                      /* Transmission types between card and device */
           DIRECT,    INVERSE,   NO_ISO
        } t_convention;

typedef enum {                             /* Types of ATR characters: TS, TA, TB, TC, TD, TK, TCK */
           TS,  /* Initial character */      T0,  /* Format character */
           TA,  /* TA character */           TB,  /* TB character */
           TC,  /* TC character */           TD,  /* TD character */
           TK,  /* Historical character */   TCK  /* Check character */
        } t_char_type;

typedef struct {                                               /* Answer To Reset characters */
    unsigned char    byte;       /* ATR character */
    t_char_type      type;       /* ATR character type */
    int              index;      /* ATR character subindex */
    } t_atr_char;

typedef struct {                                    /* Information from global interface bytes */
    t_convention    convention; /* Transmission convention */
    int             factor_F;    /* Clock rate conversion factor */
    float           max_freq;    /* Maximum frequency in MHz */
    float           factor_D;    /* Bit rate adjustement factor */
    char            max_prog_i;  /* Maximum programming current */
    float           prog_volt;   /* Programming voltage */
    int             min_delay;   /* Minimum delay between two characters = 12+N */
    } t_tx_par;

struct node_prot {                                        /* Information from one protocol */
    unsigned char    prot_type;  /* Protocol type */
    unsigned char    int_char_no; /* Interface characters number */
    t_atr_char       *int_chars; /* Interface characters */
    struct node_prot *next;       /* Pointer to next protocol */
    };
typedef struct node_prot t_node_prot;
typedef struct {                                        /* Information from all the protocols */
    unsigned char    prot_no;     /* Number of protocols */
    t_node_prot      *first_prot; /* Pointer to first protocol */
    t_node_prot      *last_prot;  /* Pointer to last protocol */
    } t_protocols;

typedef struct {                                                              /* ATR data */
    unsigned        char_no;     /* Number of ATR characters */
    t_atr_char      atr_chars[MAX_ATR]; /* ATR characters */
    t_tx_par        tx_par;      /* Tx parameters */
    t_protocols     protocols;   /* Protocol data */
    unsigned char   hist_bytes_no; /* Historical bytes information */
    } t_atr;

/* Function prototypes */
t_err_atr AllocProt (t_atr        *atr);                          /* Pointer to ATR structure */

void FreeAllProts ( t_protocols *prots);                     /* Pointer to protocols structure */

void StringAtr (     t_atr_char  *atr_char,                      /* ATR char structure */
                     t_char_type char_type,                     /* Type of ATR character */
                     unsigned    ind,                               /* Character index */
                     unsigned char character);                       /* Character to add */

t_err_atr DefaultATR (t_atr       *atr);                          /* Pointer to ATR structure */

void AnalyzeTS (     char        Ts,                             /* Character to analyze */
                     t_atr       *atr);                             /* ATR information */

void AnalyzeT0 (     char        TZero,                          /* Character to analyze */
                     t_atr       *atr);                             /* ATR information */

void AnalyzeTA1 (    char        Ta1,                            /* Character to analyze */
                     t_atr       *atr);                             /* ATR information */

void AnalyzeTB1 (    char        Tb1,                            /* Character to analyze */
                     t_atr       *atr);                             /* ATR information */

void AnalyzeTC1 (    char        Tc1,                            /* Character to analyze */
                     t_atr       *atr);                             /* ATR information */

void AnalyzeTD1 (    char        Td1,                            /* Character to analyze */
                     t_atr       *atr);                             /* ATR information */
```

```
void AnalyzeTB2 (      char      Tb2,              /* Character to analyze */
                       t_atr     *atr);            /* ATR information */

void WrNoGlobalIn (    t_atr     *atr,             /* ATR characters information */
                       t_char_type char_type,     /* Type of ATR character */
                       unsigned char character,    /* Character to add */
                       unsigned   ind);            /* Character index */

t_err_atr AnInterfaceChars (char *string,         /* ATR characters */
                       t_atr     *atr);            /* ATR information */

t_err_atr AnRestGlobalIntChars (char *string,     /* ATR characters */
                       t_atr     *atr,             /* ATR information */
                       unsigned   ind);            /* Character index */

void AnHistChars (     char      *string,          /* ATR characters */
                       t_atr     *atr);            /* ATR information */

void AnTCK (           char      Tck,             /* ATR characters */
                       t_atr     *atr);            /* ATR information */

t_err_atr AtrIso (     char      *string,          /* String to analyze */
                       t_atr     *atr);            /* Result of ATR analysis */

#endif
```

Listing 6.14
atr_iso.c Analyzes the ATR Information

```
/*-------------------------------------------------------------------------*
 * File:           atr_iso.c                                               *
 * Description:    interprets the information included in smart card ATRs   *
 *-------------------------------------------------------------------------*/

#include    <alloc.h>

#include    "atr_iso.h"

/*-----------------------------------------------------------------*
 * AllocProt:  Auxiliar function to reserve memory for a protocol   *
 *             structure.                                          *
 *-----------------------------------------------------------------*/
t_err_atr AllocProt (t_atr *atr)
{
t_protocols *prots = &(atr->protocols);
t_node_prot *new_prot;
t_atr_char *data;

if (!(new_prot = (t_node_prot *) malloc (sizeof(t_node_prot)))) return ERROR_ATR;
if (!(data = (t_atr_char *) malloc (sizeof(t_atr_char)*MAX_BYTES))) {       /* Allocating memory */
    free (new_prot);
    return ERROR_ATR;}
if (!(prots->prot_no))                                          /* Adjusting pointers */
    prots->last_prot = prots->first_prot = new_prot;            /* First protocol */
else
    prots->last_prot = prots->last_prot->next = new_prot;       /* Other protocols */
prots->last_prot->int_chars = data;
new_prot->int_char_no = 0;                                      /* Initializing values */
new_prot->next = NULL;
(prots->prot_no)++;
return OK_ATR;
}

/*-----------------------------------------------------------------*
 * FreeProt:   Internal function to free memory of protocol structures.  *
 *-----------------------------------------------------------------*/
void FreeProt (t_node_prot *protocol)
{
if (protocol){
    if (protocol->int_chars) free (protocol->int_chars);
    free (protocol);}
}
```

```
/*------------------------------------------------------------------*
 * FreeAllProts: Frees memory of all protocols.                     *
 *------------------------------------------------------------------*/
void FreeAllProts (t_protocols *prots)
{
int i;
t_node_prot *pr1;
t_node_prot *pr2 = prots->first_prot;                                   /* Internal pointers */

if (prots)
    for (i = 1; i <= prots->prot_no; ++i){
        pr1 = pr2->next;
        if (pr2){
            if (pr2->int_chars) free (pr2->int_chars);
            free (pr2);}
        pr2 = pr1;}
}

/*------------------------------------------------------------------*
 * StringAtr:  Puts ATR characters in t_atr_char structure.         *
 *------------------------------------------------------------------*/
void StringAtr (t_atr_char *atr_char, t_char_type char_type,
                unsigned ind, unsigned char character)
{
atr_char->byte = character;
atr_char->type = char_type;
atr_char->index = ind;
}

/*------------------------------------------------------------------*
 * DefaultATR: Sets ATR to default values, and initializes some     *
 *             elements of atr structure.                           *
 *------------------------------------------------------------------*/
t_err_atr DefaultATR (t_atr *atr)
{
atr->tx_par.factor_F = DEF_FACTORF;
atr->tx_par.max_freq = DEF_MAXFREQ;                                     /* TA1 doesn't exist */
atr->tx_par.factor_D = DEF_FACTORD;
atr->tx_par.max_prog_i = DEF_MAXPROGI;                                  /* TB1 doesn't exist */
atr->tx_par.prog_volt = DEF_MAXPROGV;
atr->tx_par.min_delay = DEF_MINDELAY;                                   /* TC1 doesn't exist */
atr->protocols.prot_no = atr->char_no = 0;
if (!AllocProt (atr)) return ERROR_ATR;                                 /* Other protocol */
atr->protocols.first_prot->prot_type = DEF_PROTTYPE;                    /* TD1 doesn't exist */
return OK_ATR;
}

/*------------------------------------------------------------------*
 * INTERFACE CHARACTERS ANALYSIS                                    *
 *    AnalyzeTS:  gets TS character information.                     *
 *    AnalyzeT0:  gets T0 character information.                     *
 *    AnalyzeTA1: gets TA1 character information.                    *
 *    AnalyzeTB1: gets TB1 character information.                    *
 *    AnalyzeTC1: gets TC1 character information.                    *
 *    AnalyzeTD1: gets TD1 character information.                    *
 *    AnalyzeTB2: gets TB2 character information.                    *
 *    WrNoGlobalIn: gets non global interface characters information.*
 *    AnInterfaceChars: general analysis function for interface      *
 *                 characters. This function calls the former functions. *
 *------------------------------------------------------------------*/
void AnalyzeTS (char Ts, t_atr *atr)
{
StringAtr (atr->atr_chars+atr->char_no, TS, 0, Ts);      /* Assigning values to atr_char structure */
switch (Ts) {                                                   /* Getting the information */
    case DIR_CONV: atr->tx_par.convention = DIRECT; break;
    case INV_CONV: atr->tx_par.convention = INVERSE; break;
    default : atr->tx_par.convention = NO_ISO; break;}
(atr->char_no)++;
}

void AnalyzeT0 (char TZero, t_atr *atr)
{
StringAtr (atr->atr_chars+atr->char_no, T0, 0, TZero);   /* Assigning values to atr_char structure */
atr->hist_bytes_no = TZero & MASK_HIST;                       /* Getting number of historical bytes */
(atr->char_no)++;
}

void AnalyzeTA1 (char Ta1, t_atr *atr)
{
```

```c
float fr, fD;
int fF;                                                        /* Internal variables */

StringAtr (atr->atr_chars + atr->char_no, TA, 1, Ta1);
switch (Ta1 & MASK_FI) {                                        /* Getting FI for F factor */
    case '\x00' : fF = INT_CLOCK; break;   case '\x10' : fF = 372;  break;
    case '\x20' : fF = 558;  break;        case '\x30' : fF = 744;  break;
    case '\x40' : fF = 1116; break;        case '\x50' : fF = 1488; break;
    case '\x60' : fF = 1860; break;        case '\x90' : fF = 512;  break;
    case '\xA0' : fF = 768;  break;        case '\xB0' : fF = 1024; break;
    case '\xC0' : fF = 1536; break;        case '\xD0' : fF = 2048; break;
    case '\x70' :                          case '\x80' :
    case '\xE0' :                          case '\xF0' : fF = RFU;  break;}
atr->tx_par.factor_F = fF;
switch (Ta1 & MASK_FI) {                                        /* Getting FI for maximum frequency */
    case '\x00' : fr = INT_CLOCK; break;   case '\x10' : fr = 5;    break;
    case '\x20' : fr = 6;    break;        case '\x30' : fr = 8;    break;
    case '\x40' : fr = 12;   break;        case '\x50' : fr = 16;   break;
    case '\x60' : fr = 20;   break;        case '\x90' : fr = 5;    break;
    case '\xA0' : fr = 7.5;  break;        case '\xB0' : fr = 10;   break;
    case '\xC0' : fr = 15;   break;        case '\xD0' : fr = 20;   break;
    case '\x70' :                          case '\x80' :
    case '\xE0' :                          case '\xF0' : fr = RFU;  break;}
atr->tx_par.max_freq = fr;

switch (Ta1 & MASK_DI) {                                        /* Getting D factor */
    case '\x01' : fD = 1;     break;       case '\x02' : fD = 2;    break;
    case '\x03' : fD = 4;     break;       case '\x04' : fD = 8;    break;
    case '\x05' : fD = 16;    break;       case '\x0A' : fD = 1/2;  break;
    case '\x0B' : fD = 1/4;   break;       case '\x0C' : fD = 1/8;  break;
    case '\x0D' : fD = 1/16;  break;       case '\x0E' : fD = 1/32; break;
    case '\x0F' : fD = 1/64;  break;       case '\x06' :
    case '\x07' :                          case '\x08' :
    case '\x09' :                          case '\x00': fD = RFU;   break;}
atr->tx_par.factor_D = fD;
(atr->char_no)++;
}

void AnalyzeTB1 (char Tb1, t_atr *atr)
{
char VPP;                                                       /* Maximum programming voltage */

StringAtr (atr->atr_chars + atr->char_no, TB, 1, Tb1);
switch (Tb1 & MASK_II) {                                        /* Analyzing maximum programming current */
    case '\x00' : atr->tx_par.max_prog_i = 25;   break;
    case '\x20' : atr->tx_par.max_prog_i = 50;   break;
    case '\x40' : atr->tx_par.max_prog_i = 100;  break;
    case '\x60' : atr->tx_par.max_prog_i = RFU;  break;}

if (!(VPP = Tb1 & MASK_PI1)) atr->tx_par.prog_volt = NO_VPP;               /* Analyzing PI1 */
else atr->tx_par.prog_volt = (VPP <= 25 && VPP >= 5)? VPP : RFU;   /* Getting programming voltage */
(atr->char_no)++;
}

void AnalyzeTC1 (char Tc1, t_atr *atr)
{
StringAtr (atr->atr_chars + atr->char_no, TC, 1, Tc1);
atr->tx_par.min_delay = (Tc1 == '\xFF') ? 11 : (12+Tc1);                   /* Guardtime */
(atr->char_no)++;
}

void AnalyzeTD1 (char Td1, t_atr *atr)
{
StringAtr (atr->atr_chars+atr->char_no, TD, 1, Td1);
atr->protocols.first_prot->prot_type = (Td1 & MASK_T);                    /* Protocol type */
(atr->char_no)++;
}

void AnalyzeTB2 (char Tb2, t_atr *atr)
{
StringAtr (atr->atr_chars + atr->char_no, TB, 2, Tb2);
atr->tx_par.prog_volt = (Tb2 >= 50 && (unsigned char) Tb2 <= 250)?(.1*Tb2):RFU;   /* TB2 information */
(atr->char_no)++;
}

void WrNoGlobalIn (t_atr *atr, t_char_type char_type, unsigned char character, unsigned ind)
{
t_protocols *prots = &(atr->protocols);
t_node_prot *prot  = prots->last_prot;
```

```
    StringAtr (atr->atr_chars+atr->char_no, char_type, ind, character);
    StringAtr (prot->int_chars+prot->int_char_no++, char_type, ind, character);
    (atr->char_no)++;
    }


t_err_atr AnRestGlobalIntChars ( char *string, t_atr *atr, unsigned ind)
{
char prot;                                                          /* Internal variable */
unsigned char TDi = string[atr->char_no - 1];                       /* TDi char */

if (TDi & MASK_TAi) WrNoGlobalIn (atr, TA, string[atr->char_no], ind); /* More interface characters */
if (TDi & MASK_TBi && atr->protocols.prot_no == 1)                  /* TB2 exists */
    AnalyzeTB2 (string[atr->char_no], atr);
if (TDi & MASK_TBi && atr->protocols.prot_no != 1)                  /* TBi, i <> 2 */
    WrNoGlobalIn (atr, TB, string[atr->char_no], ind);
if (TDi & MASK_TCi) WrNoGlobalIn (atr, TC, string[atr->char_no], ind);
if (TDi & MASK_TDi)
    {
    if ((prot = string[atr->char_no] & MASK_T) && (prot != atr->protocols.last_prot->prot_type))
        {
        if (!AllocProt (atr)) return ERROR_ATR;
        atr->protocols.last_prot->prot_type = prot;
        }
    if (!AnRestGlobalIntChars (string, atr, ++ind)) return ERROR_ATR;
    }
return OK_ATR;
}


t_err_atr AnInterfaceChars (char *string, t_atr *atr)
{
AnalyzeTS (string[atr->char_no], atr);                              /* "TS" character */
AnalyzeTO (string[atr->char_no], atr);                              /* "TO" character */
if (string[OFF_TO] & MASK_TAi)                                      /* "TA1" character */
    AnalyzeTA1 (string[atr->char_no], atr);
if (string[OFF_TO] & MASK_TBi)                                      /* "TB1" character */
    AnalyzeTB1 (string[atr->char_no], atr);
if (string[OFF_TO] & MASK_TCi)                                      /* "TC1" character */
    AnalyzeTC1 (string[atr->char_no], atr);
if (string[OFF_TO] & MASK_TDi){                                     /* "TD1" and remaining characters */
    AnalyzeTD1 (string[atr->char_no], atr);
    if (!AnRestGlobalIntChars (string, atr, 2)) return ERROR_ATR;}
return OK_ATR;
}

/*--------------------------------------------------------------------*
 *  HISTORICAL CHARACTERS ANALYSIS                                    *
 *     AnHistChars: analyzes ATR historical characters.               *
 *--------------------------------------------------------------------*/
void AnHistChars (char *string, t_atr *atr)
{
unsigned i;

for (i = 1; i <= atr->hist_bytes_no; ++i) {
    StringAtr (atr->atr_chars+atr->char_no, TK, i, string[atr->char_no]);
    (atr->char_no)++;}
}

/*--------------------------------------------------------------------*
 *  TCK CHARACTER ANALYSIS                                            *
 *     AnTCK: analyzes TCK character.                                 *
 *--------------------------------------------------------------------*/
void AnTCK (char Tck, t_atr *atr)
{
t_protocols *prots = &(atr->protocols);

if (!(prots->prot_no == 1 && !(prots->first_prot->prot_type))) {
    StringAtr (atr->atr_chars + atr->char_no, TCK, 0, Tck);
    (atr->char_no)++;}
}

/*--------------------------------------------------------------------*
 *  ATR ANALYSIS                                                      *
 *     AtrIso: gets ATR card information.                             *
 *--------------------------------------------------------------------*/
t_err_atr AtrIso (char *string, t_atr *atr)
{
if (!DefaultATR (atr)) return ERROR_ATR;                /* Setting ATR structure to default values */
```

```
f (!AnInterfaceChars (string, atr)) return ERROR_ATR;      /* Analyzing interface characters */
nHistChars (string, atr);                                  /* Analyzing historical characters */
nTCK (string[atr->char_no], atr);                          /* Analyzing TCK */
eturn OK_ATR;
```

Listing 6.15
look_atr.c Main Program

```
*-------------------------------------------------------------------------------------*
* File:          look_atr.c                                                           *
* Description:   Uses the functions of atr_iso.c and the definitions of               *
*                atr_iso.h for ATR analysis. The results are displayed                *
*                by several functions included here.                                  *
*-------------------------------------------------------------------------------------*/
include       <stdio.h>
include       <conio.h>

include       "wru_guti.h"
include       "atr_iso.h"

*--------------------------------------------------------------------*
* DisplayType: Displays the type of ATR characters                   *
*--------------------------------------------------------------------*/
har *DisplayType (t_char_type type_char)

witch (type_char)
    {
    case TS:   return "TS";
    case TO:   return "TO";
    case TA:   return "TA";
    case TB:   return "TB";
    case TC:   return "TC";
    case TD:   return "TD";
    case TK:   return "TK";
    case TCK:  return "TCK";
    default :  return "UNK";
    }

*----------------------------------------------------------------------------*
* DisplayProt: Displays interface characters associated to one protocol.*
*----------------------------------------------------------------------------*/
oid DisplayProt (t_node_prot *prot)

nt i;

rintf ("Protocol type: %d\n", prot->prot_type);
rintf ("Number of interface characters: %d\n", prot->int_char_no);

or (i = 0; i < prot->int_char_no; ++i)
    printf ("Character %02X  %s%d\n", ((prot->int_chars)+i)->byte,
        DisplayType (((prot->int_chars)+i)->type),  ((prot->int_chars)+i)->index);

*----------------------------------------------------------------------*
* DisplayProts: Displays information of all the protocols              *
*----------------------------------------------------------------------*/
oid DisplayProts (t_atr *atr)

nt i;
_node_prot *pr1 = atr->protocols.first_prot;

or (i = 1; i <= atr->protocols.prot_no; ++i)
    {
    DisplayProt (pr1);
    pr1 = pr1->next;
    }

*----------------------------------------------------------------------*
* DisplayChars: Information of ATR characters                          *
*----------------------------------------------------------------------*/
oid DisplayChars (t_atr *atr)

nt i;
```

```c
printf ("ATR characters:\n\n");

for (i = 0; i < atr->char_no; ++i)
    printf ("Character %02X  %s%d\n", ((atr->atr_chars)+i)->byte,
        DisplayType (((atr->atr_chars)+i)->type), ((atr->atr_chars)+i)->index);
}

/*-------------------------------------------------------------------*
 *  StringConv: Convert transmission convention into a string        *
 *-------------------------------------------------------------------*/
char *StringConv (t_convention conv)
{
switch (conv)
    {
    case DIRECT:  return "direct";
    case INVERSE: return "inverse";
    default :     return "unknown";
    }
}

/*-------------------------------------------------------------------*
 *  DispTxParam: Displays transmission parameters                    *
 *-------------------------------------------------------------------*/
void DispTxParam (t_atr *atr)
{
t_tx_par *param = &(atr->tx_par);

printf ("Transmission parameters:\n\n");
printf ("Transmission convention: %s\n", StringConv (param->convention));
switch (param->factor_F)
    {
    case INT_CLOCK: printf ("Internal clock card\n");
                    if (param->factor_D != RFU) printf ("Work etu: %.3f ms\n",
                        1/(param->factor_D)/9600*1000);
                    break;
    case RFU:       printf ("Warning: F factor is RFU\n");
                    printf ("Maximum frequency undefined\n"); break;
    default:        printf ("F factor: %d\n", param->factor_F);
                    printf ("Maximum frequency: %.1f MHz\n", param->max_freq);
                    if (param->factor_D != RFU) printf ("Minimum work etu: %.3f ms\n",
                        1/(param->factor_D)*(param->factor_F)/(param->max_freq/1.0e6)*1000);
    }
if (param->factor_D == RFU) printf ("Warning: D factor is RFU\n");
else printf ("D factor: %.4f\n", param->factor_D);
if (param->max_prog_i == RFU) printf ("Warning: Maximum programming current is RFU\n");
else printf ("Maximum programming current: %d mA\n", param->max_prog_i);
if (param->prog_volt == RFU) printf ("Warning: Programming voltage is RFU\n");
else if (param->prog_volt == (float)0) printf ("Programming voltage not required\n");
else printf ("Programming voltage: %.1f V\n", param->prog_volt);
printf ("Extra guardtime: %d etu\n", param->min_delay - 12);
}

/*-------------------------------------------------------------------*
 *  DisplayATR: Displays the ATR information                         *
 *-------------------------------------------------------------------*/
void DisplayATR (t_atr *atr)
{
clrscr ();
DisplayChars (atr);              /* Displaying characters and their corresponding types */
getch (); clrscr ();
DisplayProts (atr);                        /* Displaying protocol information */
getch (); clrscr ();
DispTxParam (atr);                              /* Displaying tx parameters */
}

/*-------------------------------------------------------------------*
 *  Main program                                                     *
 *-------------------------------------------------------------------*/
int main ()
{
char card_ans [MAX_ATR];
t_sc sc;                                                        /* Card type */
t_atr atr;

printf ("ATR ANALYSIS\n");
if (!SetSerPort (COM1, DATA_BITS_8, STOP_BITS_1, NO_PARITY, 19200, NO_INTERRUP))
    {                                                    /* Setting serial port */
```

```
    printf ("Bad port\n");
    return 0;
    }
printf ("Please, insert your card\n");                                    /* Inserting card */
if (PowerOnCard (&sc, card_ans))
    {
    switch (sc)
        {
        case GC1_CARD:
        case GC2_CARD:
        case GCJ_CARD:
        case ASY_CARD: if (!(AtrIso (card_ans, &atr))) return 0;
                DisplayATR (&atr);
                FreeAllProts (&(atr.protocols));
                printf ("Please, remove your card\n");                    /* Removing the card */
                break;
        case SY_CARD:
                printf ("Synchronous card inserted. Analysis not implemented.\n");
                printf ("Please, remove your card\n");                    /* Removing the card */
                break;
        case NO_CARD:
        default:
                printf ("Unknown card.\n");
                printf ("Please, remove your card\n");                    /* Removing the card */
        }
    }
else {
    printf ("Transmission error\n");                                      /* Maybe wru not connected */
    return 0;
    }
PowerOffCard (&sc);
return 1;                                                                 /* Returning OK */
}
```

Glossary

A	In digital binary communications, low-voltage state
ABA	American Bankers Association, who defined the content and bit density of the second track of magnetic stripe cards for on-line financial transactions. Also American Bar Association, who is supporting the regulation of digital signatures for document and user authentication.
ABS	Acrylic butadiene styrene: a plastic substrate for magnetic stripe and chip cards; used in many cards from France and Germany.
ac	Alternating current
ACK	Procedure byte sent by the card for acknowledging command reception and warning on further actions.
Active smart card	See *Super smart card*
AIM	Advanced Informatics in Medicine
ANSI	American National Standards Institute: a U.S. standards organization
APDU	Application protocol data unit. Data units employed in ISO 7816/4 for describing the structure of messages in the communications between smart cards and hosts. APDUs may contain commands or response messages.
ASCII	American Standard Code for Information Interchange: a set of 128 characters (eventually extended to 256) for coding letters, numbers, orthographic symbols, and control signals in computers and electronic storage media.
ASN.1	Abstract Syntax Notation One
Asymmetric cryptosystem	Cryptosystem based on (at least) two keys, one public, one private. Messages encrypted with the public key can be only decrypted with the private key, and vice versa.

ATM	Automatic teller machine. Bank services, such as cash withdrawal and deposit, are offered by these machines after checking the user identity by any method (e.g., a financial card).
ATR	Answer to reset. Hexadecimal string sent by chip cards when a reset signal is sent from the outside (e.g., right after inserting the card). The ATR contains information concerning the card working conditions (coding convention, frequency, etu, communication protocol, and so on) and optional data on the card manufacturer and model. ATRs are defined in ISO standards.
Authentication	See *User authentication, message authentication*
Barium ferrite	See *Ferrite*
Bar code	A series of parallel lines, usually black on white, whose width and spacing can be translated into binary data by optical means. Bar codes are commonly used for labeling goods.
Batch card	A smart card containing prepersonalization information for a given batch of cards. Different batch cards produce different cards. Batch cards produce a permanent "seal" in the card memory; they are usually employed by card manufacturers.
Behavioral feature	Biometric aspect not based on anatomic features (e.g., signature)
BER	Bit error rate: a measure of the correctness that storage media show in recording and retrieving information. BERs in communications and computers are typically below 10^{-9} (i.e., 1 bit per billion).
Biometric test	Any test for proving the identity or eligibility of a person based on permanent biological attributes (e.g., fingerprints, retina patterns, vein check, voice). Signature recognition is also considered a biometric test.
Buffering	In magnetic stripe financial cards, fraud consisting of storing card data elsewhere, so that these data can be restored into the card when the card limit is reached.
CAFE	Conditional Access For Europe: a three-year EC R&D project for definition and demonstration of high-security techniques in international payments.
Capacitive coupling	In contactless cards, system for interchanging data with an external device.
Card mask	In smart cards, functions permanently stored in the card memory for carrying out incoming commands; also known as Smart Card Operating System (SCOS).
Carte Bancaire	French Bank Card Association. Its partners include *Carte Bleue* (VISA) and *Carte Verte* (MasterCard). *Carte Bancaire* conducted many smart card financial trials in France.

Case	In T = 0 protocol, instructions are divided into cases, depending on whether the instruction carries no data (case 1), carries data from the WRU to the card (case 2), carries data from the card to the WRU (case 3), or both (case 4). Case 4 is described in ISO 7816/4; ISO 7816/3 accepts only three cases.
CEN	*Comité Européen de Normalisation* (European Committee for Standardization): a standards organization composed of the national standards organizations of 18 European countries, including all EC countries. TC 224 of CEN is involved in all card-related CEN standards.
Challenge	Procedure for a smart card to assess that the WRU into which it has been inserted is authorized to operate with it or vice versa.
Charge-a-plate	Metal plate issued by a retailers' association in the U.S., containing the name and account number of selected, credit-worthy clients and considered one of the precursors of current credit cards.
Chip card	Any plastic card containing one or more integrated circuits embedded in the plastic substrate; also known as integrated circuit card
CLA	In protocol T = 0, byte indicating the instruction class
CLK	Clock: chip card contact C3, carrying timing signals
Clock circuit	Optional circuit of chip cards: if the card lacks clock circuit, synchronization from an external clock is obtained through contact CLK.
CLS	Card life status: a new status byte, other than SW1 and SW2, introduced in ISO 7816/4
CNAM	*Caisse Nationale d'Assurance Maladie* (French National Health Insurance Service)
Coercivity	In magnetic media, magnetic field required to demagnetize a previously saturated material. The intrinsic coercivity of any magnetic material is measured as the half width of its hysteresis loop.
Confidential zone	Smart card UAM zone protected by any secret code. Confidential and free zones are mixed in current cards.
Contact	Any of the external metallic connections of chip cards, allowing the card to obtain power from, and to communicate with, the WRU. Standard cards have eight contacts, though some manufacturers use only six, since the function of the two remaining contacts has not been defined yet.
Contactless card	Chip card without contacts that are powered by batteries or induction and communicate with external devices by inductive or capacitive coupling.
CPS	*Carte du Professionnel de Santé*
CPU	Central processing unit

Credit card	Any card allowing its owner to spend money with no immediate reimbursement. Credit cards in EPOS generate electronic loans. Credit cards are used as debit cards in EFT-POS.
Cryptosystem	Any enciphering system
Curie point	Transition temperature of ferromagnetic materials: above Curie point, ferromagnetic materials become paramagnetic. The transition temperature of ferrimagnetic materials is called the Neel point or Neel temperature.
Danmønt/Dancoin	Nationwide multipurpose financial application conducted in Denmark with prepaid cards.
Data storage card	Any card with little or no control on stored data: magnetic stripe and optical cards are data storage cards.
dc	Direct current: electrical signal whose polarity is not reversed with time
Debit card	Financial card whose owner is immediately charged for the total amount spent in the transaction; used in EFT-POS as electronic checks.
Decryption	Procedure for deciphering a previously encrypted message by applying the required keys.
Degaussing	In magnetic materials, data erasing by applying ac fields
DELA	Drexler European Licensees Association: has prepared standards for laser optical cards
DES	Data Encryption Standard: a commercially available symmetric cryptosystem launched by NIST
Design rule	In microelectronics, distance between integrated components of the chip. The smaller the design rule, the larger the integration scale.
DF	Dedicated file: a file type in the ISO 7816/4 hierarchical file structure
Digital signature	Authentication of a document as being emitted by a given sender. Digital signatures are the electronic equivalent of handwritten signatures. They also provide proof of integrity and nonrepudiation.
Direct convention	In chip cards, transmission convention in which the character LSB comes first, and logic 1 is Z (high state).
DIS	Draft international standard
Discrimination level	In decision-making, threshold for separating accepted and rejected items.
Domain	See *magnetic domain*

DRAM	Dynamic random access memory: a volatile RAM which needs to be periodically refreshed. Internal computer memory is usually RAM. Smart cards use RAM for scratch pad memory.
DRIVE	An EC R&D program devoted to improving road transport
Drop-in	In optical storage media, detection of a nonexisting bit
Drop-out	In optical storage media, failure to detect an existing bit
EBT	Electronic benefit transfer: smart card applications in the U.S. with the intention of replacing food stamps and other social benefit services.
EC	European community, also called EEC, European Economic Community
EDAC	Error detection and correction: a series of error-recovery techniques based on storage of redundant information. The use of EDAC reduces the media storage capacity and improves BER.
EEPROM	Electrically erasable, programmable ROM: the usual permanent memory employed in current cards for UAM
EF	Elementary file: a file type in the ISO 7816/4 hierarchical file structure
EFT-POS	Electronic fund transfer at the point of sale: transactions resulting in an immediate transfer of funds from the customer's account to the retailer's account; performed with debit or prepaid cards.
Electronic purse	See *purse file*
Embossing	Card area where data (usually name, expiry date, and account number of the user) are represented in relief, which allows mechanical transfer of these data to paper copies (e.g., receipts).
EN	European norm: employed in standards from CEN
Encryption	Enciphering procedure to make a message meaningless to everyone except those who have the required keys
EPOS	Electronic point of sale: any attended or unattended position where payments are charged to credit cards, the reimbursement being confirmed by local (off-line) or remote (on-line) electronic means.
EPROM	Erasable, programmable ROM: unlike PROM, EPROM is erasable, usually under ultraviolet exposure. However, EPROM and PROM are equivalent in a smart card, since EPROM cannot be erased by ultraviolet light when the chip is embedded in plastic. Old smart card models employed EPROM in the user/application memory (thus, the memory ran out with card use).
etu	Elementary time unit: roughly, the time required for the card to send a bit, as defined in ISO standards. Any card declares its etu in the first byte of the ATR.

EXEC function	Executable routine stored in smart card's UAM. Some smart card chips allow the storage of programs in the UAM, thus enhancing the SCOS. This feature is never available to users, and seldom to issuers.
F/2F	Two-frequency binary encoding system for magnetic stripes. 0s are represented as regions with the same magnetization. 1s have a flux reversal in the middle of the region. Any bit, either 0 or 1, has opposite magnetization as its leading and trailing contiguous bits.
FA	False acceptance: in decision-making tests, fraction of ineligible items or persons that the test system considers eligible
Faraday effect	Change in light polarization when transmitted through a magnetic material
Ferric oxide	(Gamma phase) Low-coercivity magnetic material usually employed in magnetic stripes
Ferrite	High-coercivity magnetic material
Ferromagnetism	Property of some materials by which the magnetic moments of their atoms have the same direction—may result in permanent magnets.
File data zone	Smart card RAM zone containing the card's file structure
Flux reversal	In magnetic stripes, magnetization inversion between two adjacent regions
FNMT	*Fábrica Nacional de Moneda y Timbre* (Spanish National Factory of Coins and Stamps): now also involved in the manufacture of memory and smart cards
FR	False rejection: in decision-making tests, fraction of eligible items or persons that the test system considers ineligible
Free zone	Smart card UAM zone whose access does not require any secret code. Free and confidential zones are mixed in current cards.
French standard	Former chip card *de facto* standard, in which the card contacts were located near the upper left corner of the card, overlapping the magnetic stripe zone. After ISO standard approval, French standard was accepted until 1991.
Gamma ferric oxide	See *Ferric oxide*
GEC	General Electric Company
GIM	GEC Imprint Magnetic cards: trademark of special magnetic stripe cards provided with patches of high-coercivity magnetic material to avoid counterfeiting
GMPTE	Greater Manchester Passenger Transport Executive
GND	Ground: chip card contact C5, used as reference voltage

GSM	Global System for Mobile Communications: a cellular phone system in which the phone number and user identity are not associated with a specific telephone, but stored in a smart card which is inserted into any GSM phone. GSM handsets employ plug-in smart cards.
Guard time	Extra time between incoming characters solicited by the card through ATR interface characters.
GUTI	*Grupo Universitario de Tarjeta Inteligente* (Smart Card University Group): used throughout the book for describing simulated or fictitious smart cards and devices.
Hand geometry	Biometric test based on the features of the hand
HF	High frequency: in contactless cards, it is loosely located in the megahertz range.
High-coercivity stripe	Magnetic stripe made of new materials such as barium ferrite, which is only magnetized by high (several thousand Oe) magnetic fields.
Historical character	Any ATR character besides TS, T0, TCK, and interface characters. Manufacturers often include ID of their products in the ATR historical characters.
IATA	International Air Transportation Association: magnetic stripe cards were first proposed by IATA, who defined the content and bit density of the cards' first track.
IC	Integrated circuit
IC card	See *Chip card*
ID	Identification
IDEA	International data encryption algorithm
IMSI	International management subscriber identity
Inductive coupling	In contactless cards, system for obtaining power supply from an external source and/or for data communications. Data transfer may be also achieved by capacitive coupling.
INS	In protocol $T = 0$, byte indicating the instruction code within the instruction class CLA
Integrity	Proof for the recipient that a message has not been altered, so that the content is the same as that sent by the sender. Integrity proofs are achieved by encryption techniques.
Interchange	In financial cards, information sharing between financial companies for reciprocal compatibility of ATMs and EPOSs.
Interface character	Any ATR character containing information for communication between the chip card and the WRU. See also *Protocol parameter*.

Interleaving	Storage strategy in which sequential data are not sequentially stored. Interleaving is used in hard disks for optimizing reading/writing operations. In other media, such as optical cards, it is used to avoid error clustering (accumulation of errors) in the same data set.
Intersector communications	Data sharing between different applications of the same smart card
Inverse convention	In chip cards, transmission convention in which the character MSB comes first and logic 1 is A (low state)
I/O	Input/output, also the name of chip card contact C7, which is used for communications
IPSO	A major pioneering smart card trial which was carried out in three French cities
ISO	International Standards Organization (officially named International Organization for Standardization): one of the main standards organizations worldwide. Several ISO standards, especially ISO 7816, are applicable to smart cards.
Issuer key	Any card secret code owned by the card issuer. The master key is usually an issuer key.
JEIDA	A Japanese standards organization, which launched the first standards on IC memory (PCMCIA) cards.
Jitter	In magnetic materials with F/2F encoding, inaccuracy in the position of flux reversals
Kerr effect	Change in light polarization upon reflection in a magnetic material
Key	Generally speaking, a set of alphanumeric characters required to perform an operation which otherwise is not allowed. See also *Private key, Public key, Master key, Issuer key, Manufacturer key, Secret code.*
Laser card	See *optical card*
LED	Light-emitting diode: sometimes used for reading optical cards and for positioning hybrid magnetic-optic storage media
LD	Laser diode: used for writing (and quite often for reading) optical cards
LF	Low frequency: in contactless cards, it refers to kilohertz range
Light polarization	Light property describing the orientation of the oscillating transversal electrical field component of the electromagnetic wave.
Linear recording	In optical cards, recording system where the information is stored in straight parallel lines, as opposed to circular tracks of magnetic and optical disks.

Low-coercivity stripe	Regular magnetic stripes made of gamma ferric oxide are called low-coercivity stripes, as opposed to new, high-coercivity materials. Low-coercivity stripes are magnetized with 300-Oe magnetic fields.
LSB	Least significant bit
LSI	Large-scale integration
LSN	Least significant nibble of a byte
Lucifer	Cryptosystem developed by IBM, from which DES was derived
MAC	Money Access Service. U.S. ATM network system from CoreStates Financial Corp.
Magnetic domain	Any zone of a magnetic material in which the magnetization of its particles points toward the same direction.
Magnetic stripe card	Plastic card with a magnetic stripe, usually in the upper part of the rear surface. The stripe is divided into three tracks, where data are magnetically stored. These cards are commonly used in financial applications.
Magneto-optical storage	Reversible optical storage system based on the Kerr effect
Manufacturer key	Secret code known only by the card manufacturer. It is used to access restricted memory areas, such as the secret zone and the manufacturer zone.
Manufacturer zone	Smart card UAM zone where manufacturer data concerning the microprocessor and card ID are stored. It is written during manufacture and usually accessed only with the manufacturer key.
Mask	See *Card mask*
Master key	Main secret code of a smart card. Depending on the card model, this key may have some privileges, such as card reactivation or erasing. The master key is usually owned by the card issuer.
Memory card	Chip card without microprocessor. It may still have some data access control based on wired logic or other preset instructions. Telephone chip cards are memory cards.
Message authentication	Procedure to ensure the origin of a message, usually through encryption techniques.
MF	Master file: a file type in the ISO 7816/4 hierarchical file structure. A smart card may not have more than one master file.
Minicard	Any of the reduced-size chip cards, not yet standardized, that eventually will be applied to ticketing and related applications. See also *Plug-in card*.
MK	Master key
MSB	Most significant bit

MSI	Medium-scale integration
MSN	Most significant nibble of a byte
Multiapplication card	Smart card offering several applications (which may be developed by the same issuer or by different issuers) in the same chip.
Multipurpose card	Smart card offering several services or applications (usually from the same issuer) in the same chip.
MW	Microwave: spectral region in the gigahertz frequency range
Nibble	Half of a byte (4 bits)
NIST	U.S. National Institute of Standards and Technology
Nonrepudiation	Procedure by which the recipient of a message can demonstrate the message origin to a third party.
NTT	Nippon Telegraph and Telephone Company (Japanese PTT)
NULL	In chip cards, procedure byte sent by the card, asking the WRU to wait for another byte. It is used to avoid timeout in lengthy computations. The standard NULL byte is 60 hex.
OCR	Optical character recognition: computer programs capable of identifying letters and symbols from scanned images of printed or handwritten text.
Oe	Oersted, the measuring unit of magnetic fields. Regular magnetic stripes require 300 Oe to be magnetized. High coercivity stripes require several thousand Oe.
Off-line	In financial transactions, operations locally confirmed (i.e., without remote authorization from a host computer). Off-line transactions of magnetic stripe cards are approved by the terminal, whereas smart cards may confirm the transactions by themselves.
On-line	In financial transactions, operations confirmed by remote (e.g., card issuer) authorization
Optical card	Data storage card where data writing and reading is performed by optical signals. Optical cards are usually nonerasable (WORM). Low-capacity optical cards are used in pay phones. High-capacity (MB) optical cards (also called laser cards) may store digitized images as well as text. They are mainly used in health care applications.
P1, P2	In protocol T = 0, reference address completing INS
P3	In protocol T = 0, number of bytes to be transferred
Parent card	A smart card containing personalization information splitting a card batch into several groups. Each group has its own parent.
Passive card	Name given to regular smart cards, as opposed to active, or super smart, cards.

PCMCIA	Personal Computer Memory Card Industry Association: has prepared a standard card connector, mainly for portable computers, which can be used by a number of computer peripherals, including PCMCIA cards, IC memory cards storing several megabytes.
Personalization	Procedure performed by the manufacturer or the issuer on smart cards, mainly related to secret codes for cryptographic facilities (e.g., random number generation, encryption keys). Further steps may be added for linking the card to an application or to a customer.
PET	Polyethylene terphthalate: a plastic substrate for magnetic stripe and chip cards, especially for thin flexible cards; used in Japanese phone cards.
PIN	Personal identification number: in magnetic stripe cards, the secret number entered by the card user for performing transactions. In smart cards, the term is applied by extension to the principal secret code of the user.
PLA	Programmable logic array: some memory cards use PLAs for access control.
Plastic card	Any card with plastic substrate: credit, magnetic stripe, and smart cards are plastic cards.
Plug-in card	Tiny card designed for being permanently inserted in another device. Plug-in cards have been developed for use in GSM handsets.
Polarization	See *light polarization*
POS	Point of sale
Prepaid card	Any card containing a specified amount of money which has been previously paid by the owner. Usually employed in low-value transactions, prepaid cards are considered electronic cash. Telephone cards are prepaid cards.
Prepersonalization	Procedure performed on smart cards by the manufacturer in order to prepare different batches from the same card model. The card's serial number and some security features are set up in this step.
Private key	One of the two keys in asymmetric cryptosystems, known only to the user.
PROM	Programmable ROM: a WORM technology, used for storing permanent information in smart cards.
Protection circuit	Any circuit inside a chip card for protection against fraudulent access or environmental aggressives.
Protocol parameter	ATR interface character describing any relevant parameter (e.g., maximum programming voltage, clock rate, guard time) for the WRU to control the chip card.

PTS	Protocol type selection: a procedure by which the WRU and the card negotiate the transmission protocol.
PTT	Public telephone company: sometimes interpreted as public telegraph and telephone and as post, telegraph, and telephone.
Public key	One of the two keys in asymmetric cryptosystems: made public so that other users may utilize it.
Public key certificate	Encrypted document for assessing the validity of a public key
Purse file	A special type of card file allowing financially related operations such as credit, debit, and balance.
PVC	Polyvinyl chloride: a plastic substrate for magnetic stripe and chip cards
PVCA	Polyvinyl chloride acetate: a plastic substrate for magnetic stripe and chip cards, similar to PVC
R/O	Read only
R/W	Read and write
RAM	Random access memory, usually found in computers: smart cards use RAM for intermediate results of calculations.
Reset circuit	An optional circuit in smart cards for resetting the microprocessor when requested from the outside. When a smart card has a reset circuit, the external reset signal triggers it.
Retinal pattern	Biometric test based on distinctive features of the retina
RFU	Reserved for future use
ROM	Read-only memory: strictly speaking, memory whose data have been wired in during manufacture. Nevertheless, the term is usually applied to any kind of nonerasable memory. See *PROM*.
RSA	Rivest, Shamir, Adleman: a well-known asymmetric cryptosystem
RST	Reset: chip card contact C2, used by the WRU to reset the card upon insertion
SANTAL	A major French health care project involving cards for health care and administrative data.
Saturation	In magnetic materials, maximum magnetization achieved when a very strong external magnetic field is applied.
SCOS	Smart card operating system. See *card mask*.
Secret code	Any of the access codes contained in smart cards
Secret zone	Smart card UAM zone containing the card secret codes. Only the microprocessor can access this zone.
Self-block	In smart cards, state in which the card refuses to answer external commands. It is usually induced by incorrect entries of secret codes, especially PIN and master key.

SESAM	A major French health care project involving cards for administrative data.
SIM	Subscriber Identity Modules used in GSM
SK	Secret key (secret code)
Skimming	In magnetic stripe financial cards, fraud consisting of altering the stored information (e.g., credit limit).
Slotless card	Contactless card able to operate at a certain distance from the external device.
Smart card	Chip card whose integrated circuit contains a programmable microprocessor for managing and access control of stored data.
Smart disk	Device externally identical to a floppy disk, containing a microprocessor and IC memory. Smart disks mimic the behavior of floppy disks inside a computer, yet keep a tight control on data flow.
Smart key	Plastic key-shaped device containing a smart chip. Smart keys are chiefly used in pay TV descrambling.
SRAM	Static random access memory: a volatile RAM which does not need refreshing, the memory being preserved as long as the power supply is on.
SSI	Small-scale integration
Status zone	Smart card UAM zone where the status of card secret codes is stored. Incorrect secret code entries are stored for the card to self-block when the maximum allowed number of consecutive wrong attempts is reached.
Super smart card	Smart card featuring display, keyboard, and battery, thus becoming an independent computing system. The best known super smart card is SuperSmart Card, jointly developed by VISA and Toshiba. Also called very smart card and active card.
SW1, SW2	Status bytes sent by the card after accomplishing every external command. If the command has been correctly executed, then SW1 = 90 hex and SW2 = 00.
Symmetric cryptosystem	Cryptosystem in which the secret keys are shared by the sender and the recipient of the message. DES is a well-known symmetric cryptosystem. Many current smart cards include built-in symmetric encryption algorithms.
T0	Format character: second ATR character, indicating the presence and number of subsequent ATR characters.
T = 0	Asynchronous half-duplex character transmission protocol in chip cards
T = 1	Asynchronous half-duplex block transmission protocol in chip cards

TA	True acceptance: in decision-making tests, the fraction of eligible items or persons that the test system considers eligible.
TA, TB, TC, TD	ATR interface characters
TC	Technical committee. See *CEN*.
TCK	Check character: last ATR character
TFC	Thin flexible card: a group of cards which are being developed for ticketing and similar tasks.
TLV	Tag, length, value
TR	True rejection: in decision-making tests, the fraction of ineligible items or persons that the test system considers ineligible.
Track	In magnetic stripe and optical cards, the physical band within the active area where data are sequentially stored. Regular magnetic stripe cards have three tracks. Optical cards may have more than 2,500 tracks.
Track guide	In optical cards and hybrid magnetic-optic media, a series of lines having different reflectivity than the background. These lines are used for positioning the reading/writing head by optical means.
Transaction zone	Smart card UAM zone for the most variable data in the application. A separate zone in early cards, it is now mixed with free and confidential zones in current card models.
TS	First ATR character, containing information for measuring the card etu, as well as the transmission convention (direct or inverse).
UAM	User/application memory: memory (EPROM or EEPROM) area in smart cards where user and application data are stored. UAM is traditionally divided into several zones (e.g., secret, transaction, confidential, free, status, manufacturer), though many of these zones are functionally identical in current cards.
ULSI	Ultra-large-scale integration
User authentication	Procedure to demonstrate the identity or privileges of a user. Biometric techniques establish the user ID; both ID and privileges are established by encryption techniques.
VCC	Power supply: chip card contact C1, from which the card obtains the power V_{CC}. The standard V_{CC} is 5V.
Vein pattern	Biometric test based on the layout of the veins: usually taken from the wrist
Very smart card	See *Super smart card*
VITALE	Smart card employed in the SESAM project
VLSI	Very-large-scale integration. An integration range in microelectronic manufacturing. VLSI chips may have up to 100,000 gates.

VPP	Programming voltage: chip card contact C6, used for supplying the voltage required by the card for erasure and writing operations
Watermark	Patented procedure of Thorn EMI based on special magnetic stripes with nonerasable magnetic patterns. Pattern features are digitized and stored in an extra "track 0" alongside the three regular magnetic stripe tracks.
WG	Work group
Wired logic card	Memory card whose data access is controlled by a program permanently stored in the card memory. Memory cards cannot be reprogrammed.
WORM	Write-once, read-many times memory. It is applied to several kinds of permanent storage media, including smart cards' EPROM and optical cards. WORM memory cannot be erased. ROM and PROM are occasionally taken as WORMs, though the term is preferentially applied to memory written once *by the card user*, not by the manufacturer or issuer.
WRU	Writing/reading unit: any standalone unit or computer peripheral capable of commanding chip cards.
Z	In digital binary communications, high-voltage state
Zero knowledge	Cryptosystems in which neither the sender nor the recipient of the message know the key(s).

Index

The Artech House Telecommunications Library

Vinton G. Cerf, Series Editor

Jitter in Digital Transmission Systems, Patrick R. Trischitta and Eve L. Varma

Land-Mobile Radio System Engineering, Garry C. Hess

LAN/WAN Optimization Techniques, Harrell Van Norman

LANs to WANs: Network Management in the 1990s, Nathan J. Muller and Robert P. Davidson

The Law and Regulation of International Space Communication, Harold M. White, Jr. and Rita Lauria White

Long Distance Services: A Buyer's Guide, Daniel D. Briere

Measurement of Optical Fibers and Devices, G. Cancellieri and U. Ravaioli

Meteor Burst Communication, Jacob Z. Schanker

Minimum Risk Strategy for Acquiring Communications Equipment and Services, Nathan J. Muller

Mobile Communications in the U.S. and Europe: Regulation, Technology, and Markets, Michael Paetsch

Mobile Information Systems, John Walker

Narrowband Land-Mobile Radio Networks, Jean-Paul Linnartz

Networking Strategies for Information Technology, Bruce Elbert

Numerical Analysis of Linear Networks and Systems, Hermann Kremer *et al.*

Optimization of Digital Transmission Systems, K. Trondle and Gunter Soder

Packet Switching Evolution from Narrowband to Broadband ISDN, M. Smouts

Packet Video: Modeling and Signal Processing, Naohisa Ohta

The PP and QUIPU Implementation of X.400 and X.500, Stephen Kille

Principles of Secure Communication Systems, Second Edition, Don J. Torrieri

Principles of Signals and Systems: Deterministic Signals, B. Picinbono

Private Telecommunication Networks, Bruce Elbert

Radiodetermination Satellite Services and Standards, Martin Rothblatt

Residential Fiber Optic Networks: An Engineering and Economic Analysis, David Reed

Secure Data Networking, Michael Purser

Setting Global Telecommunication Standards: The Stakes, The Players, and The Process, Gerd Wallenstein

Smart Cards, José Luis Zoreda and José Manuel Otón

Secure Data Networking, Michael Purser

The Telecommunications Deregulation Sourcebook, Stuart N. Brotman, editor

Television Technology: Fundamentals and Future Prospects, A. Michael Noll

Telecommunications Technology Handbook, Daniel Minoli

Telephone Company and Cable Television Competition, Stuart N. Brotman

Teletraffic Technologies in ATM Networks, Hiroshi Saito

Terrestrial Digital Microwave Communciations, Ferdo Ivanek, editor

Transmission Networking: SONET and the SDH, Mike Sexton and Andy Reid

Transmission Performance of Evolving Telecommunications Networks, John Gruber and Godfrey Williams

Troposcatter Radio Links, G. Roda

UNIX Internetworking, Uday O. Pabrai

Virtual Networks: A Buyer's Guide, Daniel D. Briere

Voice Processing, Second Edition, Walt Tetschner

Voice Teletraffic System Engineering, James R. Boucher

Wireless Access and the Local Telephone Network, George Calhoun

Wireless LAN Systems, A. Santamaría and F. J. Lopez-Hernandez

Writing Disaster Recovery Plans for Telecommunications Networks and LANs, Leo A. Wrobel

X Window System User's Guide, Uday O. Pabrai

For further information on these and other Artech House titles, contact:

Artech House
685 Canton Street
Norwood, MA 01602
617-769-9750
Fax: 617-762-9230
Telex: 951-659
email: artech@world.std.com

Artech House
Portland House, Stag Place
London SW1E 5XA England
+44 (0) 71-973-8077
Fax: +44 (0) 71-630-0166
Telex: 951-659